ANDRÉ LaCOCQUE is Professor of Old Testament Emeritus at Chicago Theological Seminary. He is the author of *Thinking Biblically* (with Paul Ricoeur; 1998), *The Feminine Unconventional* (Overtures to Biblical Theology; Fortress Press, 1990), and *Daniel in His Time* (1988).

K. C. HANSON, the translator, is the biblical studies editor for Fortress Press. His published works include *Palestine in the Time of Jesus: Social Structures and Social Conflicts with CD-ROM* (with Douglas E. Oakman; 2002).

# Ruth

# Continental Commentaries

## Old Testament

*Genesis 1–11, Genesis 12–36, Genesis 37–50*
Claus Westermann

*Leviticus*
Jacob Milgrom

*1 and 2 Kings*
Volkmar Fritz

*Psalms 1–59, Psalm 60–150*
Hans-Joachim Kraus

*Theology of the Psalms*
Hans-Joachim Kraus

*Qoheleth*
Norbert Lohfink

*The Song of Songs*
Othmar Keel

*Isaiah 1–12, Isaiah 13–27, Isaiah 28–39*
Hans Wildberger

*Obadiah and Jonah*
Hans Walter Wolff

*Micah*
Hans Walter Wolff

*Haggai*
Hans Walter Wolff

\* \* \* \*

## New Testament

*Matthew 1–7*
Ulrich Luz

*Galatians*
Dieter Lührmann

*Revelation*
Jürgen Roloff

ANDRÉ LACOCQUE

# RUTH

## A Continental Commentary

*Translated by*
*K. C. Hanson*

**FORTRESS PRESS**
**MINNEAPOLIS**

RUTH
A Continental Commentary

*Library of Congress Cataloging-in-Publication Data*

LaCocque, André.
   [Livre de Ruth. English]
   Ruth : a continental commentary / André LaCocque ; translated by K.C. Hanson.
      p. cm. — (Continental commentaries)
      ISBN 0-8006-9515-1 (alk. paper)
      1. Bible. O.T. Ruth—Commentaries. I. Title. II. Series.

      BS1315.53.L3313 2004
      222'.3507—dc22

                          2004018130

Manufactured in the U.S.A.

08     07     06     05     04     1     2     3     4     5     6     7     8     9     10

# Contents

# Contents

# Dedication

This study is dedicated to Paul Ricoeur, poet of the generous and expansive interpretation, on the occasion of his ninetieth birthday.

# Abbreviations

## Ancient

| | |
|---|---|
| 1QM | War Scroll (*Milḥamah*) |
| 2QRuth[a] | 2Q16: fragmentary copy of Ruth |
| 2QRuth[b] | 2Q17: two fragments of Ruth |
| 4QFlor | 4Q174: Florilegium |
| 4QMMT | 4Q394: Halakic letter |
| 4QRuth[a] | 4Q104: three fragments of Ruth |
| 4QRuth[b] | 4Q105: three fragments of Ruth |
| *Ant.* | Josephus, *Antiquities of the Judeans* |
| *Apoc. Zeph.* | *Apocalypse of Zephaniah* |
| *b.* | Babylonian Talmud *(Babli)* tractates |
| *B. Bat.* | *Baba Batra* |
| *B. Qam.* | *Baba Qamma* |
| *ʿErub.* | *ʿErubin* |
| *Gos. Pet.* | *Gospel of Peter* |
| *Ḥag.* | *Ḥagigah* |
| *Jub.* | *Jubilees* |
| K | Ketib |
| *Ketub.* | *Ketubbot* |
| LXX | Septuagint |
| *m.* | Mishnah tractates |
| *Midr. Ps.* | Midrash on the Psalms |
| MS/S | manuscript/s |
| MT | Masoretic text |
| NT | New Testament |
| OL | Old Latin |
| Q | Qere |
| *Ruth Rab.* | *Ruth Rabbah (Midrash Rabbah on Ruth)* |
| *Sanh.* | *Sanhedrin* |
| *Šabb.* | *Šabbat* |
| *Sib. Or.* | *Sibylline Oracles* |

## Abbreviations

| | |
|---|---|
| Syr | Syriac |
| *t.* | Tosefta tractates |
| Tg | Targum |
| *T. Zeb.* | *Testament of Zebulun* |
| Vg | Vulgate |
| VL | Vetus Latina (Old Latin version) |
| *Yad.* | *Yadayim* |
| *Yeb.* | *Yebamot* |

### Modern

| | |
|---|---|
| AB | Anchor Bible |
| *ABD* | *Anchor Bible Dictionary,* ed. David Noel Freedman, 6 vols. Garden City, N.Y.: Doubleday, 1992 |
| *AcT* | *Acta theologica* |
| *AJBI* | *Annual of the Japanese Biblical Institute* |
| *AJSL* | *American Journal of Semitic Languages and Literature* |
| AnBib | Analecta biblica |
| *ANET* | *Ancient Near Eastern Texts Relating to the Old Testament,* ed. James B. Pritchard, 3d ed. Princeton: Princeton Univ. Press, 1969 |
| *AR* | *Archiv für Religionswissenschaft* |
| *ARA* | *Annual Review of Anthropology* |
| *ArOr* | *Archiv orientální* |
| *ASB* | *Austin Seminary Bulletin* |
| *ASTI* | *Annual of the Swedish Theological Institute* |
| ATD | Das Alte Testament Deutsch |
| *BASOR* | *Bulletin of the American Schools of Oriental Research* |
| BAT | Die Botschaft des Alten Testament |
| BBET | Beiträge zur biblischen Exegese und Theologie |
| BerO | Berit Olam |
| *Bib* | *Biblica* |
| *BibInt* | *Biblical Interpretation* |
| BibIntSer | Biblical Interpretation Series |
| BibSem | Biblical Seminar |
| *BJRL* | *Bulletin of the John Rylands Library* |
| *BK* | *Bibel und Kirche* |
| BKAT | Biblischer Kommentar zum Alten Testament |
| BLS | Bible and Literature Series |
| *BN* | *Biblische Notizen* |
| *BRev* | *Bible Review* |
| *BSac* | *Bibliotheca Sacra* |

| | |
|---|---|
| BST | The Bible Speaks Today |
| *BTB* | *Biblical Theology Bulletin* |
| *BVC* | *Bible et vie chrétienne* |
| *BZ* | *Biblische Zeitschrift* |
| CAT | Commentaire de l'Ancien Testament |
| CBC | Cambridge Bible Commentary |
| *CBQ* | *Catholic Biblical Quarterly* |
| CC | Continental Commentary |
| CComm | Communicator's Commentary |
| CCSL | Corpus Christianorum: Series latina |
| DSBS | Daily Study Bible Series |
| *EncJud* | *Encyclopedia Judaica,* ed. G. Wigoder et al. 16 vols. Jerusalem: Keter, 1971–72 |
| ErT | Erlanger Taschenbücher |
| *EstBib* | *Estudios bíblicos* |
| *EvQ* | *Evangelical Quarterly* |
| *ExpT* | *Expository Times* |
| FCB | Feminist Companion to the Bible |
| FOTL | Forms of the Old Testament Literature |
| GBS | Guides to Biblical Scholarship |
| *GCA* | *Gratz College Annual* |
| GKC | *Gesenius' Hebrew Grammar,* ed. E. Kautzsch, trans. A. E. Cowley, 2d ed. Oxford: Clarendon, 1910 |
| HAT | Handkommentar zum Alten Testament |
| *HBT* | *Horizons in Biblical Theology* |
| *HS* | *Hebrew Studies* |
| HSM | Harvard Semitic Monographs |
| HTKAT | Herders theologischer Kommentar zum Alten Testament |
| *HTR* | *Harvard Theological Review* |
| *HUCA* | *Hebrew Union College Annual* |
| *IB* | *Interpreter's Bible,* ed. George A. Buttrick, 12 vols. Nashville: Abingdon, 1951–57 |
| IBC | Interpretation: A Bible Commentary for Teaching and Preaching |
| *IDB* | *Interpreter's Dictionary of the Bible,* ed. George A. Buttrick, 4 vols. Nashville: Abingdon, 1962 |
| *IDBSup* | *Interpreter's Dictionary of the Bible, Supplementary Volume,* ed. Keith Crim. Nashville: Abingdon, 1976 |
| ISBL | Indiana Studies in Biblical Literature |
| ITC | International Theological Commentary |
| *JAAR* | *Journal of the American Academy of Religion* |

**Abbreviations**

| | |
|---|---|
| *JANES* | *Journal of the Ancient Near Eastern Society* |
| *JAOS* | *Journal of the American Oriental Society* |
| *JBL* | *Journal of Biblical Literature* |
| *JE* | *Jewish Encyclopedia,* ed. Isadore Singer, 12 vols. New York: Funk & Wagnalls, 1925 |
| *JJS* | *Journal of Jewish Studies* |
| *JNSL* | *Journal of Northwest Semitic Languages* |
| JPSV | Tanakh: Jewish Publication Society Version |
| *JQR* | *Jewish Quarterly Review* |
| *JRAS* | *Journal of the Royal Asiatic Society* |
| *JSOT* | *Journal for the Study of the Old Testament* |
| JSOTSup | Journal for the Study of the Old Testament Supplement Series |
| *JSS* | *Journal of Semitic Studies* |
| KAT | Kommentar zum Alten Testament |
| KHCAT | Kurzer Hand-Commentar zum Alten Testament |
| KT | Kaiser-Taschenbücher |
| LCBI | Literary Currents in Biblical Interpretation |
| LD | Lectio divina |
| MB | Le Monde de la Bible |
| MBS | Message of Biblical Spirituality |
| NAC | New American Commentary |
| NCB | New Century Bible |
| NEchtB | Die Neue Echter Bibel |
| NICOT | New International Commentary on the Old Testament |
| NIV | New International Version |
| NRSV | New Revised Standard Version |
| NSKAT | Neuer Stuttgarter Kommentar. Altes Testament |
| OBO | Orbis biblicus et orientalis |
| OBS | Oxford Bible Series |
| OBT | Overtures to Biblical Theology |
| *Or* | *Orientalia* |
| OTG | Old Testament Guides |
| OTL | Old Testament Library |
| OTM | Old Testament Message |
| *OTS* | *Oudtestamentische Studiën* |
| *PIBA* | *Proceedings of the Irish Biblical Association* |
| *PMLA* | *Publications of the Modern Language Association of America* |
| *RB* | *Revue biblique* |
| REB | Revised English Bible |
| *ResQ* | *Restoration Quarterly* |

| | |
|---|---|
| *RGG* | *Die Religion in Geschichte und Gegenwart,* ed. Alfred Bertholet et al., 2d ed., 6 vols. Tübingen: Mohr/Siebeck, 1927–32 |
| *RHPR* | *Revue d'histoire et de philosophie religieuses* |
| *RIDA* | *Revue internationale des droits de l'antiquité* |
| RSV | Revised Standard Version |
| *RTP* | *Revue de théologique et de philosophie* |
| SANT | Studien zum Alten und Neuen Testament |
| SBL | Society of Biblical Literature |
| SBLSCS | SBL Septuagint and Cognate Studies |
| *SBLSP* | *SBL Seminar Papers* |
| SBS | Stuttgarter Bibelstudien |
| *SJOT* | *Scandinavian Journal of Old Testament* |
| *SJT* | *Scottish Journal of Theology* |
| SNTSMS | Society for New Testament Studies Monograph Series |
| SPHS | Scholars Press Homage Series |
| STDJ | Studies on the Texts of the Desert of Judah |
| SubBib | Subsidia biblica |
| SWR | Studies in Women and Religion |
| TBC | Torch Bible Commentaries |
| TOB | Traduction oecuménique de la Bible |
| TOTC | Tyndale Old Testament Commentaries |
| *TSK* | *Theologische Studien und Kritiken* |
| *TTZ* | *Trierer theologische Zeitschrift* |
| *TZ* | *Theologische Zeitschrift* |
| UBSMS | United Bible Societies Monograph Series |
| *UF* | *Ugarit-Forschungen* |
| *USQR* | *Union Seminary Quarterly Review* |
| *VT* | *Vetus Testamentum* |
| VTSup | Vetus Testamentum Supplements |
| WBC | Word Biblical Commentary |
| WBComp | Westminster Bible Companion |
| WMANT | Wissenschaftliche Monographien zum Alten und Neuen Testament |
| *WTJ* | *Westminster Theological Journal* |
| *WW* | *Word and World* |
| YNER | Yale Near Eastern Researches |
| *ZAW* | *Zeitschrift für die alttestamentliche Wissenschaft* |
| ZBK | Zürcher Bibelkommentare |

# Editor's Foreword

With the publication of this volume, Continental Commentaries expands its horizons once more. André LaCocque is Emeritus Professor of Hebrew Bible at Chicago Theological Seminary, and so his immediate milieu has long been the American academy, Chicago, and the United Church of Christ. But one cannot fail to take into account his "Continental"—indeed international and ecumenical—context.

LaCocque was raised in the Reformed tradition in Liège—the self-proclaimed capital of the French-speaking region of Belgium. But he also served as the pastor of a Lutheran congregation in eastern France. He received the M.A. degree from Hebrew University of Jerusalem and then went on to earn the Th.D. and Ph.D. degrees at the University of Strasbourg, France.

His publishing has been in French and English, so his primary readerships have been both European *and* North American. His books—*The Book of Daniel*; *The Jonah Complex*; *Daniel in His Time* (Studies on Personalities of the Old Testament); *The Feminine Unconventional: Four Subversive Figures in Israel's Tradition* (Overtures to Biblical Theology); *Romance, She Wrote: A Hermeneutical Essay on Song of Songs*; and *Thinking Biblically: Exegetical and Hermeneutical Studies*—have established him as one of the most innovative interpreters of the biblical text on both continents. Fortress Press is honored to include his commentary in the Continental Commentaries series.

# Preface

With the middle of the twentieth century, biblical research's center of gravity has dramatically shifted to the English-speaking world. English has become the universal language of scholarship. It is thus with a great personal satisfaction that I see my commentary on Ruth—originally written on commission in French[1]—being published, almost concomitantly with the French version, by Fortress Press.

I use the term "version" here on account of the fact that the Continental Commentary presented here is not a slavish duplication of the French text, although very respectful of the original. The difference between the two versions is especially conspicuous when one turns to the bibliography. The CAT's rule in this respect is a short and highly selective list of works aiming at a practical use by non-specialists as well as scholars. As can be expected, the accent is on French books and articles. The Continental Commentary, on the contrary, aims at a certain exhaustiveness, at least as regards the multiple sources of information actually used by the commentary's author.

Now, looking at the respective bibliographies of the French and English versions suffices to buttress my initial assertion in this Preface. It seems fair, as a matter of fact, to say that, while modern French studies on Ruth are few and far between, the English-speaking scholars' preoccupation with this biblical book is extremely well documented. It is true that burning problems of actuality, such as immigration, refugees, minorities, the status of women, and so forth, have called attention to certain documents of the Bible that treat these issues in highly creative ways. Of prime importance among those, of course, is the book of Ruth, which features the exemplary model for Israel of a Moabitess. In point of fact, as I stress in the course of the present commentary, the book is the only one in the Bible carrying the name of a Gentile.

This brings me to emphasize a second point: Ruth is a subversive document. It is not without a deep sentiment of frustration about her people's ineptitude before God and the imperatives of the human condition that Ruth's female author chose as her heroine a foreigner, even a representative of a loathed nation: Moab.

---

[1] *Le Livre de Ruth,* CAT 13 (Geneva: Labor et Fides, 2004).

## Preface

How is Ruth-the-Moabite a saintly woman from among the nations? Through her *ḥesed* (goodness of heart, steadfast love and fidelity), that compels the host society of Bethlehem to interpret the Torah (the charter of Jewish identity before God) in a generous and amplificatory way. It is through this liberating breakthrough in the Law's wall of seclusion that Jesus of Nazareth's hermeneutics has blossomed.

The book of Ruth, therefore, is not just a touching and delightful story of two women, Ruth and Naomi, gaining respect and honor in a patriarchal and chauvinistic society, but is a vibrant plea for the adoption of a consciousness moved by expansive love rather than by restrictive legal definitions. Ruth today is as relevant as it ever was in its centuries-long perennial youth.

Before ending this Preface, I want to express my gratitude and friendship to K.C. Hanson of Fortress Press, more than the translator, a collaborator in the building of the present volume. May the latter interpret its readers as indeed it has interpreted the author and translator of this commentary.

# Translator's Note

It is an honor for me to translate Professor LaCocque's commentary. I had the courage (or temerity) to attempt it only because the author was willing to work closely with me to ensure I had captured his intention. This was not only an act of trust on his part, but also an act of *ḥesed* for which I am grateful. I hope the reader finds it a successful collaboration. My interest in taking on the project was due both to my longstanding respect for LaCocque's work and my enjoyment in teaching the book of Ruth over the years. But as much as I have studied the biblical text and read the research on Ruth, I found that I still had much to learn from LaCocque's deep insights.

In one sense, this work is a translation of the manuscript simultaneously published in French by Labor et Fides (Geneva). But the present edition includes a larger bibliography and more notes, and LaCocque has expanded the text at certain points as well.

The translation of the Bible included here is generally the NRSV. Divergences are identified in the textual notes. But the reader should be aware of two recurring spelling issues. The author has chosen the spelling of the divine name with consonants only—Yhwh (which the NRSV renders LORD). The second is the name of Naomi's husband. The NRSV renders his name "Elimelech"; but the Hebrew spelling is better represented as "Elimelek," and that has been used throughout.

Six other people deserve thanks and recognition for this volume: Jessica Thoreson, managing editor; Beth Wright, assistant managing editor; Becky Lowe, production editor; Paul Kobelski, typesetter at HK Scriptorium; Gary Lee, copyeditor; and Chuck John, proofreader. All publishing is collaboration, but these folks also make it a joy.

May 6, 2004
Northfield, Minnesota

# Introduction

Only woman is capable of nourishing within her an unsubstantiated hope, and inviting us to a doubtful future, which we would have long ceased to believe in were it not for women.[1]

Yet I will restore the fortunes of Moab in the latter days, says Yhwh. Thus far is the judgment on Moab. (Jer 48:47)

## Overview

The book of Ruth is the only biblical book bearing the name of a gentile. This fundamentally important point is in itself already a sign of subversion.

To say it unequivocally, whoever reads the book of Ruth as a simple novel misses the point (no offense to Goethe).[2] From beginning to end, this delicious story is based on an interpretation of the Torah in unexpected circumstances, as changes of fortune in families always are. The voluntary exile to a foreign land; the presence of a Moabite in Judah, despite the harsh ostracism of this people repeated in several texts from different eras; the precarious condition of widows without children to support them in their old age; the right to glean; the right of redemption; levirate marriage;[3] and many other important details of the book are explained by earlier biblical

---

[1] Milan Kundera, *Immortality*, trans. Peter Kussi (New York: HarperCollins, 1992), 342.

[2] Goethe called Ruth the most beautiful of all novels; see Johann Wolfgang von Goethe, *West-östlicher Diwan, Noten und Abhandlungen: Hebräer,* Goethe's Werke 21 (Stuttgart: Suhrkamp, 1820). See also James T. Cleland, "Ruth," *IB* 2:827–52.

[3] Cf. Genesis 38. "Levir" is Latin for "brother-in-law." The goal of "levirate" is to produce an heir for a brother who died without having children, by marrying his widow. We do not know the origin of the custom called "levirate marriage." It is attested in many ancient laws, for example at Ugarit and in Assyria; see Mattiyahu Tsevat, "Marriage and Monarchical Legitimacy in Ugarit and Israel," *JSS* 3 (1958) 237–43. Some cultures limited the extent of this marriage to the production of an heir; others considered it a permanent union; see Millar Burrows, "The Ancient Oriental Background of Hebrew Levirate Marriage," *BASOR* 77 (1940) 2–15. In Genesis 38 it seems to have been a matter of a levirate union, but not a marriage; Judah abstained from relations with Tamar once she became pregnant (Gen 38:26); see George W. Coats, "Widow's Rights: A Crux in the Structure of Genesis 38," *CBQ* 34 (1972) 461–66. In

texts underlying them. This is the reason I begin each section of the commentary by quoting these fundamental passages.

In general, Christian commentators have considered the linking of the book of Ruth to the Feast of Weeks (*Shevuot*)—which was established by Jewish liturgy to celebrate the gift of the Torah to Israel—as purely circumstantial. Even the targumic and midrashic insistence on all the characters in the narrative having obeyed the Law is seen as obvious in traditional Jewish writings. This blunting assumption on the part of modern readers is unfortunate, for the rabbis were willy nilly opening the way to the understanding of the true object of the story of Ruth. For it is not the liturgical use of Ruth during the Feast of *Shevuot* that drove the legal reading of the book, but its contents that drove its connection to the celebration of the gift of the Torah. In consideration of what appears to me to be a basic point for the reading of Ruth, I consider this to be a socio-legal commentary.

The book of Ruth portrays two heroines, Ruth and Naomi, and the reciprocal love between them. One might cynically notice that the affectionate relation between the two women demanded from the Israelite author that Ruth join the Judean community. But, on the one hand, their relationship begins in Moab, and, on the other hand, the emigration of Ruth is a response to a previous emigration by Naomi. Perhaps it is significant, nevertheless, that Mahlon and Chilion died without offspring. The story of Ruth not only depends on this special circumstance, but the author must have hesitated to give a future to "mixed marriages," from which the children would have been more Moabite than Israelite. The issue is so much clearer if, as is probable, the book of Ruth was written during the period of the ethnic purges under Ezra and Nehemiah (fifth century B.C.E.) or later—in an era, in any case, when this was a living memory.[4]

Besides, the emigration of Elimelek's family to Moab is, at the very least, surprising. From the perspective of the curses hurled against this country in the Torah and elsewhere, this may well be the last place that an Israelite would choose to take

---

any case, even in a levirate marriage only the first child is considered as heir of the deceased brother. The other children are de facto and de jure those of the levir. In the case of refusal by the brother-in-law of the woman, the *ḥaliṣâ* takes places, meaning release, symbolized by removing the sandal of the refuser. The meaning of the symbol is clear; see Louis I. Rabinowitz, "Levirate Marriage and Halizah," *JE* 11:122). In the NT, the levirate is mentioned in Matt 22:22-28 and par.; see K. C. Hanson, "The Herodians and Mediterranean Kinship. Part 2: Marriage and Divorce," *BTB* 19 (1989) 142–51; idem, "BTB Reader's Guide: Kinship," *BTB* 24 (1994) 183–94.

[4] The presence of a women's chorus, as in the Song of Songs ("daughters of Jerusalem"), is an additional indication of the comparatively late date of the story. Besides, one will see in the background of the story, marked by the famine, sterility, and death, a complex perfectly suiting the Judean people of the sixth century B.C.E. The alleged historical position—the period before the monarchy in Israel—also corresponds to the destruction of the monarchy by Babylon. Its resurgence with Zerubbabel in the fifth century was brief and without profound significance. The commentary by Victor Matthews goes in the same direction: *Judges and Ruth,* New Cambridge Bible Commentary (Cambridge: Cambridge Univ. Press, 2004).

refuge. Nevertheless, two reasons for this choice represent the spirit of the auth The first is that Ruth the Moabite, metaphorically, excellently represents "the oth... She was a woman in a man's world; she was a widow and without a child in a group for which infertility was a mark of shame; she was a foreigner and also an enemy— in short, she represents perfectly what psychology calls "the repressed." Her arrival in Bethlehem, inevitably, shakes the Judeans' sociopolitical foundations.

Second, Moab was historically the last stop at the time of the exodus from Egypt. This is the *transition* from the nomadic to the sedentary state. Leaving Beth-  lehem for Moab is a regression toward the prenatal, toward the unconscious. Naomi and Ruth do "return" to Bethlehem; but that was preceded by a "return" to their origins. The story of Ruth is a new beginning.

Moab also refused to help the Israelite emigrants on the road to the promised land. Ruth the Moabite, whose name means "to water," herself becomes the emigrant, soliciting welcome, food, and protection in Israel. All this while furnishing her hosts with what her ancestors had refused. This uncalculated mutuality, freely given (cf. Job 1:9: "Is this for nothing?"), assures Ruth's success. She tells her mother-in-law, from the older generation, "I will do all that you tell me" (Ruth 3:5). Also belonging to the older generation, Boaz echoes that declaration in saying to Ruth, "I will do all that you tell me" (3:11). As we shall see, Ruth's goodness is contagious, at least with those that are well born; she will transform Naomi and Boaz, and even "the whole people" (4:11).

Even the very sexual solicitations in chapter 3 are a way for Ruth to redeem her infamous ancestors (according to Num 25:1-3). Ruth the Moabite is the anti-Moabite. This is the reason the figure of Ruth—the story carries her name and concentrates on her existential options—remains a mystery. Unlike a Homeric hero, she does not exhaust her self by her actions. Three times the narrative asks the question of her identity, as if it was never certain. Boaz asks, "Who is this young woman?" (2:5). In  chapter 3, on the threshing floor, he asks the young woman, "Who are you?" (3:9). Finally, Naomi puts exactly the same question (literally) in 3:16. Ruth remains the unknown one, as one day another figure, with whom Ruth presents prophetic analogies, will ask, "Who do you say that I am?" (Matt 16:15), and will always remain a mystery (Matt 21:10 par.; Acts 9:5; 21:33; 22:8; 26:15).

It is true that one can also see in the story that occupies us an ideal picture of the Israelite mission as seen by an author of the Second Temple period. The exiled Judeans there are then considered as a net bringing back with them the "Moabite" convert. The ancient rabbis, in any case, in part based their rules for conversion to Judaism on the book of Ruth, pointing out that three times Naomi resists Ruth's desire to follow her to Judah. Note that this triple opposition is remarkable from a psychological standpoint, for it reveals Naomi's refusal "to swallow" Ruth and to possess her.

The devotion of the two women, to which it will be necessary for us to return, is such, according to the story, that they become mirrors for one another. Returning to

Bethlehem, Naomi, in her sorrow seeming to forget the presence of Ruth by her side, insists that her name henceforth is no longer "Charming" (this is what "Naomi" means) but "Bitter" (Mara). Now Ruth also could be called Mara, for she is also plunged into mourning, emptiness, and exile; and her lot is bitterness. This is the reason, moreover, that the restoration of the one occurs through the restoration of the other. There can be no joy for the one if there is no joy for the other. The entire story is on this theme.

One may compare Ruth and Naomi to another pair of same-gendered biblical characters: David and Jonathan. The parallel is clear, and nevertheless it is only partially valid. The two young men are contemporaries and compete with ambitious vitality. Here there is no sense of emptiness or bitterness, even if the end of their friendship is tragic. In the case of Naomi and Ruth, however, the affection is between two women, refuting the misogynistic pessimism of Aristotle on this subject. What is more, the two heroines are of very different ages: a mother-in-law and a daughter-in-law. Such a combination is exceptional between two women liking the same man, son and husband, respectively, and, according to the cliché, competing for his attention. Here the account turns more difficult again because of all the distinctives: ethnicity, religion, homeland, and language. One will see as we proceed, when we discuss the relations between Moab and Israel, that Naomi and Ruth theoretically could not be more foreign to one another. Their mutual devotion breaks all the social taboos.

Externally, besides incidental links, a single point connects them: their condition as widows. This is an almost hopeless condition, for, in a world dominated by men, they are without protection and their survival is in peril. What the orphans need is a father; what the widows lack is a dispenser of justice (*dayyān*). This is the reason God is called the father of orphans and the protector (*dayyān*) of widows in Ps 68:5 (MT 6).

When Ruth decides to accompany Naomi and to take care of her, Ruth becomes (in a sense) a husband for Naomi, before becoming a substitute mother for her sake. Not that Ruth loses any of her femininity or her personality. It is probably an error and an insult to imagine here the thought of incest between a mother (-in-law) and daughter (-in-law). Something "risky" is already discernible in the position of the two women before the introduction of even riskier scenes in the narrative. At a certain moment Naomi will seem to use Ruth as an intermediary, and Ruth will seem to assume the role of an immoral woman (see below for the rejection of such an interpretation).

Be that as it may, the paradox is obvious between a nourishing Ruth and a Naomi who, however, continues to call her "my daughter" (2:2)—doubtless a term of affection, but also a mask of authority. The role of husband alternates between them,[5]

---

[5] Ruth is not only Naomi's "daughter," or "husband" (Danna Nolan Fewell and David Gunn agree in *Compromising Redemption: Relating Characters in the Book of Ruth,* LCBI [Louisville: Westminster John Knox, 1990], 96, 103), or the mother of a child, she is also "a son" seven times over (4:13)! See also

which means that, when Boaz intervenes in their relation, he breaks the circ[.] nevertheless more as "redeemer" (גאל) than as husband that he is int[.] although the first condition necessarily involves the second in order to be r[.] From the outset, Boaz is assigned a role as redeemer (the one that has the [.] redeem, the mediator, the rectifier of wrongs).[6] His marriage to Ruth is more and legal than marital.[7]

On this subject Jon Berquist advances the interesting idea that, in a crisis situation, the "normal" evolution toward an ever greater variety of roles in society finds itself reversed.[8] In literature, characters see themselves constrained by events to accumulate (by "differentiation") various roles ("role addition"). Ruth, Naomi's daughter-in-law, also becomes her daughter (2:2, 22), her "husband" (1:14; cf. Gen 2:24) her "means of support" (Ruth 2:2), and mother of "her" child (4:17). Naomi, Ruth's mother-in-law, also becomes her mother and her father (3:1; in the Near East, fathers negotiate the marriage of their daughters). Boaz also becomes redeemer, Ruth's foster father (2:16; 3:15), her spouse, and the father of her child.

One notices, then, a deconstruction of the sexual roles. The women assume men's responsibilities; and in this direction also the narrative of Ruth is, as Berquist says, "subversive."[9] This point is important. It shows that, in the book of Ruth, the generous interpretation of the reality regarding a foreigner overflows the ethnic boundaries and transforms the view of the world. All the traditionally assigned roles and stereotypes are reconsidered and reinterpreted. The obliteration of curses against Moab (or on any other people judged by the community as "irretrievable") is also an obliteration of all constraining limits. Goodness (ḥesed) is liberating.

On the whole, the book of Ruth is a feminine book from beginning to end. Of course, as is necessary in a context of masculine primogeniture, the text starts by describing Naomi as "Elimelek's wife" (1:1), but very early the relationship is inverted and Elimelek becomes "Naomi's husband" (1:3). Moreover, in the story the men appear under a harsh light: they are absent at the time of the welcoming party for

---

Kristin Moen Saxegaard, "'More Than Seven Sons': Ruth as Example of the Good Son," *SJOT* 15 (2001) 257–75.

[6] Gottwald summarizes the functions of the redeemer in ancient Israel in four points: (1) in the case of the death of a relative without child, he takes his sister-in-law in levirate marriage in order to provide his deceased brother with an heir; (2) in cases of alienation of family property, he redeems it; (3) in cases of family members being enslaved for economic reasons, he redeems them and repays their debts; and (4) in cases of violent death of clan members, he is obligated to avenge it (Norman K. Gottwald, *The Tribes of Yahweh: A Sociology of the Religion of Liberated Israel, 1250–1050 B.C.E.* [Maryknoll, N.Y.: Orbis, 1979], 263–67).

[7] The rabbis recoiled at the wedding plans in the text and imagined that Boaz died on the wedding night, having accomplished his ritual function (*Ruth Zuta* 55; *Leqaḥ Ṭov* [Ruth] 4.17).

[8] True, the crisis is not produced from within the text, which is strikingly irenic, but the text is a response to an external crisis provoked by the decrees Ezra and Nehemiah. See Jon L. Berquist, "Role Differentiation in the Book of Ruth," *JSOT* 57 (1993) 23–37.

[9] Ibid., 36.

Naomi at Bethlehem; they appear as harvesters with vulgar manners in the field of Boaz; the anonymous kinsman of Naomi withdraws from his duty for shameful reasons; the child of Ruth/Naomi is welcomed exclusively by the women; and Elimelek, Chilion, and Mahlon play extremely minor roles. Introduced at the beginning of the story, they disappear until 4:9-10. Obed will not be the son and the grandson of any of them in the text. Besides, until then one did not know who had married whom, whose wife Ruth had been. Mahlon and Chilion are ghosts. When they were alive, they were already the living dead.

That leaves the town elders, who have a positive role but remain anonymous—with Boaz as the sole exception, of course. But Boaz is a more elderly man, with vague contours; in the story his personality is exhausted by his function, like a Homeric hero. As a בֵּן ("levirate son"), Obed is less Boaz's son than Naomi's (through an intermediary). "In him is strength"—that is what Boaz's name means—is the begetter, but his intervention is praiseworthy only within certain limits. Ruth had to risk her reputation and the tolerance of her community to get him to take his *gōʾēl* ("redeemer") responsibility. All this appears decisive to me for rejecting one of the suggestions of Edward Campbell according to which the narrative could have been composed by provincial Levites.[10] For the expansive interpretation of the Law (including a Moabite in the Judean community) can hardly come from this environment, even less given the description of them in 2 Chron 17:7-9. On the other hand, the other formative environment envisaged by Campbell, a group of "wise women," I find a lot more convincing (cf. Exod 15:21; Judg 5:11; 11:34, 40; 1 Sam 18:6-7; Jer 9:16-21).[11]

Ruth, one can say, is a book "in the feminine mode." Now, regarding every narrative, the reader has the right to wonder with which of its characters the author identifies (the most). There is little chance that it is with the Moabite. Boaz would be a valid candidate, but, to the extent that the book is written in opposition to the conservative party of the time, Boaz is less attractive than Naomi as a model. One can easily imagine an author seeing herself in a character that crosses a crisis of faith and emerges from this crisis thanks to the *ḥesed* of a "next of kin." Naomi, from many points of view, is the central character: Elimelek is "her husband" (1:3); Mahlon and Chilion are "her sons" (1:3-5); Ruth and Orpah are "her daughters-in-law" (1:6); Boaz is her kinsman (2:1); it is she who must be "redeemed," and she is the one who profits most at the end of the story (see 4:17). In short, Naomi sets the parameters of the whole narrative.

---

[10] Edward F. Campbell Jr., *Ruth,* AB 7 (Garden City, N.Y.: Doubleday, 1975), 21–22.

[11] Ibid., 22–23. It is even possible that the abundance of dialog is attributable to a woman author (fifty-five of eighty-five verses); see Carol Meyers, "Returning Home: Ruth 1.8 and the Gendering of the Book of Ruth," in *A Feminist Companion to Ruth,* ed. Athalya Brenner, FCB 1/3 (Sheffield: Sheffield Academic Press, 1993), 93. One will find a more detailed discussion on the question of women authors in the Bible in André LaCocque, "Methodological Presuppositions," in *Romance, She Wrote* (Harrisburg: Trinity, 1998), 39–53.

## Textual Criticism
### *Masoretic Text*

The MT offers a rather major confusion of the masculine and feminine forms (see 1:5, 8, 9, 11, 13, 19, 22; 4:11). It has been suggested that this is sometimes due to replacement of the feminine suffix by the masculine in late Biblical Hebrew.[12]

### *Qumran*

Four manuscripts from Qumran caves 2 and 4 relate to the MT: 2QRuth[a] and 2QRuth[b]; 4QRuth[a] and 4QRuth[b]. In 3:14 one has מ[רג]לתיו ("his feet"; see Q). In 3:16 one finds מה ("what") instead of the מי ("who") of the MT. These manuscripts are very fragmentary.

### *Septuagint*

The LXX closely follows the MT; it confirms reading תגאל ("you will [not] redeem") rather than יגאל ("he will [not] redeem") of the MT in 4:4; and the plural מגאלינו ("from our kinsmen") = Syr, rather than מגאלנו ("from our kinsman") of the MT in 2:20; and the singular of כנף ("wing/skirt") in 3:9 along with Q and Syr.

### *Syriac*

The Syriac offers a free translation, perhaps following the LXX, but all the while keeping an eye on the MT. The Peshitta shows serious reticence with regard to female anatomy: in 1:11, במעי ("my womb"); and in 4:16 ותשתהו ("laid him in her bosom") are lacking. In 4:5a וגם את ("and also") = Vg, rather than MT ומאת ("and from").

### *Targumim*

The Targums follow the MT. These are commentaries rather than simply translations. Their texts are twice as long as the original text.

### *Midrashim and Josephus*

*Ruth Rabbah* derives, in its final form, from the eleventh-twelfth centuries. *Ruth Zuta* is of obscure origin. Salmon ben Yeroham was a Qaraite who wrote in 940–960. The extant manuscript is from the eighteenth century in traditional Hebrew, but the author is Yephet ben Ali from Arabia, also a Qaraite, who wrote originally in Arabic. He was an opponent of the rabbis. Josephus (*Ant.* 5.6) parallels the Midrash.

---

[12] Cf. GKC §135o.

### *Rabbinic Commentators*

Rashi (1040–1105) employs *Ruth Rabbah* and the Talmud. Ibn Ezra (1092/ 1093–1167) distinguishes between *pĕšat* (first sense) and *dĕraš* (second sense). An anonymous rabbi (French, twelfth century?) follows the *pĕšat*. David Qimḥi (1160–1235) parallels Rashi.

## Style

The book is written in rhythmic prose. Ruth 1:16-17 is in poetic form, constructed in a series of bicola in the sequence of 3 + 3; 3 + 3; 2 + 2; 3 + 2; 3 + 2; 3 + 2.

Chiastic construction is frequently employed; compare the following:

- 1:3 and 1:5—husband and boys, boys and husband
- 1:8 and 1:12—goes and returns, returns and goes
- 1:9 and 1:14—kiss and cry, cry and kiss
- 1:20-21a and 1:21b—Shadday and Yhwh, Yhwh and Shadday
- 4:9 and 4:11—elders and people, people and elders
- 1:2, 5 and 4:9—Mahlon and Chilion, Chilion and Mahlon.

It is also important to note the symmetry between chapters 2 and 3 of the book. In both cases:

- Ruth leaves (2:3; 3:6)
- Ruth meets Boaz (2:5-7; 3:7)
- Boaz inquires about Ruth's identity (2:5; 3:9)
- Boaz asks Ruth to stay with him and then blesses her (or) blesses her and asks her to stay (2:8-12; 3:13)
- Boaz recognizes Ruth's *ḥesed* (2:11-12; 3:10-11)
- Boaz gives Ruth food (2:14; 3:15)
- Ruth returns and nourishes Naomi (2:18; 3:17)
- Ruth reports on Boaz to Naomi (2:19; 3:16b-17)
- Naomi advises Ruth (2:22-23; 3:18).

According to Stephen Bertman, there is also symmetry between the final genealogy and the introduction: both recount family histories.[13]

## • Literary Criticism

The book of Ruth is a unified work. Blinded by the kinship of Obed and Naomi, Hermann Gunkel imagined a rather fantastic scenario for the prehistory of the book.

---

[13] Stephen Bertman, "Symmetrical Design in the Book of Ruth," *ZAW 84* (1965) 165–68.

Naomi, a widow and past the age of fertility, gave birth to a son after the death of her husband. The character of Ruth was added later, which eventually became the novella as we know it.[14] Thus Gunkel missed the character of the book as an interpretation of the Torah.

In the same way, some have seen in Ruth a story for children, or a narrative in an oral version sung by a bard.[15] Or again, it is a folktale painted on canvas more or less comparable to the Russian narratives analyzed by Vladimir Propp.[16]

The concluding genealogy evidently presents a special problem since the preceding narrative is of a different literary genre. As we will see in the commentary proper, most commentators consider the genealogy inauthentic and added later as an appendix. But the arguments in favor of its authenticity are too numerous and important to overlook. One will notice, for example, the central place of Bethlehem in the narrative, the exact city to which the name of David is attached. On the other hand, as Kirsten Nielsen has shown in her commentary,[17] the structure of the book concludes as it begins *(inclusio)*. After ten years in Moab, Elimelek and his two sons die without children (1:1-5). Parallel to this, the end of the book counts ten generations of Israel culminating with King David (4:18-22).

As I will show in what follows, the book of Ruth is a novella, a short story where the situations and the characters occupy a more important place than the facts.[18] The story is short but includes numerous unexpected turns. There is no necessity of a villain in the story, and this allows maintaining a grand simplicity of composition. As a reminder, the potential villain in the story of Joseph has no difficulty submitting himself to Joseph's opinion or authority. In the story of Jonah, everyone converts to the God of Israel; even the sea monster is an ambiguous vehicle of deliverance.

The only rule of the novella is verisimilitude; it is a "history-like story." One does sometimes, nevertheless, reach the extreme limits of plausibility. For example:

- a fish swallows a man, who lives in its stomach for three days
- a Judean prophet speaks Assyrian
- a pagan country converts as a single person

---

[14] Hermann Gunkel, "Ruthbuch," in *RGG* 4:2182.

[15] For the former see Jacob M. Myers, *The Linguistic and Literary Form of the Book of Ruth* (Leiden: Brill, 1955); for the latter, Campbell, *Ruth*, 18–23.

[16] Jack Sasson, *Ruth: A New Translation with a Philological Commentary and a Formalist-Folklorist Interpretation*, 2d ed., BibSem 10 (Sheffield: Sheffield Academic, 1989), 18–23. See Vladimir Propp, *Morphology of the Folktale*, trans. Laurence Scott, 2d ed. (Austin: Univ. of Texas Press, 1968).

[17] Kirsten Nielsen, *Ruth: A Commentary*, trans. Edward Broadbridge, OTL (Louisville: Westminster John Knox, 1997), 2–5.

[18] If concentrating on intrigue, nevertheless one must say with Brevard Childs that this is "a highly artistic story which develops a plot through various scenes before reaching a climax" (Childs, *Introduction to the Old Testament as Scripture* [Philadelphia: Fortress Press, 1979], 562).

- an Israelite slave becomes the vizier of pharaonic Egypt
- an insignificant girl in the Judean Diaspora becomes queen of Persia
- a Moabite "stranded" in Judah goes by chance to glean in the field of the one who will, in an act of supreme generosity, become her husband in order to provide a descendant to a distant "cousin."

⬥ The novella of Ruth is clothed in a remarkable *form*, the folkloric story, as Jack Sasson has said, basing himself on the structuralist method of Propp.[19] He attributes the popular success of the book of Ruth to the literary habit that "leaves nothing that is unresolved, it becomes a self-contained entity."[20]

The resemblances between certain elements of the biblical novellas do not obscure certain intentional contrasts. Elimelek's migration toward Moab recalls Joseph's journey to Egypt, more so because of the marriages to foreign women. But in Ruth the scandal is made worse by the marriage of Boaz (an exemplary Israelite) to a Moabite immigrant, and perhaps already by the marriages of Elimelek's sons to Moabite women. Note also the parallel between the famine avoided in Egypt thanks to the wisdom of Joseph, and hunger/poverty transformed to abundance thanks to the goodness (*hesed*) of a Moabite. As in the story of Joseph, it is a famine (in Canaan/in Bethlehem) that pushed the Judeans to emigrate. The paradox, evidently, is that Bethlehem (which means "house of bread") is without food, while Moab—which had refused food and drink to the refugees coming from Egypt (Deut 23:3-4 [MT 4-5])—is the nourishing land chosen by Elimelek.[21]

In the novella of Ruth, all the names of the characters (except Boaz?) are without parallel. I will return to this in the analysis of Ruth 1:2. This is certainly a means the author uses of underlining that the narrative will show an exception that questions the rule. It begins with provocative events such as the emigration to Moab and intermarriages in a foreign and impure land. It even continues with the movement in the opposite direction of the Moabite going to Judah. Ruth speaks Hebrew (one expects that Mahlon would rather have learned Moabite). Israelite law is interpreted in a completely tendentious manner. The customs referred to are all old and obsolete (see 4:7). As I noted above, the male characters—with the exception of Boaz—are all passive, or openly hostile; in any case they show "the courage of women," while the women have "the courage of bishops," to repeat a fine retort of the Jansenist Port-Royal des Champs.[22]

---

[19] Propp, *Morphology*; Sasson, *Ruth,* 214.

[20] Sasson, *Ruth*, 216.

[21] Tod A. Linafelt, "Ruth," in Linafelt and Timothy K. Beal, *Ruth, Esther,* BerO (Collegeville, Minn.: Liturgical Press, 1999), 4.

[22] Jacob Neusner writes: "The femininity of Ruth is as critical to the whole . . . as the Moabite origin. The two modes of the abnormal (from the Israelite perspective)—outsider as against Israelite, woman as against man—are invoked, and both for the same purpose—to show how, through the Torah, all things become one." He adds: "If through Torah she can surpass her origins and gender, through Torah any born-

Following the example of other novellas with which I have already compared Ruth, this narrative is open-ended and apt to be developed further; for example, the story of the couple Boaz-Ruth, the Obed story, and the story of his descendants, in particular David. The same is true in the book of Jonah, in the story of Joseph, and others.[23] Without the genealogy, the narrative would be closed; with the genealogy, it remains open. The same applies to the patriarchal sagas—one also finds there narratives concluding with genealogies (see Gen 25:19-20; 30:20-24). It is necessary, therefore, to be cautious about making the negative argument concerning the genealogy standing at the end of the book—that this is in an unusual place. Things are not this hard and fast, and, as we have just seen, there are important precedents.

It is also necessary to recall the large proportion of recorded dialog in relation to pure narration. This phenomenon is unique in the Bible. Paul Joüon counts fifty-five verses as dialog out of a total of eighty-five verses.[24] The reason for this disproportion is the novella form. The protagonists evolve and change during the events as they interpret them: Joseph, the adolescent, is spoiled and "unbearable," but he becomes a wise and balanced adult. The young, timid Esther is moved by a determined will to act on behalf of her people. In Ruth this evolution is manifested through dialog, since the basic problem of the book is its hermeneutical agenda.

From this perspective, the ending of the book of Ruth relates the glorious outcome of events to their difficult beginnings, even if it entails presenting the astonishing detail of the quasi-shameful origins of King David, beginning with Perez having been born from an incestuous relationship between Judah and Tamar the Canaanite (Ruth 4:12; on this subject see *Jubilees* 41). Now the studies on ancient genealogies have shown that their composition depends on multiple purposes that one assigns to them in advance. So a genealogy generally reflects contemporary structures of authority.

Regarding our problem here: In what sense does the genealogy in Ruth 4 contribute to establishing the authority of David? From this vantage point, it frankly seems to go against the current. This is the reason some conclude that it could only have been created by opponents of the Davidic dynasty. One could think this way, on the contrary, if the book of Ruth was not concerned to show in this manner the divine election of the great king.

Of course, it may be that such a genealogy of David originated in an environment hostile to his dynasty—among Saul's supporters, for example. Its place now at the conclusion of the preceding edifying narrative of Ruth, however, evidently changes the perspective. One can also conclude that this is pure fiction from the author. Somehow or other, its use here is clearly subversive.

---

Israelite may become more than what he or she conceives possible" (Neusner, *The Mother of the Messiah* [Harrisburg: Trinity, 1993], 13, 111).

[23] The same situation prevails in Song of Songs—also a late composition.

[24] Joüon, *Ruth: Commentaire philologique et exégétique,* 2d ed., SubBib 9 (Rome: Pontifical Biblical Institute Press, 1986), 12.

At any rate, its center of gravity is not propaganda favoring David. David is here unquestionably the great king of an earlier era. It is precisely because he is undisputed that he serves a hermeneutical function here. The interpretation by generous amplification of the Torah, the testing as it does of characters, situations, and actions presenting huge legal difficulties, is the only correct one: the glorious culmination of what seemed to begin poorly, namely the birth of the messianic King David, is the proof of it. *Au contraire!* If one condemns Judah for his relations with Canaanites; Tamar's foreign origin and her recourse to incest; Perez as a mongrel; Rahab, ancestor of Boaz, for her "professional" activities; and Ruth for reasons similar to those concerning Tamar—then one also rejects David. For David, if one is to believe the book of Ruth, had a Moabite ancestor. In favor of the authenticity of such origins, one quotes 1 Sam 22:3-4, which shows unexpected relations between the young David, chased by King Saul, and the Moabites. Some insist on the improbability of this fictional attribution.[25] One thus disregards the polemical dimension of the book. The same is true of Jonah, a nonhistorical prophet, a fiction built on the mention of Jonah ben Amittai in 2 Kgs 14:25.[26] Ruth the Moabite is not historical, but a midrashic fiction built on the basis of 1 Samuel 22. As I have already said, such an elaboration would not be possible until a very long time after the fact.

Hence the whole genealogy of Ruth 4 is likely to be fictitious. That does not remove any of its impact, for ancient genealogies have no "historical" pretensions—as we use the term today. As I said above, they mirror a certain conception of contemporary power. That is verified here: the authority of the interpretation of the Law presented in the book of Ruth finds its foundation in the person of David. The greatness of the messianic king is not the result of impeccable antecedents, but the providential passage of history.[27] The same thesis led to the elaboration of the genealogy of Jesus in the Gospel of Matthew, which includes four "questionable" feminine ancestors, including Ruth. On this subject, one will notice that 1 Chron 2:3-15, which has a genealogy parallel to the one in Ruth 4, does not mention Ruth (but does mention Tamar, v. 4). In short, before and after the book of Ruth, there was no question of a Moabite grandmother of David.

In conclusion to this section, I note some prominent facts:

---

[25] Cf. A. A. Anderson, "The Marriage of Ruth," *JSS* 23 (1978) 172–73.

[26] See André LaCocque and Pierre LaCocque, *The Jonah Complex* (Atlanta: John Knox, 1981).

[27] At the time of the secession of the ten northern tribes, after Solomon's death, the rallying cry of the "rebels" is significant: "What do we have to do with the son of Jesse?" (1 Kgs 12:16). The apparent goal of these last words is to pull back the great king to humble station. It is not that he is selected by the Lord; he is simply "the son of Jesse." In similar circumstances, Jesus will also be designated as "the son of Joseph" (Luke 4:22). But it is remarkable that the opponents of David do not employ here a much more damaging expression, such as "the son of a Moabite." It seems evident, therefore, that such a legend around Ruth had not yet been born.

1. The genealogy of Ruth 4 is an integral part of the book.
2. The genealogy is fictitious; it wants to prove a point (*ad probandum*) and is consequently historically suspect.
3. The central fiction is the figure of Ruth the Moabite; she was invented because the case required it.
4. David is used here as the criterion of authenticity for a certain reading of the Torah, but he is not intrinsically the object of the narrative.
5. The fictitious genealogy concluding with King David corroborates the multiple indications that the narrative derives from a late date. The problem was then no longer the legitimacy of the Davidic dynasty, but an ultra-conservative interpretation of "scripture" in the service of power. Ezra and Nehemiah, for example, based their authority on such a reductionistic inter-pretation of the Law (particularly in its Deuteronomistic version).[28]
6. If the book of Ruth had been written as an apologia for David, one could have conceived of an author recruited from the members of the royal court—one scholar has even proposed the prophet Nathan.[29] But the goal of Ruth is quite different, and its author is probably a woman, a cultivated poet, on a par with the contemporaneous prophetess Noadiah, at the time of the governors accredited by the Persians (fifth century; see Neh 6:14). As such, the author of the book of Ruth is subversive.[30]
7. The theological value of the final genealogy of Ruth has been seen clearly by Hubbard. He writes that it "subtly recalled the steady, imperceptible hand of God's providence which had guided the story."[31]
8. Quite a long time necessarily had to elapse before one could dare to attribute a Moabite grandmother to the historical David—a woman who allegedly married an obscure Boaz, known only through genealogical lists (see 1 Chron 2:12). Boaz, nevertheless, is the only character's name known in the story related here. It is a historical anchorage inserted into the fic-tional narrative. To make the book into an apologia for David because his kingship "was a matter of discussion if not of outright controversy" does not rest on anything in the book of Ruth.[32] On the contrary, David is in no

---

[28] *Pace* B. M. Vellas, "The Book of Ruth and Its Purpose," *Theologia* [Athens] 25 (1954) 201–10.

[29] Cf. Murray D. Gow, *The Book of Ruth: Its Structure, Theme and Purpose* (Leicester: Apollos, 1992), 207–10.

[30] *Pace* David Rutledge, *Reading Marginally: Feminism, Deconstruction and the Bible*, BibIntSer 21 (Leiden: Brill, 1996), 26. Cf. André LaCocque, *The Feminine Unconventional: Four Subversive Figures in Israel's Tradition*, OBT (Minneapolis: Fortress Press, 1990). As Irmtraud Fischer says, the book "does not offer a revolutionary counterpart for women, but a politically realizable one" (Fischer, "The Book of Ruth: A 'Feminist' Commentary to the Torah?" in *Ruth and Esther: A Feminist Companion to the Bible*, ed. Athalya Brenner, FCB 2/3 [Sheffield: Sheffield Academic Press, 1999], 32).

[31] Robert Hubbard, *The Book of Ruth*, NICOT (Grand Rapids: Eerdmans, 1988), 22.

[32] Ibid., 42.

sense a matter of controversy here. Were it so, the whole story would be uniquely weakened: what would prevent one from drawing the conclusion that nothing good can come from a Moabite intruding on Israel in spite of the repeated legal prohibitions against Moab in every era of the people's history? On the contrary, the essential condition for the story to be effective is that David and his reign were completely glorious without question in the eyes of its first readers—in Judah (4:11) and in Israel (4:14, 17). There is not the least ambiguity in the fact that Obed becomes the ancestor of the great king. What is controversial in the book of Ruth is not David but Ruth the Moabite. The emphasis of the book is decidedly on its heroine. To demean Ruth to the level of an instrument of a superior (and masculine) cause is to reduce her to the status of a servant (see 2:13). This is to stop Ruth's progression arbitrarily at her initial level (now, the progression in the story goes from 2:13 to 3:9, then to 4:11, to 4:13, and finally to 4:17). It is probable that this process of robbing the heroine of her due and to favor a secondary masculine character (one thinks of the Song of Songs attributed to Solomon) is not to be suspected of conscious chauvinism; but the issue comes up too often in biblical research not to be irritating.

9. The ninth point is an appendix, for it exceeds the limits of the literary analysis of Ruth 4 and even of Ruth itself. If one can follow the sequence of the preceding arguments, one will consider with a certain sense of suspicion the thesis of postmodern literary critics on the subject of the claimed nonimportance of the author of a text for its comprehension. In reality, announcing the "death" of the author regarding his/her message is "greatly exaggerated." The "capital punishment" imposed on the author of a text in the name of the plurivocality of the text proceeds from ambiguity. Polysemy does not mean the absence of the author any less than implying the absence of a vector pointing toward (multiple) signification. The plurivocality must be a concert, not a cacophony; this is a series of variations on a theme, provided precisely by the author. This author reveals herself in the choice of circumstances and the sequence of her narration. It is unfair and wrong to take no account of this. One does not listen to a symphony by Beethoven without thinking about the composer, for his symphony is him! As Amos Oz writes, "The beginning of a story is always a sort of contract that the author establishes with the reader."[33]

Another argument in the opposite direction must be put aside. Some have compared Ruth from a literary standpoint to the story of David's succession, and have concluded that Ruth derives from the Solomonic era (tenth century B.C.E.). This is

---

[33] Amos Oz, *The Story Begins: Essays on Literature,* trans. Maggie Bar-Tura (New York: Harcourt Brace, 1999), 7.

what Ronald Hals did, for example.[34] But when Hals compares Ruth with the Succession Narrative of David (2 Samuel 9–20 + 1 Kings 1–2) and sees in both documents a theological reduction to providence as the modus operandi of God, a proof of their contemporaneity, he may be comparing apples and oranges. The two things being compared belong to completely different kinds, for one belongs to "history" (in the ancient sense of the term) and the other to fiction. In this last category, it suffices that the author restricts herself to verisimilitude. All sorts of elements of the story of Ruth are accumulated by the author precisely so that the reader does not mistake the fabulistic intent of the plot: the creation of a Moabite ancestress for David is one of the more flagrant ones; the migration of starving Judeans going to Moab belongs to the same historical impossibility; all the legal extravagances point in the same direction; the final genealogy is artificial; and so on. So even if the philological arguments requiring "late" constructions in the language of Ruth are dismissed one after the other (their accumulation nevertheless appears impressive to me), dating the composition back to the era of the judges fails the test.[35]

That did not prevent Campbell from drawing conclusions on philological bases. He insists on archaic language in certain parts of Ruth and dates the origins of the book to the time of the united monarchy in Israel (tenth century B.C.E.), but in written form during the ninth century B.C.E. But this suggestion is untenable. The archaizing style in the speeches of Boaz or Naomi reflects the talent of the author to distinguish between the appropriate vocabularies of the different generations. Campbell himself notices that Ruth, in 2:21, employs language of an older person in her quotation of the speech of Boaz.[36] This literary dexterity by the author is remarkable.

Here, as in the biblical novella generally, God's intervention is reduced to the strict minimum: the providential course of events. Hubbard writes: "At first glance, the book of Ruth gives a somewhat secular appearance."[37] Sasson, for his part, does not even mention any theology of Ruth.[38] God neither speaks in the book nor intervenes directly, except for the pregnancy of Ruth at the end of the narrative (4:13); again this intervention is silent. The rabbis, regarding this matter, underline that the name Esther means "hidden." This reminder is suitable here as well. *God is present*

---

[34] Ronald M. Hals, *The Theology of the Book of Ruth,* Facet Books 23 (Philadelphia: Fortress Press, 1969). The comparison in itself receives the attention of Linafelt ("Ruth," xxiv), but it seems much less convincing to me.

[35] Moreover, Bush raises eight late Hebrew examples in the book, which take us back to the era of the restoration, sixth-fifth century B.C.E. (Frederic W. Bush, *Ruth, Esther,* WBC 9 [Waco: Word, 1996], 18–30). Linafelt and Matthews find the argument convincing and insist on the transitional character of Ruth between Judges and 1 Samuel. The final genealogy introduces what follows (Linafelt, "Ruth," xx). Jean-Luc Vesco emphasizes the exact correspondence of Ruth 1:1 with Gen 12:10 and of Ruth 2:20 with Gen 24:27 and judiciously states that the anthological style is typical of the Second Temple period (Vesco, "La date du livre de Ruth," *RB* 74 [1967] 246–47).

[36] Campbell, *Ruth,* 17.

[37] Hubbard, *Ruth,* 66.

[38] Sasson, *Ruth,* 249. Contrast this with Vellas, "Book of Ruth," 204–5.

*in the narrative in the measure that the characters become his presence for one another.*[39] This theological characteristic corresponds perfectly to the interpretive conception of the Law as documented in the story. Ruth comes to God through the intermediary of her devotion toward Naomi. Such is the paradigm of Ruth.

In the same train of thought, it is Ruth's *ḥesed* (and Orpah's) that God emulates (1:8). Even the ambiguity of Ruth 2:20 reinforces this para-theological dimension of the book: one cannot decide on the basis of the text whose *ḥesed* did not abandon the living and the dead—God's or Boaz's.

Seen from another, supplementary angle, the whole book is undergirded by the idea of a fundamental change of fortunes. At the level of language, this change of fortune is expressed by the employment of the verb שׁוּב ("return"; see 1:6, 7, 16, 22; 2:6). Even the arrival of Ruth in Judah is a "return," for she participates fundamentally in the change of fortune.[40] Perceptive readers have seen in Ruth's "return" Lot's (and therefore Moab's) return to Abraham's family (Genesis 13; 19:36-37).[41] In Ruth 2:3 "chance" brings Ruth to the field of Boaz. Everywhere in the book, human agents initiate the course of the events. That the divine action is indicated indirectly led the author to employ the literary device of understatement.[42] The characters have recourse to prayer, and each is invariably granted (1:8-9; 2:12, 19, 20; 3:10; 4:11-12, 14).[43]

One will notice the consistent literary procedure of the book in the contrast of names of paired characters:

- Mahlon and Chilion (1:2-5)
- Orpah and Ruth (1:4, 14)
- "So-and-so" and Boaz (4:4-6, 9-10)
- Mara and Naomi (1:19; 4:12-17)

As McCarthy and Riley note:

> One of the outstanding qualities of the Hebrew short story is its ability to create characters who are both typical yet highly individual, who are ordinary and insignificant in

---

[39] "Each represents Yhwh for the other," says Francis Landy ("Ruth and the Romance of Realism, or Deconstructing History," *JAAR* 62 [1994] 303). From this perspective, one sees Ruth prostrate herself before Boaz (2:10) and call him "my lord" (2:13). A more exact example is again furnished by 4:13. Ruth "activates an aspect of Yhwh that is on the side of the alien, perhaps the feminine against the normative complacency Israel" (ibid.).

[40] The Midrash on Ruth 1:6 underlines this idea behind Ruth and adds that Ruth had already considered in her heart that Judah was her homeland. In 1:22, says the Midrash, it was as if she had always lived in Bethlehem.

[41] Bezalel Porten, "Theme and Historiographic Background of the Scroll of Ruth," *GCA* 6 (1977) 72. Harold Fisch, "Ruth and the Structure of Covenant History," *VT* 32 (1982) 435.

[42] Hals, *Theology*, 12: "a kind of underplaying for effect." Regarding Ruth 4:1 and the unexpected arrival of So-and-so at the gate of the town, the Midrash puts in the mouth of God, "Boaz did his part, Naomi and Ruth did theirs, I will do mine." Quoted by Yitzhak I. Broch, *Ruth: The Book of Ruth in Hebrew and English with a Midrashic Commentary*, 2d ed. (New York: Feldheim, 1983), 90.

[43] Absent in other books from the same era, such as Song of Songs and Esther.

their occupations and day-to-day existence, yet extraordinary in how they face challenge and adversity. . . . Yet it is through these very struggles that their greatness emerges.[44]

The procedure is not unprecedented in the Bible. One remembers other pairs of proper names, always with one of the two surpassing the other:

- Moses and Aaron
- Deborah and Barak
- David and Jonathan
- Esther and Mordecai
- Ruth and Naomi
- Rachel and Leah
- Deborah and Jael ~ HEAD DRIVER
- Jesus and John the Baptist

The contrasting parallel between them serves to give more color to the hero, as with Esther and Vashti, for example.

The pairs of characters find echo in a parallel theme in the dialogs. The speakers tend to employ the same terms twice (see below on 1:11-13, for example). By continuation of the principle of substitution, one often arrives at the result that, of the two, one is chosen and the other left. Mahlon will have a descendant, but Chilion will not. Ruth will have a remarkable line, Orpah will not (see 2 Sam 14:7; *T. Zeb.* 3). Boaz will be the redeemer, not So-and-so. One rediscovers influences from old sagas here in which the younger often supplants the oldest child, thus constantly placing in question the rigid application of the law.

The plan of the book is very simple. It follows the changes of fortune in the story to their conclusions as well as the movement of the characters from one place to another:

- 1:1-5     Introduction: Naomi's widowhood in Moab
- 1:6-18     First section: Naomi's return, Ruth's decision for Naomi
- 1:19-22     Interlude: arrival in Bethlehem
- 2:1-17     Second section: encounter between Ruth and Boaz (the field of Boaz)
- 2:18-22     Interlude: conversation between Ruth and Naomi
- 3:1-15     Third section: Naomi's plan and its implementation (on the threshing floor)
- 3:16-18     Interlude: conversation between Ruth and Naomi

---

[44] Carmel McCarthy and William Riley, *The Old Testament Short Story: Exploration into Narrative Spirituality,* MBS 7 (Wilmington, Del.: Glazier, 1986), 66, 69.

- 4:1-12    Fourth section: legal matters; Boaz inherits the land and Ruth (at the Bethlehem gate)
- 4:13-17    Conclusion: the birth of a son, the end of Naomi's misfortune
- 4:18-20    David's genealogy[45]

## Canonicity

Despite the mention by the Talmud that Ruth, like Song of Songs and Isaiah, "soils the hands" (= Holy Scripture)—which reveals the presence of an opposite opinion—one may consider the canonicity of Ruth as widely undisputed since antiquity (see Josephus, *Ant.* 5.9.1-4; Matt 1:5; Luke 3:32). The only problem is its location in the order of the biblical books (MT: among the "Writings"; LXX: after the book of the Judges). In favor of the MT, see *b. B. Bat.* 14b and *4 Ezra* 14:44-46 (an already testified order, therefore, in the first century C.E.). In favor of the LXX, see Origen and Jerome, who consider Judges and Ruth one book. Jerome admits that, for the Jews, Ruth was part of the Writings. In short, the order of the MT seems well established as the original.

## Date

The chronological formula with which the book begins, "in the days when the judges ruled," is quite fictitious. It nevertheless gives one pause. Why situate the story of Ruth in that era? First, this was evidently due to the final genealogy, according to which Boaz fathered Obed, who fathered Jesse, who in turn fathered David.

Second, the existence of Ruth is narratively situated shortly after the deplorable decision of Moab not to allow free passage to the Israelites coming from Egypt and the fornication of Moab's women with Israel's men. Moab is cursed. When Ruth appears, the memory of this dark incident had still not been dampened.

Third, it was necessary to evoke an earlier era when certain customs had currency, such as levirate marriage and the popular tribunal at the town gate. The atmosphere of the narrative is somewhat legendary because it re-creates an earlier customary, but exemplary, world.

Finally, the note in 1:1 transports the reader to an environment and an era marked by a certain abnormality. This point is particularly sensible if one places the book of Ruth, with Alexandrian Judeans, as the continuation of the book of Judges. That book concludes precisely on these words: "In those days there was no king in Israel; all the people did what was right in their own eyes" (Judg 21:25). Without transition, the book of Ruth then says, "In the days when the judges ruled. . . ." A very relative government! Indeed, a lawless time, which sets up a negative backdrop to a

---

[45] Rolf Rendtorff, *The Old Testament: An Introduction,* trans. John Bowden (Minneapolis: Fortress Press, 1986), 259.

story concerning the performance of the Law in circumstances particularly impervious to accept its accomplishment. "In the days of the judges," even the era contributed a certain obstacle to any creative interpretation of the Torah.

In addition to the philological arguments (the replacement of feminine suffixes with masculine, as we saw),[46] it is necessary to take into account the final genealogy that goes down to David, as well as the mention of Ruth 4:7 explaining the custom of taking off the shoe as obsolete at the time of composition.

But there is something more important. I already insisted on the main point that the book of Ruth is ultimately a commentary on the Law. To the background of the successive developments, there are legal texts: for example, on the intransigent anti-Moabite ostracism, mixed marriages, the right of gleaning, the right of redemption, levirate marriage, the zeal of Perez for the protection of priestly purity, the matriarchs of the historical people of Israel, the procedure of substitution, the adoption of a child, and so on. Now these basic passages are located in documents that are mostly (or maybe totally) exilic or postexilic. The ubiquity of Deuteronomy, in particular, in the substratum of Ruth is gripping, to the point that making an abstraction of the Deuteronomistic text would sterilize the narrative about Naomi, Ruth, and Boaz. The attitudes and the actions of the one or the others would make no sense.

- Why would a young woman exile herself to Judah when she is a Moabite?
- Why would she offer herself to a man from her mother-in-law's generation?
- Why would this man feel obliged to marry a Moabite?
- Why would this foreigner become a substitute mother? *SUROGATE?*
- Why would Obed be the son of two fathers and even of his grandmother?

Nothing is explained without the legal substratum, a legal substratum whose complexity in the book of Ruth is a sure sign of a composition during an era fascinated by this aspect of life and obliged to come to terms with rules as contradictory as Genesis 38, Deuteronomy 25, and Leviticus 18 or 22. The application of the Law according to the book of Ruth is the result of compromise motivated by an authentic desire for punctilious obedience.

Ruth 4:7 confirms this judgment. The text shows that the ceremonial custom of removing the shoe in cases of refusal by the "levir" to assume his responsibility, a custom appearing in Deut 25:9, had already fallen into disuse. If one objects that Deuteronomy 25 can reflect an ancient tradition and, consequently, one cannot depend on the date of the composition of Deuteronomy, the argument does not hold. During the era of Ruth's composition, the custom is again presented as valid and observable.

---

[46] Most of the philological arguments are not decisive. Cf. Susan Niditch, "Legends of Wise Heroes and Heroines," in *The Hebrew Bible and Its Modern Interpreters,* ed. Douglas A. Knight and Gene M. Tucker (Minneapolis: Fortress Press, 1985), 452; Hubbard, *Ruth,* 24 n. 9.

I have also indicated parallels to other (post-) exilic narratives such as the stories of Joseph, Job, Jonah, Daniel, and Esther. It is true that Ruth, in contrast to the other novellas that are fond of situating the hero in a foreign land, reverses the terms and places Ruth, the foreigner, in Judah; albeit faithful to its literary genre, the narrative of Ruth also begins as a Diaspora story, in Moab. In this case as in the others, the theme basically remains the response to a similar problem: Does God care for non-Israelites? Do they play a role in the history of salvation? To ask the question is already to break the rigidity of the religious isolationism of an Ezra or a Nehemiah. Now we have the confession of the latter that their ultranationalism did not proceed without internal opposition.[47]

The supposed Moabite origin of David is another point of contention regarding the dating of the book of Ruth. Considering the huge difficulties David had getting acceptance as the king of the united kingdom of Israel and Judah and as the essential conduit of the divine covenant with his people, it seems evident—as I have said—that his opponents would have seized such a perfect occasion to cast doubts on his origins to oppose his pretensions. Only long after David's reign, and at a time when his historic importance could no longer be minimized, did it become possible to speculate on the connection of David to Moab.[48]

The same argument holds true for the liberalism of the book of Ruth regarding foreigners. It is true that Moab disadvantageously distinguished itself during the conquest of Jerusalem by Nebuchadnezzar in the sixth century. But right after these events, Moab sinks into the shadow of insignificance. It became possible again, but with a subversive spirit, to present a Moabite residing in Judah.[49]

Those who, by a knowledgeable but vain juggling, attempt to date the book of Ruth early miss its principal dimension of subversive narrative. Its thesis, as it will appear time and again as we proceed, is that it is possible to perform the Torah in a

---

[47] Bernard Gosse even sees in Ruth an ideological parallel with 2 Sam 21:1-14 (regarding the Gibeonites "compensated" by David after their persecution by Saul). Here and there one has "value placed on openness to foreigners in the Davidic line. . . [which] was not without irony in the political context of the exclusion of foreigners, a policy adopted by the postexilic priesthood (Ezra 10:18-19)" (Gosse, "Subversion de la législation du Pentateuque et symboliques respectives des lignées de David et de Saül dans les livres de Samuel et de Ruth," *ZAW* 110 [1998] 45). Cf. also idem, "Le Livre de Ruth et ses liens avec II Samuel 21,1-14," *ZAW* 108 (1996) 430–33. Keep in mind that the dismemberment of Saul's sons by the Gibeonites with David's approval happens "on the first days of the harvest, at first harvest of barley" (2 Sam 21:9); I develop this point below on Ruth 1:22.

[48] If 1 Sam 22:3-4 alludes to deeper connections with Moab, then the harshness with which David is later supposed to have treated his "kin" (2 Sam 8:2; 23:20; 1 Chron 11:22; cf. 1 Sam 22:3-4) does not make sense. As Keith Whitelam comments: "the social practices presented in a text may not correspond to such practices in reality: they may be an attempt to subvert current social practices" ("The Social World," 40). What is true for the application of laws in the book of Ruth is also true for the genealogical tree of King David.

[49] In the same line of thought, it became possible to use ancient Near Eastern mythology in the book of Daniel, for example.

creative and flexible manner, opposing the suspicious and rigid ultraconservatism of the integration party. Moab can also have a place in Israel; the right of gleaning can apply to non-Israelites, even the right of redemption; the levirate as detailed in Deuteronomy 25 is open to a broad interpretation; and a rigid definition of feminine "modesty" is out of place. The sexual audacity of Tamar and Rahab the Canaanites; of Ruth the Moabite; and, through incest, of Lot's daughters, mothers of Moab and Ammon, must be judged leniently.

## Social Environment

One does not break down an open door. The book of Ruth arrived when its message constituted an exception. I evoked above the environment of the Second Temple as the constituent background of Ruth, a world portrayed in lively colors by the books of Ezra and Nehemiah. There the scribe became the head of the hierarchy, not only in the religious sphere but in the political and social as well. It is no accident that Ezra and Nehemiah are simultaneously religious reformers and governors of Judah. All the power is concentrated in their hands, and the measures they take to reorganize the Judean community after the exile are multidimensional. The Sabbath, for example, as they impose it, has religious, social, economic, and political repercussions (see Nehemiah 13).

In preexilic Israel, the authority of the kings rested on a right conferred directly by the Deity—especially according to the dynastic system of Jerusalem. The authority of the scribe-governor rests, as in modern Iran, on the exclusive interpretation of the sacred Scripture. Ezra is a "scribe of the law of the God of heaven" (Ezra 7:12; cf. Neh 8:1). He is able to come to the people with an interpretation of the Law that allows no divergence (Nehemiah 8). The Law is univocal, objective, and universal. Its correct comprehension dictates with precision the parameters of meticulous obedience to the divine will. All rebellious interpretation is punished by any available means, even beating or exile (Neh 13:25; Ezra 9; Nehemiah 9).

This background of Ruth is of fundamental importance. In this drama the three central characters are treated individually and in their mutual relations; but the society plays a framing role (physical, moral, and religious). Here, as in the whole Bible, the author considers as obvious the "high social context," as anthropologists call it. And this context remains so much more difficult to reach because it remains implicit. A special social experience, nevertheless, presided over the creation of the book of Ruth—in other words, a complex of self-identity, of needs and of interests; in short, a situation dictating the strategy.[50]

With Ruth we enter an agrarian economy based on production capacities, distribution, and consumption in the restricted framework of the מִשְׁפָּחָה ("family,

---

[50] John H. Elliott, *What Is Social-Scientific Criticism?* GBS (Minneapolis: Fortress Press, 1993), 54.

clan"—that of Boaz in particular).[51] As this socioeconomic framework of Ruth and Naomi disintegrated, the two women are left in a sort of emptiness, almost of nonexistence. Orpah rejoins her Moabite family structure, but Ruth chooses, against all expectation, the scarcity of Naomi (1:12-13).[52] This was, one can well imagine, a very serious decision.

One will remember that, according to a utopian but extremely significant tradition, every Israelite family had received as much cultivable land that a yoke of oxen could plow in a day (1 Sam 14:14), or as much as it was necessary to sow a certain quantity of seed (Lev 27:16). This indicates how important it was for a family to perpetuate itself and, consequently, how precarious a widow without a child was in absence of any means (agrarian or other) of subsistence.

In fact, the Hebrew term that designates a widow, אלמנה (Greek *chōra*), describes a legal position without parallel in our modern languages. This is someone who is: (a) a widow; and (b) without a son, son-in-law, or brother-in-law. The widow can inherit, according to all the codes of the ancient Near East except the codes in force in Israel. It is possible that the popular belief was that she was somehow responsible for the death of her husband. This would explain why widowhood was looked upon as something shameful. One gets an idea of the condition of the widow in 1 Kgs 17:12 (cf. Isa 54:4; Ruth 1:14, 18). Some widows were subjected to abuse, as the protests of the prophets demonstrate (see Mal 3:5).

The widow's options were the following: she could return to her father's house (see Gen 38:11), if she was allowed to return, for this was not an obligation except in the case of a priest's daughter (see Lev 22:13). She could also evidently remarry, except in the case of a daughter from a priestly family (see Ezek 44:22). Often, she lived by charity, as protected by the Law and the exhortations of the prophets (see Deut 10:18; Jer 49:11; Ps 68:5 [MT 6]). On the protection of the Law, see also Exod 22:22 (MT 21); Deut 14:29; 16:1, 11, 14; 26:12-13; 27:19. For the prophetic exhortations, see also Isa 1:17, 23; 10:2; Jer 7:6; Ezek 22:7. Certain widows found refuge in the temple (Ps 68:5-6 [MT 6-7]; Luke 2:37). In the earliest churches, widows were turned over to the care of the community (Acts 9:39; cf. Jas 1:27; 1 Tim 5:16).

This is the reason it was necessary to enact special legislation for their protection (besides the already quoted texts, see Deut 10:18; 24:17-22; Jer 49:11; Zech 7:10; Matt 23:14; Acts 6:1-6; *Apoc. Zeph.* 7:4; *4 Ezra* 2:20; *Sib. Or.* 2:76, 270-271; etc.). The abundance of passages already indicates the urgency of the relief. None of this, however, concerns Ruth. Being a foreigner, she is not covered by Israelite

---

[51] This clan system can explain a point of the popular blessing of Boaz in Ruth 4:11-12. The prosperity of Boaz is secured by the fertility of Ruth, his wife. The more the family enlarged itself in ancient Israel, the more the means of production were expanded.

[52] Orpah "is the majority of humankind living out its usualness on home ground" (Cynthia Ozick, "Ruth," in *Reading Ruth: Contemporary Women Reclaim a Sacred Story,* ed. Judith A. Kates and Gail Twersky Reimer [New York: Ballantine, 1994], 221).

"social security." The Law does not forget the foreigner, but the Moabites in particular were excluded. Ruth finally owed her survival to the personal goodness of Boaz and the shrewdness of her mother-in-law Naomi.[53]

The socioeconomic framework is therefore decisive. It will be strongly asserted in the last chapter of the book, portraying the legal gathering of the "elders" at the gate of the town. The final judgment concerning what is allowed or prohibited falls to them.[54]

This last point is important. The characters in the narrative do not constitute an archipelago of independent and autonomous individuals. Even if the spotlight is on certain of them, while the "others" remain largely anonymous, and even though they distinguish themselves from the crowd by their broader and generous interpretation of the Law, it is a matter of the Law of their people (by birth or adoption): Torah is their common wisdom and their culture. Thus to comprehend the book it was necessary to introduce Ruth the Moabite as adopting this culture, which used to be foreign to her. The book does not intend relating the story of Ruth taken individually but wants to integrate her within Israelite history (again the decisive importance of the final genealogy is thus emphasized).

Now, in the ancient world (and with a lot of contemporary peoples), common wisdom and culture are the fruit of a complex kinship system (all the Israelites "descend" from common ancestors). For the story of Ruth to make sense, it is necessary for Ruth to become the "daughter" of Naomi (בתי; see 2:22; 3:1) before becoming Boaz's wife.

The problem of the foreigner is therefore clearly central. It had become a point of contention during the fifth century and, as we shall see, divided the population into opposing parties. The Holiness Code shows a lively interest in the question of the foreigner in Israel (see Lev 19:33ff.; 25:23 par. Deut 10:14-19; Lev 25:35ff.). A *gēr* is subjected to the rites of purification, but is never considered an Israelite. It is on this basis that administrative authorities forbid and dissolve mixed marriages (see Ezra 9:11; 10:2; Neh 13:28-31; cf. 13:9). No reference is ever made to a *gēr* becoming a proselyte. Isaiah 56:1-7 envisions this possibility only as the result of a new revelation. Isaiah 56:3 ironically "consoles" Nehemiah to be a eunuch by associating the eunuch with the gentiles (whom Nehemiah attempted to expel).

In this same line, one finds in the literature of the Second Temple narratives such as Joseph marrying an Egyptian, the daughter of an Egyptian priest. He has children, Ephraim and Manasseh, who are legitimized by Jacob. Jacob blesses them and

---

[53] On this issue, those that would want to present Naomi as a procurer (see below on Ruth 3) do so in spite of the social and economic context of the period, to say nothing of what the author has herself reported as providential. See the commentary on Ruth 3.

[54] According to Erhard Gerstenberger, this is the location at the origin of all Israelite legislation ("Covenant and Commandment," *JBL* 84 [1965] 38–51; idem, *Wesen und Herkunft des 'apodiktischen Rechts,'* WMANT 20 [Neukirchen-Vluyn: Neukirchener Verlag, 1965]).

places them on the same plane as his own sons (Gen 41:50-52; 48:1-20; cf. 43:32, probably understood as an ironic and polemical point with regard to the nationalist tendencies and "racism" of Jerusalem). Another narrative, the one about Jonah, shows sailors of various countries offering a sacrifice to Yhwh. Achior in the book of Judith is an Ammonite. Nebuchadnezzar himself repents and worships the God of Daniel (see Dan 2:46; 4:1-3 [MT 3:31-33]; 6:26-27). And the incarnation of evil, Antiochus IV of Syria, recognizes his faults while on his deathbed, according to 2 Maccabees 9.

All these examples show that the Second Temple period was an era of deep polarization of the people. While the governors designated by the Persian power "cleansed" the Jerusalem community of its non-Judean elements, another tendency (some other faction?) put in question the exclusivity rights of God's election.

The book of Ruth contributes to the development of an idea already inaugurated by Deutero-Isaiah. One recognizes the audacity of this sixth-century prophet saying, for example, that God speaks "to his anointed, to Cyrus" (Isa 45:1). The prophet was imitated by priests in Exod 12:43-50; Num 9:14; 15:1-31; 19:10; 31:15; Deut 29:10-12 [MT 9-11]; and Josh 20:9. The "sojourner" (גֵר) is integrated into Israel in later editions of the Pentateuch. The term גֵר then designates the "proselyte" and a new term is invented for the foreign resident, the תּוֹשָׁב ("settler"). Through this compromise, the assimilationist party proposed to resolve the issue of the mixed marriages.[55]

It is clear that, in our reading of the book of Ruth, it is necessary to understand the term "foreigner" in its most powerful sense—not only on the geographical plane, but on the philosophical plane. The foreigner is the one that questions the habits and traditions, especially when these became purely labels. The drama of Kafka, for example, is that one is perpetually a foreigner. Even his presence is unbearable to the "native." In asking questions, "K. has already violated a taboo which the natives have the secret to without being able to reveal it. Or again, the foreigner is in the same position as the child whose curiosity is always suspected to be attracted to prohibited things."[56]

From the sociological standpoint as well, the modern reader may not make Ruth into an exceptional heroine in a heroic romance. Her story is paradoxical and edifying, but she is very much within the legal and customary system of Israel. If one makes an abstraction of this framework, it leaves nothing to Ruth. Her "heroism" is

---

[55] Cf. Morton Smith, *Palestinian Parties and the Politics That Shaped the Old Testament* (New York: Columbia Univ. Press, 1971). In the Midrash, the dispute between Doeg and Abner depends on the interpretation of the law regarding the Moabites. Doeg alleges that the Moabite ancestry of David made him inoffensive vis-à-vis Saul. Abner did not share this optimism. Samuel gives Abner reason, for the law affects only the Moabite and Ammonite men, not the women (see *Ruth Rab.* 2.5; *Shemuel* 22.109-110; *b. Yeb.* 76b; *m. Yad.* 4.4; *t. Yad.* 2.17). See Louis Ginzberg, *The Legends of the Jews,* trans. Henrietta Szold, 7 vols. (Philadelphia: Jewish Publication Society, 1909–38), 4:88.

[56] Marthe Robert, *Kafka* (Paris: Gallimard, 1960), 95 and n. 1.

MIMICRY

to become more of a Judean than those who are Judean by birth! Retrospectively, one can say that her fidelity toward the people and their God provides a lesson to those who should have been her teachers.

Is there also a lesson for the modern reader (Jew or non-Jew)? Yes. It consists in rediscovering that the essence of the Torah is love. When the Law is not interpreted according to the amplification principle that love dictates, it is stifled and dies. This is, I think, the raison d'être for the book. It rebels against a restrictive reading that attempted to prevail in this era in Jerusalem. It was a time of theological reflection. The circumstances of the return from Babylon did not correspond to the prophetic promises of the exilic era. One recourse was to examine the written testimony to see in what ways the people did not fill the conditions for realizing the prophecies. First, it was necessary to understand them well; this is the reason a new function was created, the scribe—in other words, the specialists in Scripture. Ezra is a סֹפֵר מָהִיר ("an intelligent scribe"; cf. Ezra 7:6, 12; Neh 8:1). Nehemiah 8:8 describes him as teaching the exegesis of the "book of the law of God."

As Michael Fishbane has shown, exegesis is interpretive: "When Shechaniah remarks that 'the Torah must be observed,' he is presumptuous, for what this strictly means is that the *interpretation* of the Torah *as developed in this circle of exegetes* was to be followed."[57] As one knows, this forced the expulsion of foreign women and their children from the community. Their motivation appeared to them based on a solid tradition. An important passage to which Ezra makes a "deliberate allusion" is located in Ezra 9:1-2. The list of the excluded countries increased by several members the seven mentioned in Deut 7:1 on the basis of Deut 23:3-9 (MT 2-8) with "an intentional exegetical attempt to extend older pentateuchal provisions to the new times."[58] Moab figures among these additions.

Such an exclusion of the Moabites from Israel is officially proclaimed during the time of the governorships of Ezra and Nehemiah (see Ezra 9:1; Neh 13:1). It is not certain, however, that the decision was effectively followed, for the book of Ezra concludes abruptly without telling us if the foreign women were actually expelled. Besides, we know that there was opposition from the prophetess Noadiah and "the rest of the prophets" (Neh 6:14). One can expect that they too could base their position on tradition. All exegetical opposition based on pentateuchal texts had to establish two points. First, it had to explore the Deuteronomic traditions as "the princes" had done in their complaint addressed to Ezra (9:1-2) and show the validity of their different interpretation. Second, it had to choose at least one of the other countries added to the list ("Ammonites, Moabites, and the Egyptians," Ezra 9:1) and establish the parameters of the application of the law.

Now, this is precisely what the book of Ruth does. It chooses—not the Ammonites or Egyptians as one might have done—but the Moabites. The reason is,

---

[57] Michael Fishbane, *Biblical Interpretation in Ancient Israel* (Oxford: Clarendon, 1985), 117.
[58] Ibid., 115–16.

PURITY

as Fishbane has also shown, that in the problematic era of Ezra the impurity of the country played a major role. This impurity, in particular, is the Canaanite practice of incest (Ezra 9:11 in reference to Lev 18:6-7). "The latter being precisely the outrage practiced by the daughters of Lot, who conceived and bore . . . Ammon and Moab (Gen 19:31-38)!"[59] This casts new light on what Ruth the Moabite represents. Besides the perversity of her people in the "plains of Moab" recounted in the book of Numbers, she personifies a country "stained by incest in their lineage" in the eyes of Judeans seized by "the obsession with ethnicity."[60] Ruth resumes afresh the Moabite question, as the book of Judith will do with the Ammonites and Tobit 7 with the Samaritans and Ammonites.[61] Their plea was not successful, as testified to at Qumran, where the Moabites are associated with the Ammonites, the mongrels, and those with crushed penis and testicles. The Moabites are among the eschatological enemies of the faithful, according to the War Scroll. On all this, see 4QMMT 40-53 (= fragment 2); and 4QFlor 1:4.

A book such as Ruth is subversive by definition: it insists on the role of women in the Israelite community; on the Moabite origin of its central heroine and of her illustrious descendant, David; as well as on a liberal interpretation of the Torah.[62]

What is criticized, then, is not only a certain exegesis of the Law and a certain application of order, but the very special principle of the social form of the community. The choice of a Moabite *dramatis persona* in this context is illuminating. Since, according to Ruth, the light of the Word (or public discourse) is concealed by negative internal forces, it is necessary to reintroduce an external one so that the dynamics of the text are subtended by a movement that is not merely physical, from Moab to Bethlehem.

In short, Ruth does not represent a simple dispute between different schools. Even less is it a matter of a confrontation between legalism and lawlessness. Prefiguring what will emerge as a major problem in the Gospels, what is in question here is a hermeneutical issue regarding the Law. It involves a hermeneutic of power, the socioeconomic and political system. By her nature Ruth is marginal, because she is

---

[59] Ibid., 119.

[60] Ibid., 120, 114.

[61] Bertholdt was the first one, apparently, to have suggested that Ruth is a polemic against the measures taken by Ezra and Nehemiah regarding foreign women (1816). A variation is to see in Ruth the thesis that God employs the rejected of society to bring salvation (Helmut Lamparter, *Das Buch der Sehnsucht*, BAT 16/2 [Stuttgart: Calwer, 1962], 19). Another is to see how a later narrative redeems past events and inserts them into the framework of *Heilsgeschichte*; Fisch, "Ruth and Structure," 435–36. All these suggestions are essentially correct and are not mutually exclusive.

[62] Walter Brueggemann speaks of biblical rhetoric as being entirely "the relentlessly critical, subversive, and ironic voice of the text, which sets itself endlessly against more conventional and consensual speech." It is "a political act" (Brueggemann, *A Social Reading of the Old Testament: Prophetic Approaches to Israel's Communal Life,* ed. Patrick D. Miller [Minneapolis: Fortress Press, 1994], 130, 131, *et passim*).

marginalized. This is a document for the minorities of every time and every place. Its message is revolutionary because it orients toward solutions marked by *hesed*—that is, generosity, compassion, love. According to the book of Ruth, the center of the Torah is *hesed*, love. Love redeems everything. Then the impasses open up, the foreigner is no longer foreign, the widow no longer a widow, the sterile woman (or so considered) gives birth, the lost property is returned to the family or the clan, the interrupted story resumes its course and is crowned by the advent of "David." More profoundly, the Law is no longer a means of control and power (at times of manipulation), but the instrument of peace, reconciliation, and equality. All the legal categories are transcended by an interpretation according to an amplifying and nonrestrictive norm. This is the reason the book of Ruth reminds one of the hermeneutic of Jesus.

Some have contrasted the warm reception of Ruth in Judah, even though she is a foreigner, with the uncomfortable position of Esther in Persia, for example, due to her Judean origins. But here again there is misunderstanding. In their return to Judah, the Judean women welcome Naomi, but Ruth passes unnoticed. Later, Ruth is treated with respect by Boaz and by Boaz only. The harvesters are riled up by the presence of a Moabite, that is, according to the stereotype, of a woman with loose morals, in their midst. These men represent without any doubt the popular opinion that, in chapter 4, will be illustrated, one could say, by So-and-so. Boaz's greatness is precisely his understanding, on the subject of Ruth, what the others do not understand. The elders of Bethlehem adjust themselves to his opinion, finding his "exegetical" arguments convincing. This was probably not their attitude beforehand. After this flash of lucidity on the part of these Judean men, they are totally eclipsed. Female neighbors share the joy of Obed's birth. The men apparently remain very reserved with regard to a Moabite in their midst. The parallel with the book of Jonah is again startling. In Jonah, clearly a postexilic work, the author presents the worst enemies of Israel, the Assyrians. But these people demonstrate a willingness to repent that makes Israel jealous.[63]

In short, the message of the narrative is not at all as irenic and calm as those who favor a preexilic date claim. The book of Ruth is antiestablishment. It is doubly subversive: as a "feminist" book and as hermeneutical key of the Law.

This character of the book evidently posed the problem of its canonization by a party known for its conservative tendencies. This problem is equally posed regarding the subject of other biblical books. One thinks about the books of Job or Ecclesiastes or again the Song of Songs. "The canon," say Christopher Rowland and Mark Corner, "is in one sense a domestication of awkward ideas; but in another sense, in the very process of domestication it contains within itself the minority opposition ideas. The formation of a dominant ideology involves the incorporation of the opposition

---

[63] LaCocque and LaCocque, *Jonah Complex*.

ideas—which means that they are not completely lost and are therefore recoverable by means of patient analysis."[64]

## Theology

The book of Ruth as hermeneutical method—in other words, according to an expansive interpretation of the Law—comports with a theological insight of the first order that one can summarize briefly: *God is greater than his Law.* In spite of the legal norm according to which "you shall not marry a Canaanite" (Gen 28:1; Isaac's order to Jacob), Judah marries one of them (38:2) and has several children. He also chooses a Canaanite as a daughter-in-law in the person of Tamar. The rest of the story is well known. Finally, Judah has two sons by his incestuous relations with Tamar, one of them being Perez. All this would be sordid enough if it was not for the providential passage in the background of the story: God prohibits all dealings with foreigners, but in this case his plan is accomplished through the foreigner!

In the story of Ruth, the commandment transcends the Law; or to say it differently, the haggadah is the indispensable frame of reference for the halakah.

Elsewhere I developed the astonishing biblical contrast between Law and commandment.[65] I return to it here regarding the central issue in Ruth of *ḥesed,* for the word is an opening on an interpretation of the Law that surpasses the letter. One could believe that this view is more Christian than Jewish; but, significantly, this is a virtue that the early rabbis recognized within earlier Hasidim. They proceeded "beyond what the Law asks" (לפנים משורת הדין), a technical expression applied in the Talmud to charismatic individuals whose interpretation of the texts through *ḥesed* brought them to accomplish commandments beyond the letter.[66] *Ḥesed* is the virtue of excess.

The book of Ruth is speaking of the same principle, but from a highly paradoxical standpoint: a non-Judean shows the way to the Judeans, precisely in an era where the respect of the letter had become the very condition of membership in the Second Temple community. Ruth thus appears as the essential external element able to break legal rigidity, by which the literal respect would result only in bitterness and the death. Before attaining the economy of *ḥesed* herself, it is according to the letter of the law that Naomi is thinking (1:20), at the threshold of an extraordinary evolution that will transport us to a supralegal level. Only by the transgression of the law—(לפנים משורת הדין) says the Talmud[67]—is there a future and a life. Rabbi Zeira asks,

---

[64] Christopher Rowland and Mark Corner, *Liberating Exegesis: The Challenge of Liberation Theology to Biblical Studies* (Louisville: Westminster John Knox, 1989), 145.

[65] André LaCocque and Paul Ricoeur, *Thinking Biblically: Exegetical and Hermeneutical Studies,* trans. David Pellauer (Chicago: Univ. of Chicago Press, 1998), 99–109.

[66] See *b. B. Qam.* 103b *et passim.* Campbell speaks judiciously of the "plus factor" (*Ruth,* 110). David Atkinson speaks of "love beyond the law" (Atkinson, *The Wings of Refuge: The Message of Ruth* [Downers Grove, Ill.: InterVarsity Press, 1983], 110).

[67] The expression *lipnîm miššûrat haddîn* is employed regarding Naomi by the Midrash on Ruth

"Why was the scroll of Ruth written? One does not find any laws there on purity and impurity, or on the subject of what is allowed and prohibited. It was written to tell us that the reward is great for those that distinguish themselves by their acts of compassionate acts and love" (*Ruth Rab.* 2:14). Later, Rabbi Carlebach commented: "This book . . . teaches us that we must go well beyond what is prescribed. We must crown every precept with the *gemilut ḥasadim*, compassionate love."[68]

The Mishnah of Rabbi Eliezer says that the whole book of Ruth is written on the subject of *ḥesed*, as is the whole Torah as well; this is why, he says, the book is read at the Feast of *Shevuot*, celebrating the gift of the Torah (and not for Passover, as the beginning of the book would imply). The principle is invoked again by Rashi on the subject of Ruth 2:7. Boaz orders his harvesters to go beyond the law of gleaning. In 3:11 Boaz promises Ruth to go "beyond his vows" (legal), according to *Iteret Yekutiel.* Finally, on 4:4 the Midrash underlines the succession of the verbs קנה ("buy") and גאל ("redeem"), the second qualifying the first. קנה indicates a commercial transaction, but גאל indicates a transaction implying sacrifice—even a considerable sacrifice—by the redeemer so that the property remains in the family. This act of redemption by Boaz, says the Midrash on 4:9, redeemed the disgrace of those that left for Moab and whose names are repeated here by Boaz (Mahlon and Chilion).[69]

The messianic way transcends the letter of the law. Its point of departure is Ruth the Moabite, whose *ḥesed* is the absolute beginning of a dynastic history illustrated by her great-grandson, David.[70] History continues the initial ambiguity during the reign of the great king, who is powerful in deeds in the religious and political domains but weaker of character in his personal life. This is in flagrant contrast with the person of his ancestress Ruth, except for her Moabite origins, always marred, in Israelite memory, by the amorality "in the plains [plateaus] of Moab" at the time of the exodus (Numbers 22–23; 25:1-2), and, going back even further in time, by Lot's incest with his daughters (Gen 19:30-38).[71] We find ambiguity again in the episodic prostitution of Tamar, mother of Perez, ancestor of Boaz (Genesis 38), which is clearly echoed in the scene of Ruth 3, in the adultery of Bathsheba (2 Samuel 11), in the suspicious "virginity" of the עלמה (LXX *parthenos*) in Isaiah 7 or of Mary in the Gospels. The scandal—in other words, the nonrespect of the Law by accumulated

---

1:7. The Midrash interprets the phrase בדרך ("on the way") as the holy transgression of the Passover festival by Naomi in her haste to return to Israel.

[68] Quoted by Broch, *Ruth,* 8.

[69] Campbell writes that the *gō'ēl* has the additional task to reestablish justice poorly interpreted by someone following the letter of the law.

[70] On 2:14 the Midrash says that Boaz's invitation to Ruth to share a simple meal is the beginning of Israelite messianic history. It presents the same suggestion on the subject of the enlarged ל (*lamed*) of ליני in 3:13: this is the first night of a new era.

[71] According to Fewell and Gunn, the goal of the narrative in Genesis 19 was to contrast Israel's origins, promised by God and accomplished by miracle, to the origins of Moab and Ammon harking back to incest (*Compromising Redemption,* 69). In *Jub.* 16:8-9 one finds a harsh condemnation of this incest; the peoples coming from this unparalleled infamy are sanctioned by God to annihilation.

transgressions—is emphasized precisely in the Gospel (Matt 1:1ff. mentions in the genealogy of David and Jesus four women [five, if one counts Mary], all "scandalous" regarding the letter of the law). At every level this "transgression" is sanctified, even including Moab's incestuous origins, in the person of Ruth, who redeems the promiscuity of her ancestors through her *hesed* (Genesis 19).

Regarding this subject, one will see in the continuation of this commentary other correspondences of the narrative with Genesis 19. Yair Zakovitch mentions the following parallels:

1. In both stories there is a man and two women.
2. Both mention the deaths of men: Lot's sons-in-law, who remained in Sodom, and the two sons of Naomi, who remained in Moab.
3. In both it is a question of the destiny of emigrants.
4. In both the women seek to resolve the problem of descent.
5. It is the older woman who provokes and prepares the encounter with a man.
6. Lot and Boaz drank (Gen 19:32-33; Ruth 3:7).
7. In Genesis it is Lot's daughters who take their father to bed; in Ruth the woman is called by Boaz, "my daughter" (3:10).[72]

It is necessary therefore to see Ruth as marking a detour with regard to the Torah. But it is necessary to know exactly why. Now it is precisely with respect to the Law that the "disobedience" is significant. Without the Law, the command to sacrifice Isaac is only an additional illustration of the religious mentality of the ancient Near East. It is in the name of the Law that Judah condemns his daughter-in-law to death; and, when he "forgives" her, he in turn participates in her transgression. Ruth's *hesed* is doubly extraordinary, in her origin (coming from Moab) and in its reference, since it is in the name of faithful obedience to *the commandment*, since no law obliges Ruth the Moabite to do anything (see 1:8-15). If the fiction had presented a holy woman of Judah, the story would have been clothed in totally different dress. It would then be a question of respecting the Law, maybe despite all opposition, and the reforming point of the current narrative would be missing. From parable, the story of Ruth would have become apologue. An apologue could date back to any time period, before or after the exile. On the contrary, if the current story of Ruth is to be understood in the field of tension between Law and commandment, it cannot have been composed during any other era than when such a tension was the expression of an existential problem: the legalistic period of Ezra and Nehemiah.[73]

---

[72] Zakovitch, *Das Buch Rut: Ein jüdischer Kommentar,* trans. Andreas Lehnhardt, SBS 177 (Stuttgart: Katholisches Bibelwerk, 1999), 50.

[73] This legalistic mentality is extended when the scandal of a Moabite's entry into the assembly of Yhwh (Deut 23:3 [MT 4]) is short-circuited by an ultraconservative rereading. The prohibition then concerns only the men of Moab and of Ammon, not the women. Now, not only does Nehemiah's dis-

To give priority to the commandment over the Law is absolutely subversive. Respecting the letter of the law is conservative. The audacity to consider that the true performance of the Law consists solely in transgressing its letter is revolutionary. From literary and ideological standpoints, the tension between the two options is maintained in the Israelite tradition by the dynamic relation between the halakah (the "prescriptive" in the tradition) and the haggadah (narrative). The literary richness of the book of Ruth is buttressed by the coexistence of these two components. What connects them here is *ḥesed*—in other words, that which goes beyond common or legislated morality.

Examples of *ḥesed* in the book of Ruth follow one after the other. They include Ruth's devotion to her mother-in-law, the offering of herself to Boaz at the threshing floor, Boaz's extravagant offer to marry her in the name of the *gěʾullâ*—which by legal definition in no way includes such a marriage (see Lev 25:25-30, 47-55; Jer 32:1-15; and Num 35:12, 19-27). If this ethical-religious context is ignored, the scene at the threshing floor (chap. 3) and the initial recommendation of Naomi to her daughter-in-law (3:1-4) become an episode of the worst taste (some readers have fallen into this trap).[74] *Ḥesed* alone elevates the act of Naomi and Ruth and the reaction of Boaz from the trivial to the sublime, from the sordid to the sacred.

Here again, the Law is not absent; it is even invoked by Ruth, who mentions the *gěʾullâ*—a surprising phenomenon from a non-Judean. But it is mentioned only to be surpassed; for if Boaz remains fastidious about the Law, nothing of what Ruth expects will come to pass. The dialectic is tight: Ruth reminds Boaz that he is a man of the Law, so that he may conclude that this same Law is relative! One understands Boaz's astonishment before the extreme audacity of this Moabite. If the story had presented a man indifferent to the Law, there would be no dialectic here. Boaz would be the image of all those that, before and since Henry IV, judged that "Paris is well worth a mass!" But it is nothing of the kind. Boaz is characterized in the story as a moral man, a principled man of a certain age.[75] He is without impetuosity, somewhat overtaken by the events (in any case before chap. 4), but wise, conservative, most respectful of laws and customs. What Ruth requires from him is without any doubt strange and even foreign, coming, as it were, from a "Bohemian." What changes his opinion is this young woman's *ḥesed*. He will accept her challenge, and thereby he

---

missal of foreign women become incomprehensible, but so does the Jewish tradition of Mahlon and Chilion dying because they married Moabite women (it is true before Boaz made the edict of the new interpretation of Deut 23:3-4 [MT 4-5]). The Targum says that the new law was enacted by Boaz himself in response to the question of Ruth in 2:10 (see also *Ruth Rabbah*). One will appreciate the suspicious matter of the decision of Boaz! One will also note the reduction of the profoundly moving poetry of Ruth 1:16-17 to a question of "cubits" allowed during the Sabbath (thus Talmud, Targum, *Ruth Rabbah,* Rashi). "Your people will be my people" is interpreted as meaning that henceforth Ruth will obey the 613 Jewish laws.

[74] Fewell and Gunn, *Compromising Redemption,* 69.

[75] The Midrash says that he was eighty years old (*Ruth Rab.* 6.2)!

**Ruth**

will become another man; he will go through a rebirth, signified and manifested by the birth of his son Obed.

Boaz is, in the fiction, the audience chosen by the narrator. He represents the reader of the fifth century B.C.E. The story is told to disorient and to reorient him toward a new view and life. In him effectively resides a real potential; he has "the force in him," as his name indicates. But for him to realize himself, it is necessary that he encounter Ruth the Moabite.

This is an extremely paradoxical situation for, according to biblical logic, the logic of the Law, the opposite is true. It is through contact with the Israelite that the gentile is realized. In the other novellas of the Second Temple era, the Judean is located in the Diaspora and delivers the country of his or her exile as well as its king, which is the case of the Egyptian pharaoh with Joseph, or the king of Nineveh with Jonah, or again the king of Persia with Esther, to say nothing of the kings of Babylon in contact with Daniel the sage. Ruth presents the inverse position: the foreigner is located in the "diaspora" in Judah and it is in contact with the foreigner that the Judean realizes himself! If this is not a biting response to the Ezra and Nehemiah of the fifth century, one could hardly imagine a better one.

Of course, Ruth is a Judean book addressing Judeans; its use is internal. But, since the audience was widened to the "nations," as early as the first century, nothing prevents readers from finding a parallel there to the message of Trito-Isaiah, for example, or even to the New Testament. If it is true that "salvation is from the Jews" (John 4:22), the reciprocal is also true. God also raises up the "righteous of the nations" who edify Israel. In this direction, the book of Ruth—like other biblical books such as Jonah or Esther—is an important "Judeo-Christian" point of encounter.

Ruth belongs to the extraordinary. She is characterized by *ḥesed*. Punctilious obedience to the Law is meritorious, but *ḥesed* surpasses personal merit and becomes contagious, one might say. Boaz employs *ḥesed* in response to Ruth's *ḥesed*, and one expects that God also employs *ḥesed* in return (Ruth 2:12).

# Chapter One

## Reference Passages

- "Thus both daughters of Lot became pregnant by their father. The firstborn bore a son, and named him Moab; he is the ancestor of the Moabites to this day." (Gen 19:36-37)
- "While Israel was staying at Shittim, the people began to have sexual relations with the women of Moab." (Num 25:1)
- "No Ammonite or Moabite shall be admitted to the assembly of Yhwh." (Deut 23:3a [MT 4a])
- "In those days also I saw Jews who had married women of Ashdod, Ammon, and Moab. . . . And I contended with them and cursed them." (Neh 13:23, 25)
- See also Numbers 22; Deut 7:3-4; 2:9; Ezra 9:1-2; 10:3.
- "An Ammonite or a Moabite is forbidden and forbidden for all time [to marry an Israelite], but their women are permitted forthwith." (*m. Yeb.* 8:3; see also *b. Yeb.* 76b–77b, in which the ostracism regarding the Moabites does not include the women)

## Overview

The book of Ruth stresses the theme of return; it is repeated throughout this chapter.[1] By the sixth century B.C.E. (and for a long time afterward), evidently, it became a virtual obsession among those exiled in Babylon. Regarding Naomi, the motif is perfectly understandable here, but not with regard to Ruth. The book emphasizes that, for her, this is also a return (see 1:6, 22; 2:6).

Ruth had not previously been to Judah and, consequently, it is illogical to say (three times) that she returned there. But the Hebrew verb is charged with

---

[1] The verbal root שׁוּב ("return") appears twelve times in this chapter. Another verb of movement, הלך ("go"), appears ten times.

directionality. שוב indicates a physical return, but also repentance, a spiritual movement of 180 degrees. Ruth, of course, does not "return" to Judah, but she turns her back on the plains of Moab; she repents of the ancestral sin; her movement is one of return, but not like that of Orpah, who returned "to her people and to her gods" (1:15; see below). As returns go, Ruth's return is a conversion (שוב). As André Neher states, "In biblical thinking, the *return* is not history beginning anew, but the continuation of a history whose sequence seemed to be impossible." He adds a pertinent note for our study of Ruth, "the return is one of the phases of marital history. . . . [If there is] separation of the spouses . . . separation is only temporary and does not affect the essence of the marital alliance, which has an eternal character."[2] Later in the narrative, Naomi (addressing herself to Ruth) has the elegance to talk about Boaz as being "*our* kinsman Boaz" (3:2).

The figure of Orpah attracts the attention of modern feminist critics, who occasionally take the role of advocates on her behalf. In France, as in the United States, one may compare Ruth and Orpah to the numerous contemporary immigrants, and Orpah is a model of those who do not deny their origins.[3]

On the one hand, Ruth remains "the Moabite" (המאביה) in Judah. This is not only the view of others (1:22; 2:2, 6, 21; 4:5, 10), but also how she presents herself (2:10; "a foreigner," נכריה). On the other hand, Ruth is not an immigrant in Ammon or in Switzerland, but in Israel. She is not forced there by political or economic circumstances; Israel is the land of her choice. This implies that she places herself beneath "the wings" of Yhwh. She expresses this herself (1:16-17; note the use of the name Yhwh), and her adopted compatriots recognize it as well (2:12; 3:10; 4:11-12, 14-15).

It is not a matter, therefore, of simply passing from one culture to another with, effectively, the possibility of safeguarding the values of the first one in the second. This is to misunderstand the *conversion* of Ruth. Orpah returns to "her gods" (1:15). She is not criticized, but neither is she congratulated. Structurally, she corresponds to the unnamed character in chapter 4, who would hardly find a defender among modern critics. Ruth renounced her gods, as do all those today who claim Christianity or Islam for themselves. Still among us is the horrific evidence of what a return to the Aryan and Teutonic roots means or the Slavophiles in Europe of the twentieth century. "The gods" are not benign, and their worshipers are not antiquarians. Chemosh

---

[2] André Neher, *The Prophetic Existence,* trans. William Wolf (South Brunswick, N.J.: Barnes, 1969), 257–58.

[3] See, for example, Bonnie Honig, "Ruth the Model Emigrée: Mourning and the Symbolic Politics of Immigration," in *Ruth and Esther: A Feminist Companion to the Bible,* ed. Athalya Brenner, FCB 2/3 (Sheffield: Sheffield Academic Press, 1999), 50–74. Honig cites another author, Julia Kristeva, *Étrangers à nous-mêmes* (Paris: Gallimard, 1991); idem, *Nations without Nationalism,* trans. Leon S. Roudiez (New York: Columbia Univ. Press, 1993). The rabbis were a lot less generous with respect to Orpah. According to *Yalkut* 600, Orpah (ערפה) is identified with the legendary mother of Goliath, Harafah (הרפה, MT 2 Sam 21:22).

in Moab was not softhearted (1 Kgs 11:7 and 2 Kgs 23:13; Chemosh is called "the abomination of Moab" and is put on the same plane as the horrible Moloch of the Ammonites). According to Num 25:2, the Israelites coming from Egypt offered sacrifices to the gods of Moab. Their mention here revives painful memories.

Naomi's exhortation to her daughters-in-law to return to their respective families ("mother's house," 1:8) does not imply what some have often said. One cannot build on this verse a more or less syncretistic theory. Naomi recommends a return not to the deities of Moab, but to a socially established security. When Orpah chooses this option, Naomi notes that she returned "to her gods," for this implies "security" and Orpah would have understood that. Ruth chooses radical insecurity; but, by the same token, she places herself under "the wings" of Israel's God. She loses everything in order to gain everything.

On the other hand, the literal obedience of Orpah to Naomi's orders has incalculable consequences of future deprivation for Chilion's family line. Because Orpah has missed the turning point of history in chapter 1 of the narrative, Chilion's death is a double death.[4]

Some remarks on the topography of Moab from J. Maxwell Miller will be helpful:

> The settled population of ancient Moab was concentrated on the narrow strip of cultivable land sandwiched between the ragged and steep Dead Sea escarpment and the Arabian desert (approximately 90 kms/60 miles N–S by 25 kms/15 miles E–W). For the most part this is rolling plateau about 1,000 m (3,000 feet) in elevation or 1,300 m (4,300 feet) above the Dead Sea. It is bisected by the steep Wādî el-Mūjib river canyon (the River Arnon of biblical times), and is bounded on the S by another major canyon, Wādî el-Ḥesa (the River Zered of biblical times). . . . Northern Moab is more open to the outside world, on the other hand, and was much better known to the biblical writers. . . . The general terminology of the Hebrew Bible . . . assume[s] that Moab extended as far as Heshbon and Elealeh.[5]

The term "Moab" is mentioned frequently in the Balaam passages in Numbers 22–24. In contrast to Ruth, Balaam is forced to bless Israel. As for Ruth, she is happy to bless God's people; but it is remarkable that every mention of Ruth's "return" is accompanied by "the plains of Moab." It is clear that we have a reminder of the indelible episode of the hostile attitude of the Moabites toward Israel at the time of the exodus from Egypt. The Israelite ostracism regarding the Moabites goes back to the episode on "the plains of Moab" (see, in particular, Deut 23:3-4 [MT 4-5]).

---

[4] "Such a fate would have meant the extinction of his family and his own annihilation (cf 2 Sam. xviii 18; Amos viii 10)" (Eryl W. Davies, "Inheritance Rights and the Hebrew Levirate Marriage [Part 1]," *VT* 31 [1981] 140).

[5] J. Maxwell Miller, "Moab," in *ABD* 4:882–83.

On both the spatial and temporal axes, the book of Ruth relates back to the Deuteronomistic History. First, the Moses speech addresses those who were about to take the land of Canaan. It is, in fact, a Deuteronomic parenesis for those that would soon reclaim the land after the exile. The fiction of "Moab" as the point of departure toward "the inheritance" of the land prevails just as well in the D source of the Pentateuch as it does in the book of Ruth.

On the temporal plane, the same dialectical perspective informs the interpretation of Ruth. "In the days when the judges ruled" indicates a period when the country had just been taken (or retaken), besides the evident chronological necessity to situate the narrative moving toward King David. Ruth and Naomi, according to the symbiosis that characterizes them, prepare the redemption of the land of Israel (the field of Naomi mirrors this at the end of the narrative), as well as the enthronement of King David. This twofold agenda is realized thanks to the repair of the generational chain broken by the deaths reported in Ruth 1:3, 5. The birth of Obed and Boaz's redemption of Naomi's land are signs of the land's complete redemption.

In the text of Ruth 2:14, for example, we learn that Ruth "ate until she was satisfied" in the field of Boaz. The idea expressed there is less anecdotal than it appears, for Deut 8:10, talking about the promised land (where Ruth is located now), says, "You shall eat your fill and bless Yhwh your God for the good land that he has given you." Ruth is the beneficiary of the land granted to Israel. _— Gen 17_

## Exile and Death in Moab (1:1-5)

1:1 In the days when the judges ruled, there was a famine in the land, and a certain man of Bethlehem in Judah went to live in the fields[a] of Moab, he and his wife and two sons. 2 The name of the man was Elimelek and the name of his wife Naomi, and the names of his two sons were Mahlon and Chilion; they were Ephrathites from Bethlehem in Judah. They went into the fields of Moab and remained there. 3 But Elimelek, the husband of Naomi, died, and she was left with her two sons. 4 These took Moabite wives; the name of the one was Orpah and the name of the other Ruth. When they had lived there about ten years, 5 both Mahlon and Chilion also died, so that the woman was left without her two sons and her husband.

1[a] NRSV: "country" (throughout).

### Notes on 1:1-5

These verses are in a contrastive parallel with the end of the book.

[1:1] "In the days when judges ruled." The purpose of this phrase is to situate the story of Ruth and Naomi in another era. An additional reason is that the story intends to remain within the local limits of Bethlehem, without national interference or the central authority of Jerusalem during the period of the monarchy. Lastly, the date of the composition of Ruth situates us in an era when the monarchy was gone. The rule of Ezra and Nehemiah recalls the rule of the judges rather than that of kings; and the Persian province that they governed was precisely Judah (Yehud). Now, as Johanna Bos observes, the time of the judges was one of the most disruptive periods of Israel's history.[6] To the extent that the author of Ruth intends in reality to refer to the fifth century—with its "judges" Ezra and Nehemiah—her implicit critique of the era begins with an exile to a pagan land, where death and destruction reign. These exiles will "return" to Bethlehem, but not under the best of circumstances. Foreign women could well be among them. The book takes the example of a Moabite woman performing her *ʿălîyâ* (the act of return, according to the modern Israeli expression) and provoking a serious hermeneutical dilemma. Is this foreign presence a problem or a solution? It is a solution; but for that to be true it will be necessary to exorcize several taboos and cross the limits of the "great code."

A simple chronological indication did not require the verb "judged" (שׁפט). "At the time of the judges" would have been sufficient. The redundancy introduced by the verb "to judge" is therefore probably the author winking at the reader: "at the time when judges really judged them [when we *really* had judges]."[7] If this is the case, the first words of the narrative orient us already toward the legal interpretation of the book of Ruth.

There is no issue of famine in the book of Judges, during the era when the story supposedly takes place.[8] As for the choice of Moab here, it is intriguing. In the introduction I referred to Michael Fishbane, and I go back once more to him. The narrative of Ruth addresses the forbidden relation of Israel with Moab. About the stay in this country, one thinks of the migrations of the patriarchs—it is also famine that obliges Abraham and Jacob to go into exile in Egypt[9]—but especially of the Babylonian exile and the intermarriages that resulted (see Jeremiah 29; Ezra 9; Nehemiah 9).

"Her two sons." This conjures up the motif of the two daughters-in-law of Naomi. Sasson recalls the biblical artifice of presenting the alternatives of an

---

[6] Johanna W. H. Bos, *Ruth, Esther, Jonah,* Knox Preaching Guides (Atlanta: John Knox, 1986), 14, 16. One finds this same judgment already in the Midrash (*Ruth Rab.* preface 2).

[7] Or better, to the contrary, is this an indication that the political chaos of the period has caused the famine? Thus the Midrash (see Mishael Maswari Caspi and Rachel S. Havrelock, *Women on the Biblical Road: Ruth, Naomi, and the Female Journey* [Lanham, Md.: University Press of America, 1996] 108).

[8] For the Midrash, famine was a punishment and a test, which Elimelek did not rise above. He abandoned his people, who counted on him to nourish them. "He deserted the holy land."

[9] Salmon b. Yeroḥam also refers back to 2 Kgs 8:1, where Elisha recommends to the Shunammite to go to Philistia. Gillis Gerleman sees in this parallel with the patriarchal sagas an intentional motif of the book of Ruth; cf. Gen 12:10; 26:1; 41ff. (*Ruth, Das Hohe Lied,* BKAT 18 [Neukirchen-Vluyn: Neukirchener Verlag, 1965], 13).

existential option in the form of two brothers, one of whom is gifted with the correct choice. We will need to recall this in reference to Orpah's decision (see below).

The expression "the fields of Moab" appears five times in this chapter (vv. 1, 2, 6a, 6b, 22). The frequency of another term is equally remarkable: the root שׁוּב ("return") is employed no less than twelve times (vv. 6, 7, 8, 10, 11, 12, 15a, 15b, 16, 21, 22 [2x]). Throughout this commentary, other numerical repetitions will occasionally be indicated. These numbers are important on two levels. Repetition is a simple and effective means to emphasize the extent of a motif. Moreover, numbers—like the "five" or the "twelve" here—are symbolic in the Bible. One thinks of the five books of the Pentateuch, the five Megillot, the twelve tribes of Israel, and so on. A figure that will appear soon is "seven." In the terms of Evelyn Strouse and Bezalel Porten, "seven . . . becomes, in chapter 4, a sacred number, even an oracle." The authors refer to the declaration of the neighbors that Ruth is more precious to Naomi than "seven sons" (4:15). Boaz is the seventh row in the final genealogy (4:21), which goes back to David, the seventh son of Jesse (1 Sam 16:10-13).[10]

Bethlehem is a point of departure and arrival.[11] This is the birthplace of David (1 Sam 16:1) and consequently a "messianic" place (see Micah 5). Contrast this mention with Deut 23:2-4 (MT 3-5). People from Bethlehem (which means "house of bread") leave the city for Moab in order to receive "the bread and water" there that were refused to their ancestors by these same Moabites. A Moabite in particular becomes their blessing (the motif of the blessing prevails throughout the book), while the Moabites had formerly hired the services of Balaam to curse Israel (see the introduction).

"The fields of Moab" is a motif that appears six times in Ruth (five times in chap. 1 alone). One finds "the field of Moab" in Gen 36:35. In the book of Numbers, the country is designated "the plains of Moab." The change of nomenclature in Ruth emphasizes, on the one hand, the relative fertility of Moab and, on the other hand, the constant association of Ruth with fields in the book. I will return to this later.

A feminist reading of the story directs one's attention to the so-called guiding role of the man in v. 1; secondarily, the text adds that he is accompanied by his wife and two sons. One sees here the tracks of ancient Israel's patriarchalism. But perhaps this is a misunderstanding. Apart from the fact that the author of Ruth is probably a woman, the story articulates a rather negative role for men—from beginning to end. The exception that confirms the rule is Boaz. Elimelek induces his family to go to Moab, and this is doubtless a misstep. It will be fatal to the father and his two sons. The women are saved. Besides, all the women in the narrative have a positive role. Even Orpah is not the object of criticism. The expression "mother's house" (1:8) is

---

[10] Evelyn Strouse and Bezalel Porten, "A Reading of Ruth," *Commentary* 67.2 (1979) 64.

[11] "Bethlehem in Judah"; there is also a Bethlehem in Zebulun (see Josh 19:15-16).

significant in this respect; one discovers it in another biblical book also written by a woman, Song 3:4 and 8:2.[12]

The narrative even provides the clue to the favorable conceptualization of women: they live out *ḥesed* (חסד) toward others. This not an exclusively feminine virtue, of course; but here it is the domain of women. When a man breaks out and becomes Naomi's redeemer (גאל), it is by imitation of Ruth's *ḥesed*. *Ḥesed* is a movement of love and compassion going beyond anything that could be expected.[13] This is the key to the book: the true application of the Law consists in going beyond what the Law expects, for, in its letter, it proceeds by reduction to the lowest common denominator (see Matt 19:8).

[1:2] The term "Ephrathites" (אפרתים) normally designates people from the region of Ephraim, in the north (Judg 12:5; 1 Sam 1:1; 1 Kgs 11:26); but Mic 5:1 (MT 2) combines the two names of Bethlehem and Ephrathah. One can see in "Judah" a tribal affiliation and in "Ephrathah" an interclan affiliation. More important is that David is "an Ephrathite of Bethlehem in Judah" (1 Sam 17:12). Ephraim is "cherished by God" (see Jer 31:19).

The proper names of persons in the book, as already noted, are unique in the Bible. It is probable that the author attached symbolic meanings to them.

"Elimelek" (אלימלך) means "my God is king." This name is without parallel in the Bible, but is a typically Hebrew name. One should note that Yhwh receives royal epithets in Exod 15:18 (eleventh century?). "Elimelek" would be, according to Campbell, the sole name in the series without symbolic value.[14] That may be, but the author certainly wants to indicate that the spouse of Naomi was a pious man, by which his name, in this context, fits the bill. His "defection" to Moab is therefore shocking; his name's promise was not accomplished. The Jewish tradition imagines that Elimelek left Bethlehem with bag and baggage to avoid dividing his wealth with the remaining population who were victims of the famine. Moreover, his name fits the temporality of the book of Ruth, since the period of the judges precedes the Davidic monarchy.

"Naomi" (נעמי) is also recognizable as a Hebrew name. The Talmud implicitly identifies her with Naamah the Ammonite (cf. *b. B. Qam.* 38a), which calls Ruth the

---

[12] Genesis 24:28 is a special case. On Song of Songs see LaCocque, *Romance, She Wrote: A Hermeneutical Essay on Song of Songs* (Harrisburg: Trinity, 1998).

[13] Katherine Doob Sakenfeld, *The Meaning of Ḥesed in the Hebrew Bible: A New Inquiry,* HSM 17 (Missoula, Mont.: Scholars Press, 1978). André Neher talks about "a voluntary act of goodness . . . . love beyond the call of duty . . . . passing over the strict line of justice" (*Prophetic Existence*, 263, 264, 266). Leila L. Bronner speaks of "superabundance" ("A Thematic Approach to Ruth in Rabbinic Literature," in *A Feminist Companion to Ruth,* ed. Athalya Brenner, FCB 1/3 (Sheffield: Sheffield Academic Press, 1993), 148.

[14] Campbell, *Ruth,* 52.

Moabite and Naamah "two good turtledoves that serve their respective nations." On Naamah see 1 Kgs 14:21, 31; 2 Chron 12:13 (the mother of Rehoboam). In this case, the two incestuous descendants of Lot would be united in the book of Ruth: Moab and Ammon.

"Mahlon" (מחלון) and "Chilion" (כליון) are united in a game of words, though the verbal roots of their names elicit nothing joyous, for, as the Midrash says, they were "obliterated" and "eliminated" from the world. Their names conclude with a particle—a diminutive according to J. J. Stamm.[15] One could translate them as "Weak" and "Sickly." One finds a similar formation in, for example, 2 Sam 8:18: Kerethites and Pelethites; Num 11:27: Eldad and Medad; Gen 4:20-22: Jabal, Jubal, Tubal; Ezekiel 38–39: Gog and Magog. The names continue in Ruth 1:4.

"Ruth" (רות). Commentators have derived her name from various verbal roots, without a solid basis. The simplest and most convincing is to see it as a form of the verb רוה ("satisfy"). The basic passage is Isa 48:20-21, which draws a parallel between redemption and quenching thirst. This equation explains the allusion by the prophet to the crossing of the desert during the exodus. Other passages to place on the list are:

- Isa 55:10b: the rain and snow "do not return there until they have watered [הרוה] the earth, making it bring forth and sprout";
- Ps 23:5b: "my cup overflows [רויה]";
- Ps 36:8 (MT 9): "they feast [ירוין] on the abundance of your house, and you give them drink from the river of your delights" (in parallel with Eden watered by the primordial river);
- Ps 65:10a (MT 11a): "you water its furrows abundantly [with rain]" (תלמיה רוה).

Rabbi Yoḥanan (one of the Amoraim, c. 180–279 C.E. and founder of the Tiberian academy) is in agreement (b. Sanh. 19b). Compare the use of terms such as "empty," "full," and "after she herself had been satisfied" (Ruth 2:18).[16] The Talmud (followed by Rashi) says that Ruth was the daughter of King Eglon (b. Soṭah 47a; Sanh. 105b).

"Orpah" (ערפה). One generally thinks about the Akkadian root *arruppu* with the sense of "mane, nape of the neck." The name could also refer to "cloud" (ערפים, "clouds"), and therefore in contrast with Ruth, this name would then indicate "little water."

Later in the book one finds yet other names, such as "Boaz" (בעז). One inevitably thinks about the two pillars at the entry of the temple, Yakin (Jachin) and

---

[15] J. J. Stamm, "Zum Ursprung des Namens der Ammoniter," in *Beiträge zur hebräischen und altorientalischen Namenkunde,* ed. Ernst Jenni and Martin A. Klopfenstein, OBO 30 (Göttingen: Vandenhoeck & Ruprecht, 1980), 5–8.

[16] For this reference, see the article by Hans Bruppacher, "Die Bedeutung des Namens Ruth," *TZ* 22 (1966) 12–18. Sasson (*Ruth,* 21) and D. R. G. Beattie (*Jewish Exegesis of the Book of Ruth,* JSOTSup 2 [Sheffield: JSOT Press, 1977], 192) arrive at the same conclusion.

Boaz (1 Kgs 7:21; 2 Chron 3:17). Yakin appears as a proper name in Gen 46:10; Exod 6:15; and Num 26:12. This is also the name of a priest in Neh 11:10; 1 Chron 9:10; and 24:7. According to Henri Lusseau, בעל עז = בעז is a comparable formation to the name of שלם בעל = שלמבו.[17] The Midrash, for its part, does not try to provide a meaning for this name. Now, since all the other names of the book carry symbolic meanings, it is necessary to follow the identification of the personage Boaz with the pillar of the temple and/or its priests. All the more so, as one of my students pointed out to me, since Ruth 3 purposefully situates Boaz on the threshing floor; the Jerusalem temple was, according to tradition, built on Araunah's threshing floor (2 Sam 24:16).[18] This association with the priesthood is provocative in a book protesting the measures taken by Ezra–Nehemiah with regard to foreign women. Etymologically, "Boaz" means "the force is in him"; this leads Strouse and Porten to comment: "Boaz is named for strength, as Ruth's late husband Mahlon was named for sickness, his brother for destruction."[19] Boaz is called *Boos* in the LXX and VL.

"Such and such" or "So-and-so" (פלני אלמני). One does not speak the name of the one that is not worthy. Thus, in the talmudic texts referring to Jesus, he is called "such-and-such" (b. Ḥag. 4b; Yeb. 49; and m. Yeb. 4:13; the two texts in the Munich Codex, an unexpurgated codex despite the pressure of the Christian persecutions). This phrase is used to designate an unknown place in 1 Sam 21:2 (MT 3) and 2 Kgs 6:8.

The name Obed (עבד) without determinative (as in "Obed-edom," for example) is problematic (as is the name "Moses," which means "sons of"). Such a shortened name has the advantage of attracting more attention to him. The child born "to Naomi" is called "Servant." "Obed" reminds one of the "Servant of Yhwh." The Midrash says that Obed is an *ᶜebed,* a characteristic term for David (see Ps 116:16); God also calls David *ᶜebed* (1 Kgs 11:31; Ps 78:70). An anonymous rabbi says that Obed was going to serve Naomi (thus also Josephus).[20]

**[1:3-5]** The circumstances just get worse as we proceed, as in the book of Job (see Job 19:21; 23:2; cf. Ruth 1:20 and Job 27:2). Here Naomi is a widow with no living children and in a foreign land.[21] One needs to remember that Lot's daughters, the

---

[17] Henri Lusseau, "Ruth," in *Introduction to the Old Testament*, ed. André Robert and André Feuillet, trans. Patrick W. Skehan et al. (New York: Desclee, 1968), 447–52.

[18] Judith Phillips (personal communication).

[19] Strouse and Porten, "A Reading of Ruth," 64.

[20] Cf. Louis Ginzberg: "As examples of piety and virtue, David had his grandfather and particularly his father before him. His grandfather's whole life was a continuous service of God, whence his name Obed, 'the servant,' and his father Jesse was one of the greatest scholars of his time, and one of the four who died wholly untainted by sin" (*Legends of the Jews,* 4:81).

[21] Elimelek is described as the husband of Naomi, an unusual identification of a man in relation to a woman. The Midrash recalls the text of Gen 48:7—"Rachel is dead to me" (מתה עלי רחל). "A man is never dead, but only to his wife," writes b. Sanh. 22b (cited by Rashi).

"grandmothers" of Ruth and Orpah, were panicked by the thought that their lineages stopped with them. It is necessary also to think about the stereotype of the Moabites in the Israelite mentality: the female Moabites were no better than prostitutes (see Numbers 25). Death can appear as a just punishment striking their spouses, Mahlon and Chilion. Only when Ruth is in Judah will she become fertile and have a son, Obed.[22]

**[1:4]** Marriages. The Midrash thinks employing the verb נשׂא—instead of לקח—indicates a mixed marriage. In any case, as Jacob Myers emphasizes,[23] the construction is usually late; we find it again in a passage of the sixth century, Judg 21:23 (cf. Ezra 9:2 and Neh 13:25).

On rereading the narrative, the reader knows that Boaz will marry Ruth the Moabite. The book nevertheless begins by mentioning that Mahlon and Chilion married Moabite women. The book opens, therefore, on a scandal and finishes, prior to the genealogy, on an "antiscandal" of sorts.

Chapter 1 of the book lays out the elements of the story that will follow. It describes the three widows, mother-in-law and daughters-in-law, with no exit, and—very important for the ensuing story—whose future is blocked *according to the Torah*. Even the hypothetical intervention of a levir is unthinkable (vv. 12-13). This is the reason that Naomi concludes that the hand of Yhwh is raised against her (vv. 13, 20-21), since his Law, even in its more liberal amendment (the provision of the levirate), condemns her to "emptiness" (v. 21) and to bitterness (v. 20).[24]

Here, therefore, the story of Naomi and her daughters-in-law could end (leaving them merely in the shadows), if a totally unexpected and unthinkable event did not occur: Ruth the Moabite decides to "return" to Judah with her mother-in-law. This element becomes a springboard for raising historical and legal issues in Israel. Suddenly, the narrative becomes less Naomi's story and more Ruth's, because Naomi has been "emptied" of all hope, while Ruth is the one who wagers on abundance. The story of Ruth is a story of fertility.

It is therefore natural to see Ruth take the initiative at the beginning of chapter 2—the role of Naomi being simply to consent. In chapter 3, nevertheless, Naomi leaves her hopeless torpor and expresses her concern for the well-being of her daughter-in-law. Shortly afterward, Ruth again occupies center stage of the scene, only to be voluntarily eclipsed by Naomi in chapter 4, but not without first having accomplished her supreme act, hoped for and prepared for since the beginning: to give birth

---

[22] The traditional Jewish reading is that sterility and death in Moab are signs of divine disfavor, which is easily confirmed by an African reading, for example, cf. Musa W. Dube, "Divining Ruth," in *Postmodern Interpretations of the Bible: A Reader,* ed. A. K. M. Adam (St. Louis: Chalice, 2001), 73.

[23] Myers, *Linguistic and Literary Form,* 29.

[24] From this perspective, Campbell's argument that Naomi employs an originally legal vocabulary in vv. 20-21 makes sense (Campbell, *Ruth,* 62).

to the redeemer (*gōʾēl*) of her mother-in-law. This oscillation between the two women begins with Naomi and finishes with her. Ruth, nevertheless, has "lost everything in order to gain everything."

**[1:5]** Naomi here is called "the woman"; this emphasizes her dependence and her powerlessness. She has practically nothing or no one on which to lean. Not that her daughters-in-law count for nothing, but her husband and sons were "as arrows in the quiver" (see Ps 127:3-5; Ruth 4:13). Lois Durbin finely states that the proper name of the woman, Naomi ("pleasing"), could not figure in so sad a verse. She adds that Naomi "is without name, without face, universal in her dereliction."[25]

The expression "left of/from" (נשאר מן) also appears in Deut 3:11; Josh 13:12; Neh 1:2, 3; Isa 11:11, 16; and Jer 8:3.

Naomi's dead sons are called "children" (ילדים) here. This is surprising, but Nielsen acutely establishes the parallel with the end of the story, when Naomi holds another child (ילד) in her arms (4:16).[26]

### The Return to Judah (1:6-15)

1:6 Then she started to return with her daughters-in-law from the fields[a] of Moab, for she had heard in the field[a] of Moab that Yhwh[b] had considered his people and given them food. 7 So she set out from the place where she had been living, she and her two daughters-in-law, and they went on their way to go back to the land of Judah. 8 But Naomi said to her two daughters-in-law, "Go back each of you to your mother's house. May Yhwh deal kindly with you, as you have dealt with the dead and with me. 9 Yhwh grant that you may find security, each of you in the house of your husband." Then she kissed them, and they wept aloud. 10 They said to her, "No, we will return with you to your people." 11 But Naomi said, "Turn back, my daughters, why will you go with me? Do I still have sons in my womb that they may become your husbands? 12 Turn back, my daughters, go your way, for I am too old to have a husband. Even if I thought there was hope for me, even if I should have a husband tonight and bear sons, 13 would you then wait until they were grown? Would you then refrain from marrying? No, my daughters, it has been far more bitter for me than for you, because the hand of Yhwh has turned against me." 14 Then they wept aloud again. Orpah kissed her mother-in-law, but Ruth clung to her.

---

[25] Lois Durbin, "Fullness and Emptiness, Fertility and Loss," in *Reading Ruth: Contemporary Women Reclaim a Sacred Story,* ed. Judith A. Kates and Gail Twersky Reimer (New York: Ballantine, 1994), 132.

[26] Nielsen, *Ruth*, 44.

15  So she said, "See, your sister-in-law has gone back to her people and to her gods: return after your sister-in-law."

6ᵃ NRSV: "country."
6ᵇ NRSV: "LORD" (throughout).

### Notes on 1:6-15

**[1:6]** God has "visited" his people and returned them to prosperity (cf. Ps 85:1 [MT 2]). God's "visits" can be disastrous or favorable, according to the Bible. Here, as in Gen 50:24; Exod 4:31; 1 Sam 2:21; and Jer 29:10, the "visit" is accompanied by God's grace and prosperity.

The chronological passage from the judges to King David is also punctuated by the physical passage from Moab to Judah. On this point, the structure of vv. 6-7 is interesting. First, Moab is mentioned (6a), then alluded to (6b), followed by the allusion to Judah (7a), and then Judah is explicitly mentioned (7b).

Note the repetition of לחם ("bread") and *Bethlehem* (which means "house of bread") in this chapter. We learn that Naomi kept her eye on the land of Israel. It is thus not surprising to read Rashi's commentary on the following verse (v. 7).

**[1:7]** Why, demands Rashi, add "place"? Because the place where she had been suddenly had lost all its glory (cf. Gen 28:10: "Jacob left Beersheba").

The Targum omits: "and they went on their way to return in the land of Judah" (while the Tg gives a text twice as long as the original). Doubtless the Targum is sensitive to the fact that the Moabites accompanying Naomi were not logically able "to return" where they had never been.

**[1:8]** "Return." The biblical account has the customary narrative sequences, even to express simultaneity. The daughters-in-law of Naomi did not accompany her, *and then* Naomi recommended that they not follow her. The two events occur simultaneously.

"Mother's house" (בית אם), instead of the usual "father's house" (בית אב), we find again in Gen 24:28 and especially in Song 3:4 and 8:2 (in contrast with Gen 38:11 or Lev 22:13, for example); in Prov 31:21, 27 one finds "her household" [ביתה]).[27] But the expression here is surprising, for, in the ancient Near East, a woman was under male guardianship her entire life—whether her father, brothers, or husband. That the books of Ruth and Song of Songs were both written by women explains the choice of expression.[28]

---

[27] Carol M. Meyers, "'To Her Mother's House': Considering a Counterpart to the Israelite *Bêt 'āb*," in *The Bible and the Politics of Exegesis: Essays in Honor of Norman K. Gottwald on His Sixty-fifth Birthday*, ed. David Jobling et al. (Cleveland: Pilgrim, 1991), 39–51.

[28] For Song of Songs see André LaCocque, *Romance, She Wrote*. In the Midrash, on this verse

Naomi's vow to her Moabite daughters-in-law shows her faith that God can act in Moab as well as in Israel. This is an important point, for it throws a certain light on the emigration of Elimelek's family to Moab. Retrospectively, one can say that Elimelek deliberately went to this country usually despised by Israelites. The following verse (v. 9) again reinforces this point. So the rabbinic condemnation of Elimelek's migration to Moab is perhaps, after all, an excess of zeal on their part.

"Kindly." This central term (חסד, "goodness, loyalty") appears here for the first time in the book; it will reappear in 2:20 and 3:10. In the first two passages (1:8 and 2:20), it is a matter of God's "loyalty"; the third one refers to Ruth. This position corresponds to the basic direction of the term *ḥesed*, that it is normally "done by the situationally superior party for one who is completely lacking in present resources or future prospects."[29] *Ḥesed* does not indicate a special favor, but responds, Katherine Sakenfeld says, to an essential need,[30] for it comes from the only possible source of assistance. *Ḥesed*, in certain contexts, is employed for "the preservation of the Davidic dynasty." But this usage ends abruptly with the fall of the monarchy in the sixth century. Deutero-Isaiah also democratizes the Davidic covenant. Paul Humbert correctly states that *ḥesed* is the key word of the whole narrative.[31] The expression "may Yhwh show you *ḥesed*" appears in only one other place, 2 Sam 2:6, also in a context of separation (cf. 2 Sam 15:20 LXX).

The daughters-in-law showed goodness (loyalty) toward their deceased husbands and toward Naomi. The author does not elaborate this point, but it is clear, by the attitude of the young women accompanying their mother-in-law, that death did not mark the end of the family relations linking them to the Israelite tree.[32] Naomi recognizes that their loyalty is extraordinary.

**[1:9]** The vocabulary of this verse is reminiscent of the *Landnahmetradition* ("taking of the land tradition"; conquest of Canaan) as well as of the David traditions (cf. 2 Sam 15:21 and Ruth 1:16-17). In particular, the notion of security (מנוחה, מנוח), here and in 3:1, points in this direction (cf. Josh 21:43—22:9; 1 Kgs 8:56; Isa 32:18; Ps 95:11). One should also keep in mind expressions such as "parcel of the field/land" (חלקת השדה) in Ruth 2:3 and 4:3, and "inheritance" (נחלה) in 4:5, 10, that also recall Davidic traditions (cf., for example, 2 Sam 20:1). As a reminder, in Deut 4:38 one has נחלה, in 12:9 נחלה and מנוחה (cf. Josh 11:23; 24:32; Judg 18:1). The book's links to

---

Rabbi Meir concludes from this anomaly that a pagan (like Orpah and Ruth) never knew who his or her father was. As to Salmon b. Yeroḥam, he sets our text in contrast to Lev 22:13; but he adds that the two women had lost their fathers, an opinion expressly contradicted by Ruth 2:11 (Boaz praises Ruth for leaving behind her father, her mother, etc.).

[29] Sakenfeld, *Meaning of Ḥesed,* 12.

[30] Ibid., 234.

[31] Paul Humbert, "Art et leçon de l'histoire de Ruth," in *Opuscules d'un hébraïsant* (Neuchâtel: Secrétariat de l'Université, 1958), 86.

[32] Cf. Neher, *Prophetic Existence,* 266, 268.

the Davidic tradition (in particular in Deuteronomistic form) are tight. The security that is at issue here depends on the remarriage of the two widows in Moab, for they lost this security with their widowhood.

Here Naomi blesses the foreigners in an impure land with a Yahwistic formula, and Ruth herself takes an oath by Yhwh (1:17). One cannot draw from this a precise argument for the dating of Ruth; but such a universalism during the Solomonic era is very improbable.

**[1:10]** It is necessary to note that Orpah—and not only Ruth—wanted "to return" to Judah and live among Naomi's people. Moreover, before calling Ruth "my daughter" in Ruth 2:2, Naomi calls both of them "my daughters" (1:11, 12, 13). Now, one should not lose sight of the fact that she addresses herself to two Moabites. She even goes so far as to invoke Yhwh's *hesed* on them (as distinguished from using "Elohim"). The flipside, which contrasts with this, is that Orpah returns to "her gods" (v. 15). Hence the modern business of "saving" Orpah as someone faithful to her ancestral heritage (in contrast with Ruth, indirectly criticized for her servile mentality) is severely limited by the biblical text itself. One should clearly emphasize Ruth's extraordinary course, which abandons "her gods" to serve Israel's God in a world where "the very notion was unthinkable," as Adele Berlin states.[33] One sees that this is far more important for the biblical mentality than the loyalty to ancient but pagan traditions. Biblical religion demands a disorientation and a fundamental reorientation (see Overview above). Ruth is not afflicted with a weak character and easily influenced (see Ruth 3). Her "conversion" in 1:16 is not a sign of weakness but of courage. So it is with all conversions to the living God (cf. the last words of v. 16 and the invocation by Ruth of Yhwh in v. 17). The "weakness" of Ruth—with respect to Naomi and Israel's God—is the place of God's power. Thus it is Jesus' obedience and even slavery that Paul emphasizes in Phil 2:6-8. Would it be necessary therefore to conclude that Jesus was in reality a timid personality?

Actually, Ruth turns her back ("Orpah" could mean "[back of the] neck"), not to Naomi, like her sister-in-law, but to her own origins and to her ancestors; she adopts another history and another genealogy (as Christians and Muslims today see Abraham as their father).[34] But this costly disjuncture was preceded by a comparable movement by her mother-in-law. Naomi could have desperately hung on to her remaining attachments to her adopted country. She decides, to the contrary, to cut her last links with Moab and with her daughters-in-law (1:6-7). Without the extravagance of Ruth, who places herself deliberately in the same position, one would understand Naomi wanting to commit suicide, in any case in having a death wish. This is neu-

---

[33] Berlin, "Ruth and the Continuity of Israel," in *Reading Ruth,* ed. Kates and Reimer, 257.

[34] Ruth A. Putnam sees a parallel to Jonathan's being torn between his filial loyalty and his friendship with David. His choice, so to speak, is definitive between his country and his friend. "Friendship," in *Reading Ruth,* ed. Kates and Reimer, 48.

tralized, not by one theological argument or other—as the "friends" of Job attempt—but by Ruth plunging into Naomi's solitude—which, from that time on, is no longer solitude but communion. The "conversion" of Ruth is not the adoption of a religious system, but the choice of goodness.

In this context it is interesting to notice, with Mishael Caspi and Rachel Havrelock,[35] that the male biblical hero often cuts off links with his or her family in order to attach to the one God, while the heroines group themselves in pairs: Sarah and Hagar, Rebekah and her wet nurse Deborah, Rachel and Leah, and Naomi and Ruth (after the deconstruction of the pair Orpah and Ruth). They always finish by allying themselves regarding the perpetuation of the family/clan.

On this subject it is important to emphasize, with Athalya Brenner for example,[36] that in pairs of women there is most often mutual opposition; remarkably, this is not the case with Naomi and Ruth. The exception here is not by chance. The author, consistent with herself, shows, in a first movement, that goodness alone is able to resolve the problems that are more harmful because of their frequency and their depth. If, effectively, a mother-in-law (Judahite) and a daughter-in-law (Moabite) can treat each other like Naomi and Ruth (in v. 14 the verb "cling" [דבק] indicates an intimate communion; see below), one can expect that other potential conflicts may find their solution in the same manner. The book of Ruth will demonstrate this.

**[1:11]** This verse unquestionably shows that the issue of the levirate is at stake from the outset in the book of Ruth.[37] The Midrash agrees on the subject of this verse, but not without expressing some surprise regarding how the question can be put regarding Moabites. Additionally, we find another allusion to the levirate in this chapter, for Orpah is called "your sister-in-law" (יבמתך, 1:15). Now the term יבם designates a brother-in-law (Latin *levir*) in the law of the levirate (Deut 25:5-10) and never designates a sister-in-law aside from this verse in Ruth.

Naomi's question is purely theoretical on several levels (and in this direction the tracks of levirate marriage are merely echoes, but the continuation of the narrative will show that they are far from accidental):

1. She is no longer of childbearing age (1:12).
2. She no longer has a husband.
3. Even if she had a new child, it would arrive too late (cf. *m. Yeb.* 1:1; 2:1).
4. According to the ancient rabbis, another condition would not be filled: the יבם must be born from the same father and mother.
5. The wait of the young women would be too long (Ruth 1:13).

---

[35] Caspi and Havrelock, *Women on the Biblical Road,* 34.

[36] Athalya Brenner, "Female Social Behaviour: Two Descriptive Patterns within the 'Birth of the Hero' Paradigm," *VT* 36 (1986) 257–73.

[37] *Pace* Hubbard, *Ruth,* 109.

The theoretical problem posed by Naomi places us in the position illustrated by Genesis 38. But the story of Ruth will show that what was only irony at the start becomes concrete reality in the end. Nevertheless, it is not a baby that Ruth will marry to perpetuate the Elimelek name, but an old man. One may think about this subject with regard to the principle of "a coming together of opposites" (*coincidentia oppositorum*).

Naomi now calls the Moabite daughters-in-law "my daughters." She presses them to return to their respective families. The verb "return" (שׁוּב) is employed three times in vv. 8, 11, 12. It is important to note these triple motifs in the book; we will return to them. But note now how repetitive Naomi's speech is—as invariably that of Boaz is; thus the two people of age in the story—indicating the hesitation, seeking to make the argument convincing. "Return" (1:11, 2x), "for" (1:12, 2x), "also" (2x); הֲלָהֵן ("is this indeed," 2x), "with a man" (2x, and with the mention in 1:13, 3x), "my daughters" (2x), "sons" (2x); "your sister-in-law" (1:15, 2x); in 2:22-23, "daughter" (2x), and "harvest" (2x).

For the legalistic reading, the dismissal of the two daughters-in-law to Moab and to its gods supposes that the two women were not converted to Judaism. But then all sorts of other problems present themselves. The *Zohar Hadash Ruth* 180-82 asserts that "Ruth" was the Jewish name given to the Moabite when she married Mahlon and converted.[38] Ruth 1:16 would represent a development of this conversion. I shall spare the reader similar convolutions. One may prefer the interpretation of Rabbi Chaim Azulaï (1724–1806) on Ruth 1:8,[39] according to which the girls "went beyond this that one could await by wearing *hesed* out; Naomi blesses them while wishing that God in turn wears out *hesed* toward them and thus goes beyond this that they could await."

On the subject of the triple refusal of Ruth to follow the counsels of Naomi to return to her country, the model is probably Elisha's triple refusal to abandon Elijah, despite his admonitions (2 Kings 2).

**[1:12]** "I am too old." In a chapter that will soon explicitly refer to the vocabulary of Genesis 12 on Abraham's departure regarding Ruth's emigration, the verb זָקַנְתִּי repeats Gen 18:13 and the reflection of Sarah in this whole passage.

"This night" does not appear in the Targum, probably for reasons of indecency. Naomi imagines a parallel position to the one of Genesis 38 (Judah and Tamar) and, in a best-case scenario, even if she was fertilized that night, it would be unthinkable for her daughters-in-law to wait for the son to become an adult (supposing it would be a boy).

---

[38] Quoted by Zlotowitz, in Nossom Scherman and Meir Zlotowitz, *The Book of Ruth/Megillas Ruth*, The ArtScroll Tanach Series (Brooklyn: Mesorah, 1979), xlix–l.

[39] *Nakhal Eshkol* (a commentary on the five Megillot).

The scenario imagined by Naomi is again not directly levirate, but the allusion to this custom is clear and finds support in the preceding verse and in the remainder of the book. The goal here would be to obtain marriage security for the two women. One will note with Sakenfeld that the life expectancy in the ancient world was forty years or less.[40]

**[1:13]** "Refrain from marrying," or "abstain from being with a man"; literally, "to be an ʿāgûnâ," a woman abandoned by her husband, but not divorced. There is no other example of the verb. The substantive became common in Post-Biblical Hebrew. Myers translates: "to restrict oneself"; this leads to a reading of: "Will you restrict yourself to having no spouse?"

The book of Ruth begins, like the story of Job, with the death of almost all Naomi's kin.[41] She notes God's ineffectiveness or even hostility. There are hardly any other biblical examples where the victim dares to criticize God so directly for his or her affliction—even the communal complaints in the desert after the exodus address themselves to Moses (cf. Exod 15:24; 16:2; 17:3; Num 11:1; 14:2).[42] In a sense, in relation to Naomi, Ruth stands in contrast to Job's wife in relation to her wretched husband (Job 2:9). Here and there, however, the story begins badly, and the reader understands immediately that when things begin that way, they can well go from bad to worse. If there is change for the better, it can only be at the price of an extraordinary *peripeteia* (change of fortune), to employ the Aristotelian term. In biblical language, this is a תשובה, a 180-degree turn, a conversion, a "return." This is what is meant in Naomi and Ruth's story by the use of the verb שוב in Ruth 1:6, 7, 16, 22; and 2:6.

The comparison with the book of Job (another work from the Second Temple period) is also interesting on another level. Before the final theophany (the genealogy at the end of the book of Ruth corresponds to this), the Joban problem is conditioned by the universally accepted principle of retributive justice (see Job 8:6-7; Deut 28:7ff.). One recognizes one of the foundations of Deuteronomistic theology there. Now Job explores all its aspects from the viewpoint of his personal concern and arrives at a negative conclusion, something like: God is just but he is not good, or he is good, but is not just (Hobbes's paraphrase). The final theophany is the only thing that will cut this Gordian knot.

From this perspective, the book of Ruth seems to return to the principal question expressed in the book of Job. For here every good act is rewarded; all prayer is granted. Divine justice is retributive.

---

[40] Sakenfeld, *Ruth,* IBC (Louisville: Westminster John Knox, 1999), 27.

[41] The Midrash on 1:5 deduces from the word "also" (גם) that they had already lost all their goods, their horses, donkeys, and camels. When God punishes, God starts by depriving the guilty of their property.

[42] One may perhaps see in Naomi's complaint an echo of Isa 45:7 (antidualism).

But this is no more than the surface of things. For what is "effective" according to Ruth is not *do ut des* ("I do so that you will do in return") or "measure for measure," but excessiveness, extravagance, supreme risk, sacrifice, "to lose one's life."[43] The distance in comparison with the lesson of the book of Job is nullified: here and there, the divine response to the human quest cannot be measured in retribution, but in graciousness (לחנם in Job 1:9) or love (חסד in Ruth).

"Would you then wait?" This is an "ironic echo" of Gen 38:11, where Judah asked Tamar to wait for his son Shelah to grow up.[44]

"It has been more bitter for me than for you." The position is more serious for Naomi than for her daughters-in-law in this instance, because she could no longer give birth. Moreover, her loss is attributable to God, something Naomi does not imply regarding her daughters-in-law. (On this latter point, see above, under vv. 3-4). The expression "bitter for me" (מר־לי) we meet again only in Isa 38:17 and Lam 1:4.

"The hand of Yhwh has turned against me" (יצאה בי יד־יהוה) is literally "the hand of Yhwh went out against me"; it means, "Yhwh attacked me."

[1:14] "They raised [their voices]" (ותשנה, without ʾaleph as in Jer 9:17; Zech 5:9; plene in Ezek 23:49, תשאינה). The same linguistic phenomenon occurs in Ruth 2:9—צמת for צמאת.

"Clung." The verb דבק normally applies to devotion toward God (cf. Deut 4:4). Here, however, as in Song of Songs (another Hebrew book by a woman), the religious vocabulary is reoriented toward interpersonal relations. This is the position that prevails in Gen 2:24, which states that a man will "cling to his wife." The sense of intimacy expressed by this verb is again reinforced by the declaration of Ruth in 1:16-18, which resembles a marriage vow. Whoever claims to cling to God but bypasses their neighbor is a liar (as one might paraphrase 1 John 4:20). Women seem to understand this more immediately than men. One will also note that the devotion (דבק) comes after an abandonment (עזב) in both Gen 2:24 and Ruth 1:16: Election inevitably implies selection. One cannot attach oneself to someone without breaking attachments to others, for no one is an island (cf. 2 Sam 20:2). This is the reason Israelite monotheism rejects all other allegiances (see Matt 6:24). One will compare the course of Ruth here with Boaz's blessing in Ruth 2:12 and with the response of

---

[43] Paul writes that "God chose what is foolish in the world to shame the wise; God chose what is weak in the world to shame the strong" (1 Cor 1:27). The *Yalkut Shimeoni* (a midrashic anthology attributed to Rabbi Shimeon ha-Darshan, thirteenth century) declares, "Two women sacrificed themselves for the tribe of Judah: Tamar and Ruth" (quoted by Scherman and Zlotowitz, *Megillas Ruth,* 107). Already in the fourth century, St. Ephrem of Syria wrote, "Honorable women became . . . contemptible for you" (*Hymnes de la Nativité* 1.2; quoted by Jane Richardson, "Ruth according to Ephrem the Syrian," in *Feminist Companion to Ruth,* ed. Brenner, 174).

[44] Hubbard, *Ruth,* 112.

Ruth in 3:9: "you are a *gōʾēl*" (often the *gōʾēl* is God himself; note that the root גאל appears twenty-one times in the book).

[1:15] The movement from "my daughter (-in-law)" to "your sister-in-law" indicates a disappointment that Naomi does not succeed in hiding.[45] With יבמתך, "your sister-in-law," we are again in a levirate marriage context. The LXX has *synnymphos,* which is a hapax legomenon: "marriage partner." Naomi places herself in the context of Genesis 38 (Judah and Tamar). As one will readily see repeatedly in what follows, the parallels with Genesis 38 are numerous and loaded with importance. Correspondences between Ruth and this chapter of Genesis are articulated by Zakovitch, and following his lead, I make the following points:

1. In both cases, the spouses are foreign.
2. Er and Onan die, as do Elimelek's sons, and the problem of the preservation of the name (family) consequently arises (Gen 38:9; Ruth 4:5, 10).
3. Onan "ruins" (שחת) his semen on the ground, says the text; So-and-so in Ruth 4 does not want to "damage" (שחת) his property, he says (Gen 38:9; Ruth 4:6).
4. The verbal root יבם in Hebrew does not appear in the narrative literature outside these two texts.
5. Judah sends Tamar back to the "her father's house"; Naomi sends each of her daughters-in-law to her "mother's house."
6. The clause "Would you wait until they [the subsequent levirs] were grown" that is placed in the mouth of Naomi (Ruth 1:13) is echoed in the petition of Judah that Tamar wait for his son Shelah to grow up.[46]

The parallels between the two stories are striking. Time and again we shall discover allusions to Genesis 38 in the book of Ruth. Ruth is set in a series of "scandalous" women such as Tamar, Rahab, and even Lot's daughters. I shall return to this point in my discussion of Ruth 3.

Naomi does not present Orpah as a model for Ruth to emulate, but as an example that she could logically follow.[47] Besides, Naomi does not kiss Orpah as she departs; it is Orpah who kisses her mother-in-law.

## Ruth's Great Return/Reversal (1:16-18)

16 But Ruth said,
"Do not press me to leave you
or to turn back from following you!

[45] Yehoshua Bachrach, *The Mother of Royalty: An Exposition of the Book of Ruth in Light of the Sources,* trans. Leonard Oschry (New York: Feldheim, 1973).

[46] Zakovitch, *Ruth* [in Hebrew], Miqra le-Yisrael (Jerusalem: Magnes, 1990), 50.

[47] *Pace* Carolyn Pressler, *Joshua, Judges, Ruth,* WBComp (Louisville: Westminster John Knox, 2002), 271.

Where you go, I will go:
where you lodge, I will lodge;
your people shall be my people,
and your God my God.

17 Where you die, I will die—
there will I be buried.
May Yhwh[a] do thus and so to me,
and more as well,
if even death parts me from you!"

18 When Naomi saw that she was determined to go with her, she said no more to her.

17[a] NRSV: "LORD."

### Notes on 1:16-18

**[1:16]** The jolting style of Ruth contrasts with the rhetorical formalism of Naomi. On this, refer to the discussion on v. 10 above. As Gunkel commented on the subject of Ruth's devotion to her mother-in-law: generosity emulates generosity.[48]

"Your God will be my God." Compare 2 Sam 15:21 (the declaration of loyalty by Ittai to David). Some critics have hypothesized that the formula was part of a sort of naturalization liturgy. There may perhaps already be a hint of a conversion liturgy in the mention of a "mixed multitude" among those that departed from Egypt in Exod 12:38. It is necessary, nevertheless, to emphasize that Ruth remains "the Moabite" almost to the end of the narrative.

It is evident that Ruth realizes that God is inseparable from the person of Naomi. Not only because Ruth must have learned who the God of her mother-in-law and of her husband was, but because this knowledge is, for her, incarnate in the person of the Judean. Orpah was also exposed to this same "catechism" (etymologically, "oral instruction")—in vain from the moment when she separates herself from Naomi (Orpah did "return to her people and to her gods," says Naomi in 1:15). As for Ruth, she attaches herself in the narrative to a God that is not hers, to a woman instead of a man, then to an old man that is neither her own age nor from her own people. In other than biblical circumstances, she might be considered out of line. She is either delirious or "faint with love" (Song 2:5; 5:8).

Before saying that the God of Naomi will be her God, Ruth adopts Israel as her people: "your people will be my people." Devotion (דבק) to God comes through devotion to Israel (see Zech 8:23). This is a lesson that Christians have often attempted to forget. Ruth's decision "effects a voluntary change of identity and

---

[48] Hermann Gunkel, "Ruth," in *Reden und Aufsätze* (Göttingen: Vandenhoeck & Ruprecht, 1913), 67.

unforced submission to a new orientation. It calls forth commitment that defies the fear of the unknown and willingly accepts the consequences of the ultimate."[49]

"Your God will be my God." This God is the one that Naomi has just described as judge and executioner! Ruth prefers the exacting God of the Judeans to certain easygoing pagan idols.[50] Naomi designated "the LORD" as being the final cause of their total misfortune; Ruth takes this upon herself, but in order better to challenge this divine judgment. She will go to Bethlehem and attempt to convert emptiness into fullness. The Moabite places herself in her mother-in-law's group, but soon she will take the lead of the group. The big wager is that the God whom Ruth adopts is not defined by Naomi's quintuple accusatory declaration.

It is necessary to raise this astonishing dimension of the book of Ruth. The former pagan makes Naomi, Boaz, and her adopted people retrieve God's benevolence and love (*ḥesed*) (see 2:20). "The words of the Torah are challenged by the actions of a stranger."[51]

Ruth's decision to leave everything has often been compared to Abraham's decision in Genesis 12. Effectively, as early as Ruth 1:16, Ruth becomes synonymous with extravagance. She simultaneously leaves the security of her country, parents, and familiar gods. Her choice recalls that of Abraham. Perhaps it even surpasses his in value since Ruth chooses an enemy, or at least hostile, country.[52]

One can recognize yet another comparison, although through a contrast of terms. Ruth is a descendant of Lot; Lot who also left his city of Sodom destined for destruction. Physically and symbolically, it was forbidden to look back, but this is what Lot's wife could not resist doing; she was turned into a pillar of salt (Gen 19:17, 26). Besides the later incest, at the origin of Moab, there is already this negative issue attaching to the person of Lot. Ruth the Moabite redeems both disgraces of her origins. In contrast to Lot's wife, Ruth never looks back, which contrasts also with her sister-in-law, Orpah, whose name means precisely "the nape of the neck," regret for what has passed.

The parallel with the story of Lot and his daughters is not absent from another scene in the life of Ruth. Her offer on the threshing floor—we shall see the decisive importance that clothes play in the narrative—recalls, in a less distant echo, the incest that I have just noted. Here also, following the example of Lot, Boaz is made drowsy by an excess of food and of drink, and a woman turns the situation to her own advantage.[53]

---

[49] Ofosu Adutwum, "Ruth," in *The International Bible Commentary,* ed. William R. Farmer et al. (Collegeville, Minn.: Liturgical Press, 1998), 569.

[50] As among the monstrous gods and goddesses of the Levant, there are also domestic and protecting deities.

[51] Susanne Klingenstein, "Circles of Kinship," in *Reading Ruth,* ed. Kates and Reimer, 202.

[52] Cf. *b. Šabb.* 55a: Abraham left on God's order, but Ruth left on her own initiative.

[53] Cf. Francine Klagsbrun, "Ruth and Naomi, Rachel and Leah: Sisters under the Skin," in *Reading Ruth,* ed. Kates and Reimer, 269.

**[1:17]** "Where you die" (באשר תמתי). The preposition in Hebrew is ambiguous. Is she thinking of the instrument of Naomi's death ("in the manner in which you will die, I will die")? The unanimous Jewish tradition understands it as, "by whatever [judicial] means you die" ( = even if by stoning, burning at the stake, decapitation, or hanging)! She will also be buried in the same ground. One would expect that Ruth would live a lot longer than Naomi, given her age. But Ruth promises her that, even when Naomi is no longer living, she will not return to Moab but will choose to be buried in Judah like her mother-in-law. One can better measure the importance of burial in ancestral ground when one turns to passages such as Gen 29:29-31; 50:13, 24-26; and Josh 24:32. As a matter of fact, the grave was of immense importance. Jacob and Joseph insisted on being buried in Canaan. In the grave one "sleeps with one's fathers" (1 Kgs 2:10; 11:43; 14:31). From that time on, Ruth chooses not only a new people and a new deity, but new ancestors (!), those of Naomi and her family. Voluntary displacement cannot be any more radical.

The verse emphasizes the indirect character of faith expressed by the Moabite. The God of Naomi becomes her God, and so on. That this choice is the best is emphasized by the fact that, as soon as Naomi and Ruth put their feet on Israelite soil, events propel them toward their redemptive conclusion (toward the *gĕʾullâ;* cf. 2:1ff.).

"Do thus and so to me and more also" is an oath formula that one finds again only in the Deuteronomistic books of Samuel and Kings. However, this formula occurs elsewhere with Yhwh only in 1 Sam 20:13. This is also the only time in the book of Ruth where the heroine pronounces the divine name. The situation demands it here, for if she had employed the common "Elohim" (God) in her formula, one could have believed that she invoked Chemosh, the Moabite deity.

**[1:18]** "She said no more to her." This expression is quite surprising. The obvious meaning is that Naomi no longer attempts to convince her; but one also can understand it in a more radical sense: that she stopped speaking to her—and effectively, the dialog between the two women resumes only in Ruth 2:2. Naomi's silence—to which we shall return—does not betray her bad mood, but a deliberate discretion. Speaking with Ruth now could only encourage her, even indirectly, in her decision to abandon everything, as with Abram when he left Ur of the Chaldees (Genesis 12). Silence alone is the appropriate attitude in the face of such a sacrifice. Besides, Ruth's words are infused with such emotional importance that they cannot be followed by Naomi's replies, which could only be disappointing.

## The Welcoming Committee (1:19-22)

19 So the two of them went on until they came to Bethlehem.[a] When they came to Bethlehem, the whole town was stirred because of them; and the women said, "Is this Naomi?" 20 She said to them,

"Call me no longer Naomi,
call me Mara,
for the Almighty[a] has dealt bitterly with me.
21  I went away full,
but Yhwh[a] has brought me back empty;
why call me Naomi
when Yhwh has dealt harshly with me,
and the Almighty has brought calamity upon me?"
22  So Naomi returned together with Ruth the Moabite, her daughter-in-law,
who came back with her from the fields[a] of Moab. They came to Bethlehem
at the beginning of the barley harvest.

19[a] LXX omits: "So the two of them went on until they came to Bethlehem."
20[a] MT: שַׁדַּי (throughout).
21[a] NRSV: "LORD" (throughout).
22[a] NRSV: "country."

### Notes on 1:19-22

**[1:19]** "Is this Naomi?" About ten years had passed (see 1:4), and the intervening events had not been a source of joy for Naomi. Bitterness marks her face (v. 20).

Naomi has been reproached—in particular by feminist critics—for remaining silent on the subject of her daughter-in-law in the verses that follow. One can, however, interpret this silence in a much more positive way. Naomi comes back to the center of her "support group." This is not Ruth's support group; on the contrary, this group may appear hostile. In this sense, Naomi's silence about her daughter-in-law appears to be discretion. Cautiously, she leaves it for time and public rumor (cf. 2:11, etc.) to do their work. Musa Dube acutely observes, "even during the famine, one has full hands in Judah, while in Moab, the famine envelops you even when it seems that there is food in abundance." The author emphasizes that Judah's fertility could well be a disguised famine for Ruth, as Moab was in the past for Naomi.[54]

**[1:20]** "Call me Mara." מרא is already announced in 1:13—"bitter for me" (מַר לִי). The spelling of Mara (with final *aleph* instead of *he*) is Aramaic. This is a possible chronological index, all the more since Naomi invokes the divine name of "Shadday," an epithet that experienced a new wave of usage after the exile (see below on 1:21). The parallel with Job 27:2 is striking.

Naomi says to the women of Bethlehem, "Call me Mara." A name change corresponding to a change of social or psychological condition is not unusual in the Bible (Gen 41:45; 2 Kgs 23:34; 24:17; Dan 1:7). If it was necessary to prove that the

---

54 Dube, "Divining Ruth," 74.

proper names in the book have a symbolic value, v. 20 makes the point. Immediately after this name change comes an accusatory complaint, as it alludes to the place also called "Mara" in Exod 15:23. A little further in the text of Exodus 15, however, the bitterness of the people (corresponding to the bitterness of the waters) arises and God proclaims himself their healer (15:26); he will also reveal himself to be the healer in Ruth. The parallel is so much more striking when one remembers that "Ruth" means "the one that stems thirst" (see p. 40 above).

Note that Naomi does not allow the community to give her a name here. The contrast in 4:17 will be so much larger (see p. 144 below). This deserves reflection, for suddenly Naomi places herself in the exact opposite situation of those who return from Babylon to Zion and feel the need to establish their genealogies in order to emphasize their honor and property rights (cf. the genealogies in the Chronicler's Work). Naomi is without honor, and her right to the property will be debated in the continuation of the story. For the moment, the community has no clear sense of Naomi's identity ("Is this Naomi?" 1:19). In other words, the question of the group and the response of Naomi indicate, effectively, an "emptiness" (1:21). The history of Israel has just made a false step; it lacks a link in the chain. Now, as in similar cases, emptiness will be filled by the intervention of a foreigner, or precisely by a foreign woman. This woman substitutes herself for the Israelite failure: one thinks of Hagar the Egyptian, Tamar the Canaanite, and now Ruth the Moabite.

Thus a model is set, of which Paul in the New Testament will make the biggest case: the nations substitute themselves for the people of the promise (without replacing them, evidently). One will notice with care that, according to the model, substitution is not supersession. Ruth does not leave Naomi, but quite the opposite, returns to her all her "fullness."

Naomi attributes her misfortune to God, for she is persuaded, like Deutero-Isaiah, that God is the one who "make[s] weal and create[s] woe" (Isa 45:7). She bemoans her "emptiness"; but Ruth has no less reason to feel depleted. She too is a widow, without child; and, being a Moabite in Israel, there is little possibility for her to be married. She could even be raped by men without scruples (see Ruth 2:9, 15-16; and the commentary on those verses). It is true that in the past she had an Israelite husband in the person of Mahlon; but the circumstances were completely different: Mahlon lived in Moab. The intervention of the extraordinary will be necessary to put an end to the downward spiral of the two women. The Midrash says simply: a miracle. (See my analysis on vv. 3-4 above.)

Returning to the motif of Naomi's silence, another interpretation is possible. That Naomi does not mention Ruth and her comparable situation can only be explained by the suffering that, sometimes, renders one blind and deaf.[55] Naomi is

---

[55] Fewell and Gunn emphasize Naomi's silence in *Compromising Redemption,* 75. Effectively, when Naomi, at the turning point of the story, discovers that possibly everything is not ruined, her eyes are opened and she sees in Boaz the hand of Yhwh (2:20).

enveloped in misfortune and Ruth stands in the shadows. All things considered, though, of the two women, Ruth is still emptier—at any rate, the one more uprooted. But, in contrast, she does not protest. Her silence is as eloquent as the complaints of her companion; but she is inaudible and therefore easily overlooked. Her silence does not bear the same message as the cry of Naomi, for she chose to be the messenger of the future. When she speaks up, the verbs are in the future from beginning to end.[56] Thanks to her, the story's plot does not solely call for abandonment and despair. One could diagram it as follows:

- emptiness / famine / departure / alienation / hope;
- food / settlement / marriage / fullness;
- mourning / departure / emptiness / bitterness / arrival / nourishment / marriage / fullness.

She employs the term שׁדי (Shadday, "Almighty," not accompanied by אל, as in Gen 17:1-2; 28:3; 35:11; 49:25; Num 24:4, 16; Ps 68:14 [MT 15]; 91:1; Isa 13:6; Ezek 10:5; Joel 1:15). This is a very ancient epithet, as demonstrated by Genesis 49 and Numbers 24.[57] The shift here from Shadday (v. 20) to Yhwh (v. 21), then again to Shadday is remarkable. Shadday is the one who gives and restores offspring. Yhwh is the one that brings back (Naomi, or exiled Israel: שׁוב) after testing (or "tormenting": ענה). The twelve uses of שׁוב in chapter 1 suit the place where the return happens.

"The Almighty has brought calamity to me" (המר שׁדי לי). One sees this in Job 27:2, says Myers.[58] שׁדי, the titulary God, was not faithful to his name. As to the one who speaks here, her name is probably an abbreviation of a theophoric name: "[God is] my delight," "Naomi." She says: "Why call me Naomi ("[God is] my delight") when he has mistreated me?"[59]

[1:21] "Brought back" or "return" (שׁוב). In a section where the pivot is a movement of return—a term in Hebrew that can also be translated by "conversion," or even by "reversal"—Naomi describes to the women of Bethlehem the reversal of fortune to which she has fallen victim. From "Naomi" she became "Mara"; the one that personified fullness is now depleted. She calls herself "empty," a widow and one whose children are dead. Moab devoured everything; only she remains, but she is as a carcass emptied of all substance. The parallel to the first chapters of Job is evident.

---

[56] Avivah Zornberg, "The Concealed Alternative," in *Reading Ruth,* ed. Kates and Reimer, 65–81, with reason, insists on this.

[57] Cf. Frank Moore Cross, "Yhwh and the God of the Patriarchs," *HTR* 55 (1962) 225–59. He invokes the extrabiblical sources from the fourteenth century B.C.E. and concludes that the expression is pre-Mosaic (250).

[58] Myers, *Linguistic and Literary Form.*

[59] Pressler, *Joshua, Judges, Ruth,* 273.

"The LORD has dealt harshly with me." The Hebrew construction ב- ענה ("to testify against") is always read in this manner (once "to testify for," in Gen 30:33), as in "my sins testified against me," says Salmon ben Yeroḥam. An anonymous rabbi in *Ruth Rabbah* relates it back to 1 Sam 12:3; Exod 20:16; and Deut 5:17 (as well as to Gen 30:33). But the meaning in Ruth 1:21 is not clear. Ibn Ezra rejects the interpretation proposed by "certain ones" that ענה means "to humiliate" (this is the direction that I favor; cf. Exod 10:3). But the LXX and Peshitta seem to have read the verb as a piel and translate "to afflict." The confusion derives from the construction of the verb in the Qal (simple form) here with the preposition. ענה in the piel with Yhwh as subject appears in Deut 8:2, 3, 16; 1 Kgs 11:39; 2 Kgs 17:20; and Isa 64:11, but never with ב. As to ענה ב in the qal, it means, in fact, "to testify against": 2 Sam 1:16; Isa 3:9; Jer 14:7; Mic 6:3; Hos 5:5; 7:10 (but Yhwh never testifies against people in these texts). The context indicates the sense of "to afflict" (*pace* Ibn Ezra, Segond, TOB, etc.). Nevertheless, in one sense or another, it is clear that Naomi employs a juridical style. She pleads against an accusation of which she is unaware and a condemnation that is more or less Kafkaesque (cf. Job; Jer 12:1).

Taking account of the ambiguity of the verb, Avivah Zornberg combines the two meanings and insists on Naomi and Ruth's feelings of shame and humiliation upon returning to Bethlehem. For the populace says that if there is suffering, there is therefore guilt.[60]

The paradox in this matter is that Naomi complains about being "empty" and criticizes God for her miserable condition, while she is accompanied by someone whose name means "satisfy." In fact, God has already provided her fullness (4:15), but she does not see it and does not know it. The book of Ruth abounds with such ironies. Naomi is ungrateful for her daughter-in-law; she is as blind as Balaam in the plains of Moab (Num 22:25-31).

[1:22] "So Naomi returned." Naomi had lost everything: husband, children, and social status. She begins recovering her identity with her decision to stop being a foreigner—an option that makes Ruth an alien.

"Ruth the Moabite." This disrupting epithet reappears in 2:2, (6), 21; 4:5, 10.

"Who [Ruth] came back with her from the fields of Moab." The precision is surprising. Commentators suggest eliminating this phrase; but one finds it in all the versions. The verbal form (perfect) presents the anomaly of being constructed with the definite article! What is this sentence doing here? "Ruth the Moabite" rings negatively to Israelite ears. The author immediately makes up for this negativity with the positive side that transforms and transfigures. Ruth is a Moabite who returned from the fields of Moab. She is not Orpah, or one of the women from the country that seduced the Israelites at the time of their Egyptian exodus. Henceforth, it will no

---

[60] Zornberg, "Concealed Alternative," 68.

longer be possible in Israel to think about the Moabites in a completely negative manner. "Moab" will always evoke the "return" of "Ruth the Moabite."

"They came" (ובאו והמה). The pronoun "they" is superfluous in this Hebrew construction and adds a note of accentuation: "Now, here they are arriving in Bethlehem for the harvest of barley."

The end of chapter 1 contrasts with its beginning: famine first and harvest at the end of the section. Nevertheless, it is not necessary to conclude too quickly that the motif of the barley harvest is necessarily without ambiguity. Brian Britt establishes an interesting parallel between Ruth 1 and 2 Samuel 21, the only place in the canonical texts where the theme recurs (one rediscovers it in Jdt 8:2).[61] In each case the context is famine and death. Britt sees a "literary sacrifice" in the death of Elimelek and his sons, leading to a dead end. In Judith 8 it is also the time of the barley harvest when Manasseh, Judith's husband, dies (8:2-3); but this is again the origin of a work of salvation and, here and there, performed by a woman![62] D. F. Rauber, however, does not draw the same conclusions from this theme, but points out the *inclusio* of the "beginning of the harvest" in 1:22 and "the end of the barley and wheat harvests" in 2:23.[63]

Verse 22 is repetitive and announces what follows in chapter 2.

As I indicated above and as Malbim judiciously remarks, Naomi and Ruth return to the country at the moment of the barley harvest (Passover). He concludes that it is too late to sow Elimelek's field (which comes up only in chap. 4). That would explain why Naomi had to sell the field (see 4:3); selling it hurriedly was necessary for survival.[64]

---

[61] Brian Britt, "Narrative Sacrifice in the Hebrew Bible" (unpublished article).

[62] Britt points out another parallel between Ruth and Jdt 11:23, where Holophernes repeats the famous formula "your God shall be my God" from Ruth 1:16.

[63] D. F. Rauber, "Literary Values in the Bible: The Book of Ruth," in *Literary Interpretations of Biblical Narratives,* ed. Kenneth R. R. Gros Louis et al. (Nashville: Abingdon, 1974), 167.

[64] M. L. Malbim, *Megillat Rut* [in Hebrew] (Jerusalem: 'Eṣ ha-ḥayim, 1991), at 4:3.

# Chapter Two

## Reference Passages

- **Gleaning:** "When you reap the harvest of your land, you shall not reap to the very edges of your field, or gather the gleanings of your harvest. You shall not strip your vineyard bare, or gather the fallen grapes of your vineyard; you shall leave them for the poor and the alien: I am Yhwh your God." (Lev 19:9-10 = 23:22 par. Deut 24:19)
- **Land tenure and redemption:** "The land shall not be sold in perpetuity, for the land is mine; with me you are but aliens and tenants. Throughout the land that you hold, you shall provide for the redemption of the land. If anyone of your kin falls into difficulty and sells a piece of property then the next of kin shall come and redeem what the relative has sold." (Lev 25:23-25; see also 25:47-49)
- **Levirate marriage:** "When brothers reside together, and one of them dies and has no son, the wife of the deceased shall not be married outside the family to a stranger. Her husband's brother shall go in to her, taking her in marriage, and performing the duty of a husband's brother to her, and the firstborn whom she bears shall succeed to the name of the deceased brother, so that his name may not be blotted out of Israel." (Deut 25:5-6; see also Gen 38:8-11)

## Overview

In this chapter, one finds a sequence of five dialogues:

- Ruth and Naomi, v. 2
- Boaz, the reapers, and Ruth, vv. 4-7
- Boaz and Ruth, vv. 8-14
- Boaz and reapers, vv. 15-16
- Naomi and Ruth, vv. 19-22

The theme of this new development pivots around the recurring principle of "more than what is required [by the Law or general morality]." Campbell signals this deliberately: "emphasis on the extra, the more-than-required. Boaz will prove to be one who can give more than is legally required."[1] This voluntary act by Boaz is in response to Ruth's extraordinary initiative—one who left everything for her commitment to her mother-in-law and her people.

### Gleaning in the Field of Boaz (2:1-17)

2:1 Now Naomi had a kinsman on her husband's side, a prominent rich man,[a] of the clan[b] of Elimelek, whose name was Boaz. 2 And Ruth the Moabite said to Naomi, "Let me go to the field and glean among the ears of grain, behind someone in whose sight I may find favor." She said to her, "Go, my daughter." 3 So she went. She came and gleaned in the field behind the reapers. As it happened, she came to the part of the field belonging to Boaz, who was of the clan of Elimelek. 4 Just then Boaz came from Bethlehem. He said to the reapers, "Yhwh[a] be with you." They answered, "Yhwh bless you." 5 Then Boaz said to his servant who was in charge of the reapers, "To whom does this maiden[a] belong?" 6 The servant who was in charge of the reapers answered, "She is the Moabite who came back with Naomi from the fields[a] of Moab. 7 She said, 'Please, let me glean and gather among the sheaves behind the reapers.' So she came, and she has been on her feet from early this morning until now, without resting in the house."[a]

8 Then Boaz said to Ruth, "Now listen, my daughter, do not go to glean in another field or leave this one, but keep close to my young women. 9 Keep your eyes on the field that is being reaped, and follow behind them. I have ordered the young men not to bother you. If you get thirsty, go to the vessels and drink from what the young men have drawn." 10 Then she fell prostrate, with her face to the ground, and said to him, "Why have I found favor in your sight, that you should take notice of me, when I am a foreigner?" 11 But Boaz answered her, "All that you have done for your mother-in-law since the death of your husband has been fully told me, and how you left your father and mother and your native land and came to a people that you did not know before. 12 May Yhwh reward you for your deeds, and may you have a full reward from Yhwh, the God of Israel, under whose wings you have come for refuge!" 13 Then she said, "May I continue to find favor in your sight, my lord, for you have comforted me and spoken kindly to your servant, even though I am not one of your servants."

14 At mealtime Boaz said to her, "Come here, and eat some of this bread, and dip your morsel in the sour wine." So she sat beside the reapers, and he heaped up for her some parched grain. She ate until she was satisfied, and she had some left over. 15 When she got up to glean, Boaz instructed his

---

[1] Campbell, *Ruth*, 111.

young men, "Let her glean even among the standing sheaves, and do not reproach her. 16 You must also pull out some handfuls for her from the bundles, and leave them for her to glean, and do not rebuke her."

17 So she gleaned in the field until evening. Then she beat out what she had gleaned, and it was about an ephah of barley.

1ᵃ MT: אִישׁ גִּבּוֹר חַיִל.
1ᵇ NRSV: "family" (throughout).
4ᵃ NRSV: "LORD" (throughout).
5ᵃ NRSV: "young woman."
6ᵃ NRSV: "country."
7ᵃ NRSV: "even for a moment."

### Notes on 2:1-17

**[2:1]** This is an editorial comment, not Naomi's own reflection. She evidently does not mention Boaz, since she has no reason to think about him, as "So-and-so" is the closest redeemer (גֹּאֵל). It is by chance that Ruth goes into Boaz's field; it is not premeditated. In the absence of a plan, there is divine providence. "The two [Ruth and Boaz] meet in a fertile environment," as Levine points out.[2]

מֵידָע: "an acquaintance" works well to render the Hebrew construction, from the root יָדַע, meaning "know." But the translation hides the legal character of the term, also employed by parties to a contract. Note that the root יָדַע is employed often in the book of Ruth (see 2:10, 11; 3:2-4, 11, 18; 4:4). On the basis of this term, the kinship link with Naomi is loosened. Boaz may be portrayed as having a certain legal responsibility vis-à-vis Naomi, but it is quite secondary in comparison with the similar one of a closer kinsman, "So-and-so," in chapter 4.

Boaz is called "a prominent rich man" (אִישׁ גִּבּוֹר חַיִל). JPSV translates "a man of substance," RSV "a man of wealth," and REB "prominent and well-to-do member" (cf. 2 Kgs 24:14, with a social nuance). According to 3:11, Ruth is a "worthy woman" (אֵשֶׁת חַיִל). But the expression is not exactly the same here as there. Ruth is not exactly a "women of wealth"! In Ruth 3:11 the JPSV reads "a fine woman." The Midrash judiciously adds that David is also called a גִּבּוֹר חַיִל in 1 Sam 14:52 (as interpreted by the Midrash); for appropriate other personages, see Judg 6:12; 1 Sam 9:1; 1 Kgs 11:28; 2 Kgs 15:20. The parallel with David's dynasty is not mere chance. All the same, it is not without interest to see that the rabbis also interpreted גִּבּוֹר חַיִל applied to Boaz as designating a man versed in the Law.

**[2:2]** In order to emphasize the unusual character of what will follow, the text mentions once more that Ruth is a Moabite. Her identification as a foreigner is repeated

---

[2] Amy-Jill Levine, "Ruth," in *The Women's Bible Commentary,* ed. Carol A. Newsom and Sharon H. Ringe (Louisville: Westminster John Knox, 1992), 78–84. Therefore, it has nothing to do with a "sudden recollection" by Naomi that Boaz could be a redeemer (2:20), despite what Levine thinks (81).

seven times in the book (as "Moabite": 1:22; 2:2, 21; 4:5, 10; as "foreign": 2:10). It is an important key to understanding the book. Too often commentators have not sufficiently stressed that Ruth is someone "outside the law." This is the subversive reason the author chose a Moabite as heroine.

The tradition stresses the paradox of Ruth the Moabite asking her mother-in-law's permission to go and glean as, for the Midrash, Ruth was the daughter of King Eglon of Moab (*Ruth Rab.* 2.6), as we saw above. This legendary trait is not without interest for us, for it makes David a descendant of a Moabite dynasty (see Judg 3:12ff.). Another rabbinic tradition makes the opposite point: Ruth is described as "poor and foreign." To her are applied passages such as Lev 19:9-10; 23:22; Deut 24:19-22—the last on the right of gleaning, the first two on the rights of the stranger, widow, and orphan. But these privileges are not self-generating; it was necessary for the prophets to recall the people to apply the Law; thus Amos 5:10-15; Mic 3:1-3; Isa 1:17; 5:8-13; 18:4-6. Clearly, the authorization to glean had to be granted by the owner. This is complicated by the fact that Ruth is not a Judean and consequently is not automatically under the protection of the Torah; on the contrary, the Torah condemns making advances to Moabites. All she can hope for is "to find favor in the eyes" of the field's owner. Briefly stated, Boaz could have invoked the regulations against the Moabites and forbid his field to Ruth.[3]

"Behind someone" (אשר אחר, or "after"). One does not find this formulation except in Ezek 40:1 (sixth cent. B.C.E.). אחרי אשר is more frequent, but is not constructed with the imperfect as here.[4]

The expression "find favor" appears another thirteen times in the Bible to describe a person's position before God. In its broadest sense, it is the position of a person of lesser rank before a superior. It is necessary to understand the sentence as: "after having found favor in the eyes of someone."[5]

One rediscovers in 2:2 ("go, my daughter") a strange echo of preceding adjurations in chapter 1, "go, return" (1:8), "return" (1:11), "return, go" (1:12), "return" (1:16).[6]

One expects, ever since chapter 1, to find more emphasis on Naomi's discourse. Here, nevertheless, she says only two words (in Hebrew): "Go, my daughter." One had rather expected some warning against the dangers that Ruth might encounter (see 2:22; 3:1). The brevity of the permission given to Ruth here expresses her despondency: the two women had arrived at the bitter end—at subsistence. They have nothing more to lose.

---

[3] Linafelt ("Ruth," 38) speaks of the "rights of Ruth in the field of Boaz"; but as a Moabite she has none.

[4] Myers, *Linguistic and Literary Form,* 23.

[5] *Pace* Sasson, *Ruth,* 43–44.

[6] Cf. Fewell and Gunn, *Compromising Redemption,* 77; Phyllis Trible, *God and the Rhetoric of Sexuality,* OBT (Philadelphia: Fortress Press, 1978), 179–80.

**Ruth**

Ruth, as a character in the narrative, is strangely linked to the notion of "field." She comes from the "fields of Moab," and the mention of her Moabite origins in this verse recalls that; she gleans in Boaz's field in chapter 2, then goes to the same field in chapter 3; and finally, in chapter 4, she is closely associated with redemption of the field by the redeemer (גאל). The intention is not necessarily to make Ruth a farmer (as opposed to the townspeople of Bethlehem), but to emphasize, I think, that she cannot be considered a displaced person "with neither hearth nor home," a Bohemian without roots. In Moab or in Judah, Ruth is "connected" (דבק; see 1:14). She is rooted in her new environment as she previously was in her own country. "A wheat field in Judah is just like a wheat field in Moab," says Ostriker.[7] Moreover, the feminine symbolism of the field is very fitting here. From this perspective, Boaz's exhortation for Ruth not to glean in fields other than his (2:8) is fully sensible. (Note that 2:8 employs the same verb, "keep close, cling" [דבק], as in 1:14; see p. 67).

**[2:3]** "As it happened" or "by chance" (ויקר מקרה). As emphasized above, Ruth accidentally gleaned in the field of the one that would one day become her redeemer. He was from Elimelek's clan and fulfilled the conditions enunciated in v. 1. Luck or providence? The continuation of the narrative turns luck into providence. In vv. 11-12 Boaz leaves no doubt about this subject. Clearer yet is Naomi's comment in v. 20.[8]

The construction "as it happened" does not appear elsewhere except in Qoh 2:14, 15, which is a very late text. In Gen 24:12 one finds "please grant" (הקרה-נא). One is reminded of texts such as Wis 16:17c: "the universe defends the righteous."

**[2:4]** The verse begins with the word והנה ("Just then"), which contributes to reinforce the dimension of journey in a development that began with something like "now it happened that she came . . ." (v. 3). Berlin especially has insisted on the surprising effect that this expression introduces: "Now, it happened that Boaz arrived from Bethlehem." In 3:8 one finds "and behold, there was a woman lying at his feet," and in 4:1, "now, the redeemer . . . came passing by."

---

[7] Alicia S. Ostriker, "The Redeeming of Ruth," in *The Nakedness of the Fathers: Biblical Visions and Revisions* (New Brunswick, N.J.: Rutgers Univ. Press, 1994), 173.

[8] Hubbard says, "Since only Yahweh can do the impossible, one will recognize Yahweh's intervention when the unreal becomes reality" (*Ruth,* 111). On the other hand, some critics think that the "theology of Ruth" is virtually nonexistent, and it is evident that it appears only faintly. Yet it remains that God is mentioned 23 times in the book, of which 21 are in the dialogs (17x as Yhwh). Cf. Hals, *Theology.* Hals, nevertheless, thinks that the choice of different designations for God is without importance. But if one adds the two mentions of Yhwh by the narrator, there are 15 references to Yhwh, or *Yah* in Hebrew (an abbreviation often employed for Yhwh), which has a numerical value of fifteen. Elohim appears 4 times, but only 3 times does it designate the living God. One knows the biblical insistence on the figure three, the symbol of fullness. Shadday, on the other hand, appears only twice (= incompleteness); but Naomi invokes this name precisely in order to blame him for his disappointing work as far as she is concerned (cf. 1:20-21).

Boaz is a pious man. This is important for the continuation of the narrative, which demonstrates his fidelity to the divine law, but also his willingness to adopt a broader interpretation of it. From this perspective, one could not reproach him as someone whose laxity toward the Law would permit him to take the Moabite in marriage. An atmosphere of holiness pervades his person and everything around him, which will show itself repeatedly in the verses that follow (see Ps 129:8).

**[2:5]** "To whom does this young woman belong?" One does not run across this question except in Gen 32:18 and 1 Sam 30:13 (in these two texts the expression is used of male servants): the question refers to persons of humble origins belonging to a master. In relation to this one, their own identity matters little. Indeed, in the two cases mentioned, the men remain nameless. An anonymous rabbi in *Ruth Rabbah* was astonished by the bluntness of the question and comments, "It is as if he reproached [his foreman] for allowing gleaning." Boaz naturally considers her a servant. The foreman's response mentions the family links with Naomi, which, of course, changes Boaz's perspective. Ruth has a certain accreditation because of her links with Boaz's relative. He noticed her in the midst of the gleaners perhaps because she was not one of the regular workers, because her ethnic characteristics distinguished her from the Judeans, as did her natural beauty (for it is clear that she does not leave Boaz unaffected as a man). One cannot exclude a combination of these three possibilities.

The foreman comments on two additional important elements: she accompanied Naomi at the time of her return to the country, and she is a tireless worker. Far from living off of Naomi, she took charge of their subsistence. If Boaz's question to the foreman of the harvest disguises his reproach, the foreman's response fully justifies his decision to allow this "maiden" to glean in the field.

On the designation of Ruth as a "maiden," here and elsewhere, one will find a fitting development at 4:13. It is enough here to underline, along with the author of the story, that Ruth is nubile. She is a young widow, and her age contrasts with that of Boaz. It is remarkable how skillfully the author chooses vocabulary. This is revealed in seemingly insignificant details (see also, for example, v. 14 and the commentary). The whole narrative is very brief (eighty-five verses); but, at each step of the way, the reader is invited to reflect, for the text is constantly allusive.

Ruth's work without rest retrospectively confirms her determined spirit already demonstrated in chapter 1. It was certainly not because of her deficient will power that she left everything to follow her mother-in-law. From start to finish, Ruth appears as a woman of strong character (אשת חיל), like the woman described in Prov 31:10-31 (see Ruth 3:11). Boaz's foreman is the first to be impressed, before his patron. But Boaz will not be left behind, as the rest of the chapter demonstrates.

**[2:6]** Boaz's foreman corresponds to Abraham's servant in Genesis 24. Ruth, a young woman or a girl (!), is said to have "returned" to the country, as in chapter 1, and her arrival is assimilated to the return of her mother-in-law. But this fact is balanced by Ruth's point of departure (also Naomi's)—namely, "the fields of Moab." On the one hand, describing the young woman as going from one field to another seems like an innocuous detail; but more disturbing is the implicit allusion to the "fields of Moab," where Israel was seduced by the Moabite women (see Numbers 25). That Ruth is a Moabite is the first thing said about her. Her name is not even mentioned; her origins obliterate everything else.

**[2:7]** The first difficulty in this verse is the emphasis given to "glean among the sheaves"; this was unusual for a gleaner. In any case, Ruth does not claim a right but asks a favor (see above on v. 2, pp. 62–63).[9] But the favor is rather extraordinary: instead of gleaning what was left by the harvesters, Ruth asks permission to glean "among the sheaves," that is, what was put in piles by the workers for winnowing. In other words, Ruth's request was beyond what was ordinarily granted—in short, beyond the "letter."

The immediate object of her request is clear. As the end of the chapter shows, what she will harvest will be infinitely more abundant; furthermore, she will be able to nourish her mother-in-law. But, in a deeper sense, Ruth represents a hermeneutical imperative. If one sticks to the strict interpretation of law and custom, she dies and so does Naomi (see 1:17: "where you die, I will die."). Only a generous interpretation can save them both. This is for Boaz to decide.

Note how much the psychology of Ruth is mistaken if one considers her a young, coy, and humble woman—even self-effacing (the book of Ruth as a rural romance!). One is dealing with a strong and determined woman, as will be shown again in chapter 3. Her self-denial in order to benefit her mother-in-law attains the heights of human courage. As the TOB says, "The translation of this verse is widely debated." It renders the text thus: ". . . this is her residence, the house is hardly it!" In this case, the foreman's use of the demonstrative pronoun זֶה ("this") designates the field and not the person of Ruth, as the LXX implies. It is followed by numerous commentators (one compares then the despising word of 2 Sam 13:17, where Amnon says of his sister Tamar, "Put this [זֹאת] [woman] out of my presence!)."

Avi Hurvitz suggests that the text reflects the foreman's confusion; he is uncertain of Boaz's approval.[10] This idea is not without interest when one sees the author's stylistic mastery in reports of speeches. Be that as it may, Ruth clearly conquered the foreman's heart before she conquered that of the owner of the field.

The difficulty of the verse is complicated by the ambiguity of the term "a little, hardly" (מְעָט). Ibn Ezra interprets it as "a little time"; an anonymous rabbi in *Ruth Rabbah* interprets it as "a little grain," a reading that is also suggested by Bertrand

---

[9] Cf. Nielsen, *Ruth*, 57.
[10] Hurvitz, "Ruth 2.7—'A Midrashic Gloss'?" *ZAW* 95 (1983) 121–23.

Zimolong.[11] The LXX already interpreted the term in a temporal sense: "she did not rest a bit in the field," reading שבתה (*šibtah*, "she is seated") as being שבתה (*šabtah*, "she stopped, rested") and introducing a nonexistent negation in the MT. For LXX perhaps, Ruth took a moment's rest (when Boaz arrives in the field?), which permits the dialog between the two of them (vv. 8-9).

Another major difficulty is the term "the house" (הבית). Perhaps this is haplography with the word שבתה (thus Rudolph). Or was there a shelter in the field for resting (thus Tg)? For the Vg, she "did not return to the house for a moment," implying a negation absent in the MT and the improbable derivation of the verb from the root שוב ("return"). In an interesting note, Lys changes the pointing of the MT and suggests the translation, "This [the field] is her residence, the house hardly so."[12]

**[2:8]** Boaz's exhortation not to go into another field is rather surprising. One can understand that Boaz acts here to surpass everyone in generosity. But his directive takes its full meaning from the context of the exclusion of foreign women by Ezra and Nehemiah. Boaz's field symbolizes the land of Israel. Ruth's assimilation among Boaz's "young women" is her integration in Israel.[13]

This socioreligious milieu is the only likely one to clarify the use in 2:9 of the verb נגע ("molest"), which connotes major violence (Gen 26:11, 29; 32:25, 32 [MT 26, 33]; etc.) or illegitimate sexual relations (Gen 20:6; Prov 6:29). From this perspective, one thinks of a text such as Neh 13:25. Let us add, with Hubbard, the motif of the protection of the "elect woman" (Sarah in Gen 20:6; Rebekah in 26:29).[14] Eventually, Ruth will be equated with the matriarchs of Israel (Ruth 4:11-12).

What is extraordinary in Boaz's attitude is that it implicitly broadens the interpretation of the law regarding the protection of the foreigner to a Moabite (see infra, on v. 10). The insistence of Boaz that Ruth remain in his fields and not to go anywhere else is again underscored by employing the verb דבק ("keep close"), here as in 1:14, at the time of Ruth's "conversion" (see also 2:21, 22). Subtly, the text insinuates that Ruth's loyalty to Naomi becomes real by her loyalty to Boaz (or to intermediaries in his service, for these are the extension of Boaz and also a screen that protects him from an engagement that would then be judged to be too radical). Matthews's note that ancient Near Eastern hospitality transforms a stranger into an ally is correct.[15] But he never takes seriously the fundamental fact that Ruth is a Moabite. Without this aspect of the issue, Ruth's surprise at Boaz's benevolent attitude (in 2:10, for example) becomes incomprehensible.

The verb normally takes the preposition ב ("to") as in 1:14, but Boaz employs

---

[11] Bertrand Zimolong, "Zu Ruth II,7," *ZAW* 58 (1940–41) 156–58; cited by Campbell, *Ruth*, 96.

[12] Daniel Lys, "Residence ou repos? Notule sur Ruth ii 7," *VT* 31 (1981) 497–501. This reading of Lys finds confirmation in the same use of זה that designates the field in v. 8, which follows.

[13] Hubbard, *Ruth*, 156.

[14] Ibid., 160.

[15] Matthews, *Judges and Ruth*, 228.

the preposition עִם ("with"). And when Ruth quotes Boaz in 2:21, she repeats this unique abnormality in the Hebrew Bible. One has already seen that the author makes an idiomatic distinction between the speeches of different generations.

"To glean in another field." The verb here, לקט, is in the Qal (basic form), while the eleven other appearances of the word in the book use the intensive form (Piel). To conclude with Jenni that it indicates a comparatively easy gleaning is not convincing.[16] Why would it be easier for Ruth in another field? On the other hand, the change to the Qal form clearly avoids a total of twelve uses of the verb, at a time when the attraction to "another" field would bring Ruth to miss her destiny.

What follows in 2:9 and 16 reminds one of the same scene in chapter 1. There one has the verb נגע ("touch, abuse"), while one finds פגע ("urge [to do]") in 1:16 ("do not urge me to leave you"). On נגע see above.

On the subject of Boaz's speech here (2:8-9), one will note again, as in the speech of Naomi in chapter 1, the repetition of certain words: הלא (lit. "is this not," 2x); הנערים ("young people," 2x); נערותי ("my young women"); בשדה ("in the field," 2x); והלכת ("and you will go," 2x; plus 1x תלכי, "go"). When he resumes speaking in v. 11, Boaz says, הגד הגד לי ("it was told [in detail] to me"), and the reader is not surprised by this repetition. Boaz speaks with the rhythm reflecting an older man. He is also conscious to say unusual things in an exceptional situation. He weighs his words, which sometimes leads him to stammer.

Different people seem to like calling Ruth "daughter," and they are, by the way, all pleasant people. "My daughter" (בתי) is found again in Boaz's mouth in 3:10, 11; in Naomi's in 2:2, 22; 3:1, 16, 18; a total of eight times. But, as Ostriker rightly says, the seduction scene with Boaz, a paternal figure, is like a pastoral repetition story (a redemption?) of Lot's daughters (Genesis 19). For, as she adds, "the Torah loves the breaking of boundaries."[17]

**[2:9]** Boaz gives the order not to bother/scold/harass Ruth: was this a common practice in ancient Israel? Or rather is it a question of hurling jibes at this poor Moabite? As a reminder, Ruth is known not to have a male protector. Boaz becomes her protector anticipatorily. This is a first step in the general direction of the narrative that climaxes with the marriage of these two people.[18]

Ruth will be able to keep her eyes on her work without being obliged to watch the young men, fearing to be bothered by their advances. The young men could be attracted to this young woman with whom a sexual relation would not be considered as adulterous (Lev 20:10; Deut 22:22) or as reprehensible seduction (Exod 22:16 [MT 15]; Deut 22:28-29).

---

[16] Ernst Jenni, *Das hebräische Pi'el: Syntaktisch-semasiologische Untersuchung einer Verbalform im Alten Testament* (Zurich: EVZ, 1968), 188–89; cited by Sasson, *Ruth,* 96.

[17] Ostriker, "Redeeming of Ruth," 175 n. 1.

[18] Cf. Sakenfeld, *Ruth,* 43.

In the introduction above, I emphasized the inverted position of Ruth the Moabite in comparison with the usual novella, where one finds a (young) Israelite or Judean becoming a counselor or chancellor in a foreign country, like Joseph in Egypt, Daniel in Babylon, Ahikar in Assyria, or Mordecai in Persia, where Esther is queen.

This inversion finds a special echo in the motif (at first blush inconsequential) of Ruth going to drink water drawn by the young men (2:9), in contrast to the typical scene of the traveler given water by girls, among which the traveler often finds a wife (see Genesis 24; 29; and Exod 2:15-22). One must consider this overturning of generically determined conventions from the vantage point of the subversion presented in the book (see above, in 1:8: "mother's house"). This subversion expresses itself on the ethnic or racial plane on one hand, and on the sexual plane on the other. There is, in fact, a double reversal in that a Judean serves a Moabite and a woman drinks water drawn by men. Ecclesiastes would not be happy. For him it was outrageous to see slaves on horseback and princes walking (Qoh 10:7). We are only up to chapter 2 of Ruth and already we find an overturning of traditional values.[19] Ruth will soon talk about herself as a servant (v. 13), but one will not miss the irony of the point after Boaz's declaration in v. 9. Starting now, neither Ruth nor Boaz will be the same as before their meeting.

In the background of this whole scene is the text of Deut 23:2-4 (MT 3-5), which denounces the Moabites' refusal to provide the Israelite exiles "bread and water." In the same train of thought, Boaz's blessing of Ruth is in opposition to the report of Balaam's "cursing" Israel on the "plains of Moab."

The mention of drinking water recalls, as I already said above, the encounter scenes between future partners in biblical narratives (see Genesis 24; 29; Exod 2:15-22). But here Ruth has a parallel role to Abraham's servant (Gen 24:17-20) or to Moses (Exodus 2). One will note that Abraham's servant prostrates himself before Yhwh when he understands that he found a woman for Isaac. In Ruth 2:10 there is also a prostration, but in front of a man!

**[2:10]** Ruth prostrates herself in front of Boaz. The scene recalls a similar one, with a non-Judean prostrating himself in front of a Judean, such as Nebuchadnezzar in front of Daniel (Dan 2:46; see also, in a negative sense, Acts 14:11-18).[20] In his turn, David, a descendant of Ruth according to our story, will see Abigail prostrate herself in the same manner in front of him (1 Sam 25:23).

"I found favor in your eyes." This repeats, in an affirmative form, the vow formula of Ruth in v. 2. A third mention of this expression is located a little further on, in v. 13. Biblical authors gladly repeat three times the same motif.

---

[19] This literary procedure, also emphasized by Alter, is, so to speak, "a means of attaching that [narrative] moment to a larger pattern of historical and theological meaning" (Robert Alter, *The Art of Biblical Narrative* [New York: Basic Books, 1981], 60).

[20] On this motif see André LaCocque, *The Book of Daniel,* trans. David Pellhauer (Atlanta: John Knox, 1979), 53–54.

There is a wordplay in Hebrew that Segond translates with a French wordplay: "être reconnue, moi qui ne suis qu'une inconnue," נכריה . . . להכרני. On the latter term, which I translate "foreigner," see Gen 31:15; Ps 69:8 (MT 9); Job 19:15; this is a person from a foreign country (Exod 21:8).

The notion of the foreigner is among the most important in the Bible. The Israelites themselves are "foreigners" in their own country (Lev 25:23), as they were in Egypt (Exod 2:22; 22:21 [MT 20]), as they will be in exile in Babylon and in the Diaspora. Israelite ethics concerning the foreigner are based on this basic trait of their identity. The idea is picked up again in the New Testament (see 1 Pet 2:11).

But Biblical Hebrew carefully distinguishes between two different terms for designating the foreigner: גר and נכרי. In French, one hardly has a choice without employing the pejorative term *métèque* for נכרי. English distinguishes between "foreigner" and "alien." For the נכרי is not simply the foreigner, but one who is strange and different.[21] The biblical Israelite was very aware of having been a גר in a נכרי country ("an alien in a foreign land" is the NRSV translation in Exod 2:22 = 18:3; cf. 22:21 [MT 20]; 23:9; Deut 10:18, 19; 23:7 [MT 8]). The "nations" are נכרים (see, for example, Exod 21:8).

גר became a technical term in Post-Biblical Hebrew for designating a convert to Judaism. Within the Bible, the גר can be a foreigner with the right to refuge in Israel (Lev 16:29; 25:47); and, consequently, Ruth could avail herself of this status with Boaz. Rather she chooses the term נכרי, "foreigner." Is this humility? Of course, but there is also another important reason. The socioreligious "purges" of Ezra and Nehemiah had as their object, according to the texts, foreign women (נשים נכריות; see Ezra 10:2, 10, 11, 14, 17, 18, 44; Neh 13:27). In this context of the Second Temple, Boaz sees that Ruth confronts him with a challenge: will he seize this pretext, offered by the young woman herself, to reject her in the name of the letter of the Law (see Deut 15:3, נכרי)? Or else, in this concrete case that puts in question the legal theory, will he understand that "the Torah loves the breaking of barriers," as Ostriker says?[22]

The response of Boaz is "gospel-like" before the fact (see Matt 5:23-24). To employ the Pauline expression, "the letter" would kill Ruth, "the spirit" gives her life—literally (see 2 Cor 3:6).

But Ruth is not simply a foreigner, she is a Moabite; and, at that time, one legal prescription of inclusion—by which a נכרי would become a גר—collides with another: the exclusion of Moab from all alliances. To which of the two is one to give priority? The book of Ruth is entirely stretched by this bipolarity of the "prescriptive" that is open to a bipolar interpretation of the Torah. Ruth is prostrating herself in front of Boaz, the interpreter. Just as chapter 1 of the book sketches the structure of the

---

[21] The Tg paraphrases, "while I am of a foreign country . . . [that is] impure."

[22] Ostriker, "Redeeming of Ruth," 175 n. 1.

whole narrative, the decision of Boaz in favor of Ruth announces his role as redeemer in the remainder of the book.[23]

Boaz bases his attitude on the recognition of the experience suffered by the foreigner. When one situates Ruth 2:10 in the historical and social context of the expulsion of foreign women by Ezra and Nehemiah, the irenic words of Boaz are set much more in relief. The inherent suffering due to change is not recognized by the governors of Judah in the fifth century. Boaz, by contrast, establishes a parallel by alluding to Abraham (Gen 12:1) in the following verse. If it is necessary to choose between Nehemiah and Abraham, his choice is already made.[24]

**[2:11]** Regarding Ruth's migration paralleling Abraham's, see above on Ruth 1:16. The vocabulary closely recalls Gen 12:1; but the addition in Ruth of "and your mother," whom the Moabite also left, is significant (see 1:8 and p. 44). The intertextual references are mixed here. One should also refer to Gen 2:24, which states that a man leaves his father and his mother to attach himself to his wife—the verb דבק is employed also in Ruth to describe Ruth's devotion to her mother-in-law. This intertexual connection to Genesis 2 is quite remarkable. Man and woman become one flesh; Ruth and Naomi have one destiny together. And this is certainly an iconoclastic trait on the part of the book. The tenacious stereotype according to which the friendship between two women is impossible (thus, Aristotle)—in particular a mother-in-law and her daughter-in-law—is debunked here.

"And your native land," or "the country of your birth." This expression is not employed exclusively in the Hebrew Bible in the context of the Babylonian exile, it is true; but this is its privileged usage (see Jer 22:10; 46:16), after a description of the patriarchs' migrations (Gen 11:28; 12:1; 24:7; 31:13). In a book that insists on genealogical continuity or discontinuity as Ruth does, Boaz's declaration comes to fill the absence of genealogy regarding Ruth. Boaz "establishes that Ruth's courage and her loyalty to her mother-in-law will amply serve in place of a genealogy."[25]

It is clear that the arrival of the two women at Bethlehem was a sensation. On "has been fully told me," see above on Ruth 2:8 (p. 68). Boaz continues to speak in a bombastic stream, employing here a double Hophal (passive causal form; something like, "It was told to me saying," or "It was made to be told to me").

Boaz mentions Ruth's mother-in-law in passing, but he does not reveal how close his kinship is with Elimelek, therefore with Mahlon, Ruth's deceased husband. This revelation will come from Naomi at the end of the chapter. Thus Boaz will show himself generous but prudent, open but only up to a certain point—*in medio virtus* (middle-of-the-road virtue). In order to drive this petty bourgeois from his

---

[23] Thus Moses already rescued Jethro's daughters before liberating his people from Egypt (Exod 2:17).

[24] In the Jewish tradition, Abraham is the host par excellence. His tent was open on all sides so that travelers coming from all directions were welcomed (*Midr. Ps.* on Ps 37:1 [126 b, par. 1]).

[25] Alter, *Art of Biblical Narrative*, 59.

comfortable but completely predictable rut, nothing less than a dramatic and properly shocking confrontation will be necessary (3:8).

"Before" renders the Hebrew expression תְּמוֹל שִׁלְשׁוֹם ("yesterday, third day"). This phrase is also used in case laws (see Exod 21:29, 36; Deut 4:42; 19:4, 6). Boaz is a man of law and well-read (see Ruth 4).

**[2:12]** Linafelt notices that Boaz's invocation of Yhwh can be a "deflection of Ruth's distinctively 'worshipful' posture toward Boaz" (v. 10).[26] In this case, Ruth does not seem to have grasped the complete extent of this exclamation of Boaz, for she persists in calling him "my lord" (v. 13). A similar weakness of Ruth, doubtless due to the fact that she was inexperienced in the faith of Israel's God and in the culture that developed in this context, is met again at the vv. 21-22. There Ruth also does not seem to understand that a woman in Israel does not mix freely in the company of men (see below on 2:21-22).

But there is more. Boaz's demonstrative piety could easily become a subterfuge, to which Ruth, politely but firmly, makes an obstacle. She wants "to find favor in his eyes"—Boaz's rather than God's? Ruth's speech brings the level in any case back to earth, contrasting strongly with the unctuous term "my lord." While Boaz talks about "Yhwh's wing" (see Ps 91:4), Ruth places herself under Boaz's wing (Ruth 3:9). That does not mean, in contrast to Linafelt, that Ruth has a "manifest lack of interest in the Lord";[27] but she knows that pious words do not replace a personal commitment. There is evidently a huge difference between invoking the presence of the Lord and becoming this presence for others.

One will note that here Boaz shares the conviction of most biblical authors, according to which Yhwh remunerates both good and bad human actions in an equitable way. Boaz speaks to Ruth about retribution; and, effectively, the principle that he enunciates is one of distributive justice (see Jer 25:14; Ps 28:4; Job 34:11 [in the Elihu speeches]; Prov 24:12b). The book of Job, after developing the same idea at length, smashes it to pieces in the end. But Boaz is not there yet in chapter 2 of Ruth. His piety rests on the judicial (or economic, in this verse) principle of equivalence—a long way from the principle of overabundance (*hesed*).

Concerning the "pietism" of Boaz, one does not have to wonder why the author chose to present the character in this manner. In my reading, Boaz represents the conservative party of the fifth century. The author does not circulate in that environment and describes Boaz as a bit ridiculous. But I do not see how she would render his piety suspect, as the eyes of modern commentators commonly see her. Boaz remains worthy of respect from start to finish, especially at the end, evidently; but he lost nothing, in chapter 4 of the book, of his legalist and somewhat pompous style.[28]

---

[26] Linafelt, "Ruth," 37.
[27] Ibid.
[28] One finds the same idea expressed in Humbert, "Art et leçon."

The use of מַשְׂכֻּרְתֵּךְ ("your reward") is just like that in relation to Abraham in Gen 29:15, where the word appears for the first time. In Gen 15:1 the term שָׂכָר is the same verbal root, but indicates a soldier's pay; see also 30:16, 18; 31:7, 41. In Genesis the reward is especially in terms of offspring; the allusion here is elucidated by this parallel with Genesis.

כְּנָפָיו ("his wings") may allude to the divine presence between the wings of the cherubs on the ark of the covenant (see 1 Kgs 6:23-28; 8:6). On כָּנָף, "protection, wing," see Exod 19:4; Deut 32:11; Ps 17:8; 36:7 (MT 8); 63:7 (MT 8); 91:4. Boaz seems to project upon God the responsibility that he himself should assume and, effectively, will assume in the future. If that is the case, Boaz represents at this level the piety of the well-meaning of every era, a surface piety that Jesus denounces with indignation. Boaz will have to take himself to the Moabite school and learn that piety proceeds from goodness (*ḥesed;* see Matt 8:10; Luke 7:9). Ruth finely indicates this in her response (v. 13, where one finds the ambiguous "though I am not, I shall be one of your maidservants"). But perhaps this is too much suspicion on my part. Rabbi Arama (1420–1494) paraphrases the declaration of Boaz: "God alone can adequately reward you for your acts of *ḥesed.*"[29]

The term is clearly a wordplay on כָּנָף, the edge of Boaz's clothing (3:9). One could say that the whole theology of Ruth is in this parallel between the divine wings and the edge of Boaz's clothing. The divine action is inseparable from the human action. The human agent is the essential vehicle for the divine direction of this story (collective and individual). Ruth's marriage to Boaz will effectively be the expression of divine protection. The reader will appreciate the refreshing absence of a deus ex machina.

"Full reward." The TOB provides a note: "The root of this word, used twice, marks fullness and also peace (*šlm*)."

**[2:13]** The obvious meaning of Ruth's declaration is that she received Boaz's consolation as if she was a servant while she is not. But the Hebrew is again ambiguous and can be understood in the sense that Boaz treated her as a servant while she will never be one.

According to *Ruth Rab.* 5.5, Ruth says to Boaz, "I am not like one of your servants" (the term here is שִׁפְחָה), to which Boaz replies, "God forbid! You are not one of the servants [*haʾămāhôt*] but one of the matriarchs [*haʾimmāhôt*]."[30] שִׁפְחָה is probably allusive, as Campbell remarks, for there is an analogy with מִשְׁפָּחָה ("clan") in 2:1, 3. Ruth chooses her words carefully; Boaz must understand that she uses שִׁפְחָה with several levels of meaning.

---

29. "Commentary on the Five Megillot," Salonique 1573; cited by Zlotowitz, in Scherman and Zlotowitz, *Book of Ruth,* 96.

30. One might note, with Beattie, that this explanation would have fit better at 3:19 (*Jewish Exegesis,* 215).

Sasson discusses the difference between the use of שפחה here and of אמה in 3:9. The first would designate a very inferior level, the second a servant apt to become the spouse or the concubine of a freeman.[31] After what we saw above on the subject of Ruth's use of the term נכרי (fem. נכריה) to describe herself (2:10), it may well be, in fact, that שפחה is used to situate her on the same social rung.

Ruth calls Boaz "lord" (just as God is Lord) and thanks him for his "consolation" (as God is comforting; see Isa 12:1; 51:12; 52:9; 66:13; Ps 71:21; 119:82). We are quite in the spirit of the book (see Ruth 2:12 and p. 73).

"To speak to the heart" (דברת על־לב). One rather expects דברת אל־לב. The note in TOB is judicious: "The heart is not simply the organ of emotional life (it is not a matter of a declaration of love from Boaz to Ruth!), but the center of the being where intelligence and decisions are located." But the expression, whatever TOB thinks, is somewhat ambiguous. It appears nine times in the Bible with the meaning "console" (for example, Gen 50:21; Isa 40:2), but also several times meaning "to seduce a woman" (Gen 34:3; Judg 19:3; Hos 2:16).

**[2:14]** Boaz's generosity is evident. Ruth is poor and she is hungry. But there is more. Ruth is invited to eat with men (the harvesters), which is unusual. She, a Moabite, will eat with the Judeans, which is scandalous in the eyes of conservatives.[32] Boaz has just taken a step in the direction of liberalism. His evolution has begun. Besides, Ruth's gleaning is transformed by Boaz's wishes. She now has access to the very harvest, no longer just to what the harvesters leave behind. An act of generosity again, but especially surpassing the letter of the law; Boaz goes "beyond what the Law asks" (לפנים משורת הדין).

"And at mealtime," and before that, Boaz does not say a word, like Naomi after Ruth's speech in 1:17.

The חמץ ("tart wine") is a desirable drink (see Num 6:3). The word is translated in Greek by *oxos* (with the same sense) in the Gospels, as already in the LXX of Ps 69:22 (Eng. 21); this is a red table wine drunk by the Roman soldiers. It seems that pious women banded together in Jerusalem to reduce the sufferings of the crucified ones offering some of them this wine as quenching thirst and intoxicating (see Mark 15:36; Matt 27:48; John 19:29; *Gos. Pet.* 5:16-17).

Ruth sits "beside" (משד) the harvesters in contrast with the other gleaners who, evidently, are not integrated into the circle of the official workers or engaged by the owner of the field. She received a social and moral promotion from Boaz.

תשבע ("he tended [to her]") is a hapax legomenon in the Bible, but the term is employed in the Mishnah (*m. 'Erub.* 10:1). Ibn Ezra translates "he gave her." Myers

---

[31] Sasson, *Ruth,* 53.

[32] Salmon bar Yeḥoram cannot prevent himself from protesting: she sits at the side of the harvesters, but she does not have the right! (He adds something like, "but such are women!")

compares תשׁבּע to the Akkadian *ṣabatû*, "to hold." The LXX perhaps has reason to translate it with "to pile up."

Boaz feeding Ruth is already a marital act, as Ruth also feeds Naomi, to whom she attached herself as a husband attaches himself to his wife (see above, 1:14 and 2:11).

"She ate and had some left over." We meet all these terms together again in 2 Chron 31:10 (on the subject of King Hezekiah's reform; see also, by contrast, Mic 6:14). The problem of survival, so evident in the narrative of Ruth, is best explained in the context of the restoration in the sixth-fifth centuries. The former exiles, who idealistically returned to Zion, know severe famine due to various circumstances (political, climatic, and—as the prophets Haggai and Zechariah say—religious). In support of this thesis of the prophets, the priestly author of the book of the Chronicles rebuilds the story of Hezekiah's reform that, according to him, changed the famine into fullness thanks to his piety. The evident message for those repatriated during the era of the Second Temple was that a sincere return to Yhwh would resolve all the problems, including that of daily bread (see Neh 9:25).

The scene of Ruth eating to satiety and having "some left over" (as in 2 Chron 31:10) is less a marker of the abundance of Boaz's table than an anticipatory response to the priestly "solution" of the Chronicler, who echoes the ritualism of the leaders of the people in Zion. Ruth receives everything in abundance, no thanks to her ritual fidelity—which would have no meaning as far as she is concerned—but because of her goodness (*ḥesed*; see vv. 11-12 above). As the aphorism says, "A word to the wise is sufficient."

**[2:15]** This verse implies more than it seems at first sight. The promotion of Ruth goes "well beyond the letter of the law," as David Jackman says.[33] According to rabbinic legal instruction (halakah), the poor do not have the right to glean among the sheaves. In the following verse, Boaz pushes generosity to the extreme, according to the central principle of the book: overabundance, "how much more"—again, very much a "gospel" principle (see Matt 7:11 and Luke 11:13; Matt 12:11-12; Rom 11:12, 24; Heb 9:14; etc.).

**[2:16]** An initial remark concerns Boaz's style. He employs here an oldish form of conjugation (with an infinitive absolute followed by the conjugated form of the same verb).

The insistence of the text on the prohibition to scold Ruth (see 2:9, 15) is justified by a general tension between harvesters and gleaners, the latter being considered rapacious, but also because Ruth is a Moabite in the middle of hostile Israelites (see 2:9 above).

---

[33] Jackman, *Judges, Ruth,* CommComm 7 (Dallas: Word, 1986), 336.

שׁל ("pull, remove"). This is the same verb as in Exod 3:5—Moses must remove his sandals.

צבתם ("handfuls/armfuls"?). This is a hapax legomenon. Even though the last radical is a ת and not a ט as in v. 14, one sees a parallel with Akkadian *ṣabātu,* "hold" (see v. 14 above).[34]

[2:17] An ephah is approximately 40 liters, evidently a large quantity after gleaning. Compare the reaction of Naomi in v. 19. The figure is exaggerated, but one evolves, since the beginning of the chapter, in overabundance, from every point of view.

### Ruth Reports to Naomi (2:18-23)

18 She picked it [the grain] up and came into town, and her mother-in-law saw how much she had gleaned. Then she took out and gave her what was left over after she herself had been satisfied. 19 Her mother-in-law said to her, "Where did you glean today? And where have you worked? Blessed be the man who took notice of you." So she told her mother-in-law with whom she had worked, and said, "The name of the man with whom I worked today is Boaz." 20 Then Naomi said to her daughter-in-law, "Blessed be he by Yhwh,[a] whose kindness has not forsaken the living or the dead!" Naomi also said to her, "The man is a relative of ours, from our redeemer."[b] 21 Then Ruth the Moabite said, "He even said to me, 'Stay close by my [male] servants, until they have finished all my harvest.'" 22 Naomi said to Ruth, her daughter-in-law, "It is better, my daughter, that you go out with his young women, otherwise you might be bothered in another field." 23 So she stayed close to the young women of Boaz, gleaning until the end of the barley and wheat harvests; and she lived with her mother-in-law.

20[a] NRSV: "Lord."
20[b] NRSV: "one of our nearest kin"; LXX and Syr: "one of our redeemers."

### Notes on 2:18–23

[2:18] Ruth gives Naomi the grain and the leftovers of her meal. One may choose to see in "what was left over after she herself had been satisfied" an assertion, from Ruth, of her personality—a sort of "me first, you afterward, if anything is left."[35] But this idea is so foreign to Ruth's totally generous character that it borders on the ridiculous. Not only is it evident that Ruth could not materially do otherwise than eat her meal on the spot, but, as we saw above, the motif of abundance and surplus reflected

---

[34] As Hubbard says, "Certainly, the law never called for such a thing (cf. Deut 24:19)" (*Ruth,* 178).

[35] Fewell and Gunn, *Compromising Redemption,* 98.

a nagging problem for those repatriated to Zion in the sixth to fifth centuries. By her *ḥesed*, Ruth became a source of abundance and a fountain of hope for others. Moreover, the insistence of the text on Ruth's satiety (vv. 14, 18) refers back to her name (Ruth = satiety) and to what she represents with respect to Naomi: the return to fullness. Verse 18 expresses this; anything else would have been subtly selfish.

[2:19] Naomi asks Ruth, איפה (*ʾēpōh,* "where?"); two verses above, Ruth had gleaned two ephahs (איפה, *ʾēpâ*) of barley. The assonance is a literary device typically used in the book.

The incidental blessing is parallel to those in 1 Kgs 10:9 (= 2 Chron 9:8) and Prov 5:18. It corresponds to Boaz's blessing. Naomi is clearly on the same wavelength as Boaz. Moreover, she uses the term "to recognize" (נכר) that Ruth had used in 2:10 with Boaz.

מכרך relates back to the wordplay in v. 10 above (see Gen 24:27). The one that has well received Ruth has "distinguished, recognized her,"[36] in other words, he had consideration for her (and allowed her to glean in his field). The blessing in Naomi's mouth in vv. 19 and 20 measures the distance since her lamentation in 1:21, accusing God of tormenting her. Ruth did not only bring her sustenance. One saw above the transformation of Boaz and Ruth (see 2:9). Now Naomi enters into the circle. Soon the whole town of Bethlehem will benefit from this change.

"Boaz." Ruth delayed as long as possible to reveal the name of her benefactor, thus increasing the excitement of Naomi by teasing her. Suddenly, there is in the text of chapter 2 a magnificent *inclusio* with the name of Boaz in v. 1 and here at the end of the chapter. Four verses below, the name of Naomi will also be in an *inclusio* with its mention in v. 1. Boaz and Naomi never meet face-to-face in the narrative, but they are, so to speak, twinned from afar, a gap filled by Ruth.

[2:20] One finds several expressions illustrated in this verse in other texts: ברוך הוא ליהוה ("blessed is he by Yhwh") in Gen 14:19; אשר לא עזב חסדו ("the one that does not abandon his loyalty") in Gen 24:27 (Yahwist source). One will note that קרב ל- ("near to") is always constructed elsewhere with the preposition אל, except here and in Neh 13:4, another text from the Second Temple period (cf. Lev 25:25; Ps 15:3; 38:11 [MT 12]).

Ruth mentions Boaz's "favor" (חן; 2:10, 13), but Naomi translates it as "fidelity" (חסד), which raises the stakes to a higher level. Boaz showed *ḥesed* toward Ruth.[37] He gave her beyond what could be expected by gleaners from the owner of

---

[36] "Recognized as his," says Humbert, is implicitly in antithesis to 2:10, which has the same verbal root. "Art et leçon," *Opuscules,* 94 n 3.

[37] There is some ambiguity in the text regarding the subject of the verb "to abandon." Is it Yahweh or is it Boaz that has not abandoned his goodness? The problem seems resolved by the parallel to 2 Sam 2:5, judiciously noted in this regard by Hubbard, *Ruth,* 186.

barley fields (see Lev 19:9-10; 23:22; Deut 24:19-22). What goes beyond the letter is called *ḥesed,* as we have often seen (see the introduction, pp. 28–30). Boaz thus shows his predisposition to understand and to accept the next challenge of the Moabite (chap. 3; see the overview to that chapter, p. 87). We met the same excess as early as their departure in the attitude of the two Moabites, Ruth and Orpah, whose *ḥesed* was praised by Naomi (1:8). Their fidelity toward their mother-in-law went beyond all normal expectation.

"Or the dead." In other words, this concerns Naomi since he had consideration for her death, said Salmon bar Yeroḥam. One may, in fact, suppose that Naomi subtly alludes to reckoning herself among the "dead" since she is "Mara" and "empty" (1:20-21). But, no less subtly, the text follows the thread toward fullness and the restoration of the line of "the dead ones." God began the work of re-creation, and Naomi blesses his progress. She may even underline the implicit promise of the protection of the young woman, declared by Boaz in 2:9 (see above).

"The man is a relative of ours." An anonymous rabbi in *Ruth Rabbah* says that Naomi notices right away that the quantity of grain retrieved by Ruth cannot be simply gleaning (לקט). From her question (v. 19) and her blessing, Naomi guesses that the owner of the field is a kinsman. Ibn Ezra is justified in specifying that it is a question not of levirate here, but of redemption (גאלה), "a different custom."[38]

מגאלנו (which I would translate "one among our *gōʾēl*") has problems. If Naomi describes him as "one of our *gōʾēl*s," it would necessarily be a plural substantive (as in LXX and Syr). The Masoretes perhaps understood it differently: "This one is a near kinsman rather than our *gōʾēl*." In this case, Naomi would be indicating to Ruth that she knows that another person is the *gōʾēl*, as we shall see effectively portrayed in chapter 4, where he is designated as "So-and-so." The text of the verse remains intentionally imprecise as to the function of the *gōʾēl* in relation to the two women. For this is again a legal issue, likely the question of a minimalist interpretation or of a broad interpretive amplification. Which one Boaz will choose is left unresolved.

**[2:21-22]** It is necessary first to emphasize that one can infer nothing from the fact that Ruth does not repeat Boaz's words quoted earlier in the narrative. It is not logically necessary to repeat word for word something that is implicit.[39]

In the conversation between Ruth and her mother-in-law, there is a rhetorically subtle game. The text indicates from the outset that the difference of views between the two women is due to the fact that Ruth is a Moabite and, therefore, has a different sensitivity than Naomi, who is a Judean. Ruth candidly says that Boaz invited her

---

[38] Just because "redeemer" (גאל) can designate God in certain texts (see Gen 48:16; Exod 6:6; 15:13; Isa 41:14; 43:1; 52:3; Hos 13:14), it is not neccessary to conclude that, for Naomi, men are the representatives of heaven on earth (see Levine, "Ruth," 82).

[39] Let us note, on this subject, that the text of v. 14 does not give any indication that Ruth was going to take her mother-in-law the leftovers of her meal.

to "stay close to my servants," which Naomi in the following verse kindly corrects to "go out with his young women." Elsewhere, I drew attention to the women's liberation in a seminomadic population such as the country of Moab (she was not veiled, for example, and participated in male occupations due to necessity).[40] In Ruth 2:7 the foreman noted that "this [kind of people] does not rest even for a moment!" Here Naomi explains to Ruth: "It is better, my daughter, that you go out with his young women."[41] Ruth's error is attributed directly to her Moabite origins; the text finely states it: "Ruth the Moabite says. . . ."[42] Beforehand, to the very "Israelite" request of Boaz, "To whom does this young woman belong?" he was answered allusively, "This is a young Moabite." That is to say that she does not belong to anyone. This time Naomi's lesson is not lost on her. The next verse says that Ruth attached herself (the same term, דבק, that previously appeared in 1:14) to the young women, Boaz's servants.

Ruth begins her response with the two particles גם כי, which are a rather rare combination in Hebrew (see Hos 8:10; 9:16; Isa 1:15; Ps 23:4; Prov 22:6; Lam 3:8). Here it is necessary to translate, "He *even* said to me. . . ."

The construction עד אם ("until") is very rare (only in Gen 24:19; Isa 30:17). Ruth quotes Boaz, whose vocabulary remains florid. That explains (and excuses?) the redundancy of "my servants" (lit. "the servants who belong to me") and of "all my harvest" (lit. "all the harvest that belongs to me"). Boaz is somewhat rambling and seems disturbed by the presence of the young woman. One will notice the insistence in chapter 2 on the *young* people in contrast to Boaz's implicit seniority.

[2:22] "It is better, my daughter, that you go out." Compare 3:13, which uses the same term, טוב ("Good!").

Naomi's fears for her daughter-in-law express themselves through the term פגע ("bothered"—instead of נגע, "bother, molest," in the mouth of Boaz in v. 9), which implies violence (but not rape, it seems). In a milder sense, see 1:16 (quoting Ruth): "Do not press (פגע) me." But the distance is short to the sense we saw of נגע in 2:9, to which I refer the reader (p. 68).

Whatever the degree of violence that is referred to several times in this chapter, Ruth is clearly living dangerously. The motif is emphasized too frequently (see vv. 9, 15, 16) for it to represent only a habitual side issue in the existence of the gleaners in general. We saw above that a young widow could constitute an even stronger temptation, since having intercourse with her was not punishable by any legal means. But it is necessary, here again, to be sensitive to the social and religious context of the narrative, written in the sixth to fifth century. The hostility with respect to the

---

[40] LaCocque, *Feminine Unconventional,* 108–9.

[41] On this subject, see Broch, *Ruth,* 68.

[42] This specification here about Ruth is lacking in LXX, OL, Syr; but there is an *inclusio* with 2:2: "Ruth the Moabite says to Naomi. . . ."

foreigner is transparent. Certain ones in Judah would gladly put her in harm's way in the name of the Torah (the harvesters are pious people; see v. 4).

Ruth crosses the minefield thanks to her generosity, perhaps also to her innocence, but certainly equally thanks to the protection of enlightened persons such as Naomi and Boaz. It is on their side that the author places herself.

Ruth is sheltered in two places: the field of Boaz and the house of Naomi (v. 23). This situation can be only provisional. It will last just through the time of the two harvests, barley and wheat. This is the reason, as we will see, that at the end of the chapter, when she "attached herself to Boaz's servants" and "lived with her mother-in-law," this does not constitute a "happy ending," but is the expression of a malaise.

[2:23] This verse situates the narrative in its internal chronological framework. The two harvests are separated by a period of seven weeks, between Passover and *Shevuot* (Pentecost).[43]

Passover celebrates the "return" to the promised land (after the Egyptian exile); *Shevuot* celebrates the gift of the Torah (on Sinai). The author of Ruth could not have better situated the events that she describes if, effectively, she envisions the situation of the fifth century, after the return from the (Babylonian) exile and before what is for her the veritable rediscovery of Torah through the exercise of *ḥesed*.

The mention of Ruth's residence retrospectively recalls the promise to Naomi in 1:16 and, prospectively, announces the abnormality of chapter 3 on the threshing floor. Boaz's foreman had already noticed that the field was her residence (v. 7).

As Auld points out, chapter 2 begins with Naomi and ends with her as well. The same is true in chapter 3. But here the end of the harvest acts as an "ominous counterpoint. . . . Their sources of sustenance are depleted, the two widows remain alone together."[44]

---

[43] But the Midrash mentions three months, which would correspond to the waiting period for a proselyte to be allowed to marry.

[44] Judith A. Kates, "Women at the Center," in *Reading Ruth,* ed. Kates and Reimer, 193. Cf. A. Graeme Auld, *Joshua, Judges, and Ruth,* DSBS (Philadelphia: Westminster, 1985), 270.

# Chapter Three

## Reference Passages

- "About three months later Judah was told, 'Your daughter-in-law Tamar has played the whore; moreover she is pregnant as a result of whoredom.' And Judah said, 'Bring her out, and let her be burned.' . . . And [the midwife] said, 'What a breach you have made for yourself!' Therefore he was named Perez." (Gen 38:24, 29b; see also Gen 19:31-38, quoted with respect to chap. 1 above)
- "You shall also say to the Israelites, 'If a man dies, and has no son, then you shall pass his inheritance on to his daughter. If he has no daughter, then you shall give his inheritance to his brothers. If he has no brothers, then you shall give his inheritance to his father's brothers. And if his father has no brothers, then you shall give his inheritance to the nearest kinsman of his clan, and he shall possess it. It shall be for the Israelites a statute and ordinance, as Yhwh commanded Moses.'" (Num 27:8-11)

## Overview

Boaz does not pursue what had begun so well with Ruth. Naomi becomes nervous and decides to push him to make a decision. The new speech of Naomi is naturally hesitating and somewhat rocky. One finds repetitions of words, as noted in Ruth 2:8, 11 ("do not" twice [vv. 1, 2], followed by הנה־הוא or והוא [vv. 2, 4]) without counting the pronominal confusions (1st person singular instead of 2nd person), as already noted.[1]

Ruth's response is, as usual, brief. The older characters in the story speak at length, the younger ones get directly to the point. The opposite would be surprising.

Naomi's plan is particularly ambiguous and open to misunderstanding. I will return to this. One senses a certain embarrassment, for example, in the Jewish tradition. Nevertheless, Naomi's intentions were pure. The most serious misunderstanding, evidently, would be to think that Naomi uses her daughter-in-law for personal

---

[1] Mona DeKoven Fishbane, "Ruth: Dilemmas of Loyalty and Connection," in *Reading Ruth,* ed. Kates and Reimer, 303. She attributes these confusions to Naomi's "overidentification" with Ruth.

ends. This is the reason she distances herself from this interpretation at the outset: she suggests that this is above all for Ruth's own good, so that she does not remain a widow. Now this declaration of intention immediately follows the note in 2:23 that Ruth continued to live with her mother-in-law. Naomi could selfishly perpetuate this situation, which is not displeasing to her (cf. 2:18). But such is not her duty, as she says. She must first of all think about Ruth's well-being (see the repetition of the root טוב, "good, well"] four times in this chapter: 3:1, 7, 10, 13). Other repetitions in the chapter include:

- ידע ("know"): 3:2, 3, 4, 11, 15, 18
- שכב ("lie down"): 3:4a, 4b, 7a, 7b, 8, 13, 14
- גרן ("threshing floor"): 3:2, 3, 5, 14
- עשׂה ("do, act"): 3:4, 5, 6, 11, 16
- מרגלת ("feet"): 3:4, 7, 8, 14
- גאל ("redeem"): 3:9, 12a, 12b, 13a, 13b, 13c, 13d
- בקר ("morning"): 3:13a, 13b, 14

Pressler points out that, while Naomi has a field to sell (cf. chap. 4), Ruth has absolutely nothing to assure her future. Naomi has the intention of repaying Ruth for her tokens of affection.[2]

Naomi talks about "security, rest" (מנוח), which is rather unexpected in this context for the modern reader. But one finds the motif already in 1:9, to which I refer the reader, and we will meet it again as an *inclusio* in v. 18 (Boaz will not have any rest [שׁקט] that night). An anonymous rabbi in *Ruth Rabbah* comments that the husband of a married woman is called "security."

Naomi's approach in this matter is still troubling. It would even be obscene if the story had not taken the approach from the start that the perspective is the obedience to the Torah. Of course, the exegete cannot mitigate the roles of Naomi and Ruth in this matter. This scene is as risqué as the one described in Genesis 38. It would nevertheless be an error to conclude that, for the author, the end justifies the means. For the action of the two women, just like that of Tamar, is justified not only teleologically but already in its intention. It is not a matter of Ruth prostituting herself, or of Naomi playing the procurer, but taking the direction of the events that *must result* in the continuation of Elimelek's line (just like that of Judah with regard to Tamar). This is the reason for Ruth's coming to Israel.

The contrast to the beginning of chapter 2 is obvious; there it is said that Ruth arrived "by chance" in the field of Boaz (2:3). Now, nothing more is left to chance. Hoping that luck will happen again is naive or foolish, and Naomi is neither naive nor foolish. One remembers that the author presented the character of Naomi as gifted

---

[2] Pressler, *Joshua, Judges, and Ruth*, 285.

with an exceptional moral force. When her husband and two sons died, her daughters-in-law chose to remain with her (cf. 1:7), and even to leave their country to follow her to Judah (cf. 1:10). Naomi also had the nobility of soul to bless in advance the remarriage of her daughters-in-law instead of judging them harshly as "unfaithful" toward their former husbands (cf. 1:9). Nor is she reckless for daring to confront God as she does in 1:13.

Nevertheless, in both Ruth 3 and Genesis 38, there is a total wager, a dangerous double or nothing. One may lose her reputation (Ruth) or her life (Tamar). In any case, the faint heart will never be able to understand such risks; they will always find it preferable to render the talent intact at the end that they received at the start.

Faithful to its penchant for understatement, the biblical narrative provides no indication about the protagonists' mood. We are not told that Naomi's and Ruth's hearts were pounding during this whole escapade, but one may easily guess that they were.[3] Everything would be played out on the threshing floor. In this increasing suspense, Naomi was possibly sending her daughter-in-law to her destruction—or at least to the confirmation for witnesses that one can expect nothing more than promiscuity from a Moabite. Ruth was perhaps going to be mistaken for a prostitute. Boaz was perhaps going to commit irreparable harm. For, with Pressler, it is necessary to emphasize Ruth's independence as a woman without male support, but also without legal responsibility to anyone at all ("legally, she was a free agent").[4] But Boaz could take advantage of Ruth's offer without risking any consequences, even if she became pregnant by him.[5] In short, Ruth places herself in extreme danger, so that if there was a trap on her part, as several commentators indicate, it will snap shut more surely on her than on Boaz.

Indeed, from then on everything depended on him, and one can infer from Naomi's decision to send Ruth to the fields at night that she had more faith in this kinsman than in the other one, who was, however, closer—this So-and-so, to whom she pointedly did not send Ruth. After all, Boaz was presented to the reader as אִישׁ גִּבּוֹר חַיִל, which may be paraphrased "a noble-hearted man" (2:1), and apparently Naomi knew enough about him to know that he was a man of action (3:18). The story proves that she was judicious in her judgment, which is a retrospective compliment to her intuition. Besides, without Naomi's active role in this turn of events, she would have been completely passive within the story.

Chapter 3 of Ruth is perfectly congruent with the mentality of the author. She likes extreme situations—a migration to Moab, marriages with "questionable" women, unlimited love for a mother-in-law, and so on. With the scene in chapter 3, we arrive at the point of maximum tension. This is "the night of Ruth" after which the

---

[3] In Ruth 1:14 Orpah, in tears, kisses her mother-in-law and leaves without a word. Her silence says more than words.

[4] Pressler, *Joshua, Judges, and Ruth,* 287.

[5] Ibid.

tension can only attain its breaking point or relax itself. This is a case of what Søren Kierkegaard called a "teleological suspension of the ethical." If one misses this turn, one evidently can cynically write on the low instincts of Naomi and her manipulation of Ruth. On the contrary, if one takes seriously the biblical exception—Moses' killing the Egyptian (Exod 2:12; cf. Acts 7:24; Heb 11:27); Lot's incest with his two daughters (Genesis 19; their motivation is never put in question); Abraham sacrificing Isaac on Mount Moriah (Genesis 22); Tamar's posing as a prostitute with Judah (Genesis 38); and Jacob usurping the right of the elder brother and taking shameful advantage of his father's blindness (Gen 27:1, 19), an action specifically condemned by the law (Lev 19:14; Deut 27:18)—then the message becomes particularly important for the reader confronted by an existential decision: either the sordid, or the sublime.[6]

There is undeniably a succession of "improper" events in salvation history (*Heilsgeschichte*). To a certain extent, they constitute the backbone of this history, for they all depend on a determinative *vision*. In the name of this (covenantal and eschatological) vision, Jacob is moved by a consuming passion, Rachel demands children or death (Gen 30:1), and Tamar forces events (Genesis 38). Errors of incalculable proportion are committed: Sarah puts Hagar in Abraham's bed, Lot commits double incest, Jacob "hates" Leah. Other alternatives will always remain ambiguous. Abraham committing infanticide? Moses committing murder? Rahab an opportunist? Tamar a nymphomaniac? And what does one say about David? Everything about this exceptional man is subject to caution.

These examples will allow us better to probe the anguish of the heroines in chapter 3 of Ruth. Not only could their "plan" fail with more moral, social, and economic consequences than one knows, but more profoundly, their vision itself can be misleading. It is risky for them to let go of a false *Heilsgeschichte,* a hollow history, in short, to reach not to the sublime but to the lamentably trivial, for they chose to go beyond ethics.

The scene on the threshing floor is punctuated with words with double meanings. Ruth tells Boaz to spread his "wing" (כָּנָף) over her (3:9). Now this term can, just like the Hebrew word for "feet" (3:4, 7, 14), designate the penis (see 1 Sam 24:4-12; Deut 23:1 [MT 2]). On this subject it is important to emphasize that, lacking Ruth's offer, Boaz would be a simple object of manipulation, an average dupe, a means to arrive at different ends. One could equally accuse Tamar of the same insensitivity if she had not personally compromised herself so much in order that through her the law might be fulfilled. A lot of authors psychologize the characters in the book of Ruth and speak easily of Naomi and Ruth as cold manipulators, and of Boaz as only looking out for his own interests. They thus forget the legal and social issue of the whole matter. The issue is returning life to an Israelite clan obliterated by the death of its progenitors. Only a combination of the laws on redemption (גְּאוּלָה) and on the levirate is able to revive the clan of Naomi from the dead. Boaz will be the

---

[6] "Who do you say that I am?"

agent and, at the right moment, Naomi and Ruth do realize it. But that does not imply that Boaz is relegated to the status of an instrument without a soul in their eyes. Ruth marries Boaz—not the better part for Ruth, as Boaz himself admits (3:10)—and it will not be on the insistence of this man that she consents (3:9). It is she that proposes marriage, a suggestion seen by Boaz as the ultimate sign of *hesed* toward him. This is finally what transforms Boaz and brings him first to what one could call a new life. If one again insists on the use of the word "manipulate," then Boaz is manipulated to his greater gain, as a disciple is "manipulated" by a master.

It is evident that the book of Ruth does not technically belong to law or to wisdom, even if elements of the narrative recall one or the other type. One thinks about "mixed" texts such as Deut 23:3 (MT 4); Lev 25:23-55; Deut 25:5-10; and Proverbs 31, to cite only the most obvious. But the haggadah in Ruth 3 uses these nonnarrative nuances; it does not serve them. Naomi and Ruth are too extreme to comport with the sapiential definition of the "prudent woman," and Boaz becomes too audacious juridically to be a model of the man faithful to the Law. The oscillations of the tradition on this subject are significant. Is it to honor him, or to accuse him of opportunism, that the rabbis say that Boaz himself enacted a new law modifying Deut 23:3 (MT 4) and stipulating that the objectionable marriages are the ones with the men of Moab and Ammon, not with their women?

It is important to underline that in Ruth 3 it is the women who take the initiative to advance story and history. The fact is emphasized in the book by the allusions to Tamar and the matriarchs. There is in this story a generic dynamic that undergirds its sequence. It begins, moreover, in chapter 1, with the impressive dialog between women that the author situates in Moab, and by Ruth's moving declaration, expressing her love for her mother-in-law. In chapter 3 Ruth succeeds with her plan due to her extraordinary devotion to her mother-in-law. Before being faithful to the one that will be her second husband, she first proves her *hesed* (constant love, fidelity, devotion) toward another woman. She accompanies her mother-in-law for her good and in a total abandonment of herself. By contrast, the men, with the exception of Boaz, are beset with hostile sentiments regarding her. Fortunately, the noble character of Boaz sees in her something other than a Moabite: he appreciates her courage and fidelity. The women of the community appear in Ruth as the stabilizing elements in the society. They are also the most intuitive ones, the ones most open to creativity in their relationship—through the intermediary of Naomi—with Ruth. They are all presented as welcoming, compassionate, and likable. Moved from beginning to end by the extraordinary destiny of Naomi, they are the only ones to understand that, for Naomi, Ruth "is better than seven sons" (4:15). This is not the case of the elites, blinded by Ruth's Moabite origins, insensitive to her *hesed*, her fidelity toward the Israelites first, and then toward God. The men have been more conservative than the women, immobilized in their ideology, which leaves no room for the unexpected. The institution stifles the event.

In a certain sense, the same is true of Boaz: despite being the best of his generation, he must be pushed by Ruth and Naomi to move beyond himself to reply to the call of the extraordinary. It is why Naomi incites her daughter-in-law to take advantage of a situation that Boaz, who has just celebrated the end of the harvest, does not control completely. At night, the young woman will therefore go to the threshing floor, uncover the lower part of Boaz's body, and stretch out by his side (3:4). At this point, Naomi is sure that the man will take the initiative. The scene is scandalous. One can see a certain parallelism with the conduct of Judith in Holophernes's camp; but here, Naomi and Ruth are confident right from the beginning in the nobility of Boaz's heart. Nevertheless, the situation in which Ruth puts herself is so much more compromising since failure would again, in an irreparable way, place Ruth's goal in question: to get married and provide an heir to her deceased husband and, indirectly, to her mother-in-law.

Modern critics have been sensitive to this state of affairs. Trible notices that if Ruth 1:1 refers to "his wife" (referring to Elimelek), the story quickly passes to the woman's point of view and speaks of "Naomi's husband" (1:3). Similarly, "his two sons" become "her two sons," and the two foreign daughters-in-law are surprisingly related back to the houses of their mothers (1:8).[7] Berlin adds that the story constantly emphasizes the advantageous situation of Naomi. The characters exist only in reference to her, even though Ruth quickly becomes the principal center of attention. In fact, the Moabite does not stop climbing the social ladder: she first calls herself "the foreigner" (2:10), then "your servant" (2:13; 3:9), and finally becomes "the woman who is coming into your house" (4:11). Boaz addresses her progressively as "a young woman" (2:15), "my daughter" (3:11a), and finally "a worthy woman" (3:11b)—the equal, in a way, of the "noble-hearted man" (2:1), as he has been called.[8]

If we return to the scene in chapter 3, it is clear that when Naomi puts Ruth in a compromising situation, it is obviously with the bet that the *gōᵓēl* will act with the utmost kindness toward her and that, to this excess of *ḥesed* from Ruth, he will reply with an "overabundance" that will go beyond the letter of the law. Once more, confusing Naomi's action with procuring would be to miss the partially sapiential character (secondary, but clear) of this pericope. The message communicated is that Naomi had a deep intuition about the future. Her advice to Ruth is not at all dubious, but demonstrates a finesse of spirit.

Ruth's arrival at the threshing floor is an act of *goodness* (this is the translation of חסד required here), as Boaz says when he awakens, when he could take advantage of the occasion offered by this woman in his "bed." It is an act of charity from the one

---

[7] Trible, *God and Rhetoric,* 169–70. See also Meyers, "To Her Mother's House"; idem, "Returning Home."

[8] Adele Berlin, "Poetics in the Book of Ruth," in *Poetics and the Interpretation of Biblical Narrative,* BLS 9 (Sheffield: Almond, 1983), 84–85.

that has no other resource to attain the world of a rich man than humbly to offer her own body. An act of charity toward a man whose age, obviously, does not correspond anymore, say, to the ideals of youth and who therefore has decided to remain without a wife—in any case, without offspring.

The *ḥesed* of the offer is really superior to the preceding act of goodness (3:10). For after having sacrificed "her father and her mother and the country of her birth for a people that she did not know beforehand" (2:11), Ruth is now ready "to die" socially on behalf of her mother-in-law.[9]

Fewell and Gunn trivialize the issues.[10] Now, on the basis of 3:12 in particular, where Boaz makes Ruth aware of the existence of a nearer kinsman ("So-and-so" in chap. 4), Sasson judiciously had concluded that Naomi's sending Ruth to Boaz sufficiently shows that "she was not concerned about resolving her own problem."[11] One can always imagine that St. Mary the Egyptian, for example, who prostituted herself to pay her crossing from Marseilles to the Holy Land, found a good pretext to conceal her carnal desires. Some have pushed the morbid further by casting doubts on the actual relationship between Jesus and Mary Magdalene.[12]

Remove the sacred and everything becomes suspect or otherwise despicable. It is important to distinguish clearly between how things appear to the modern reader and what the author intended. Naomi can appear to play a role close to procuring, but that is certainly not the intention of the narrative. The "appearance" of Naomi's actions is part of the polysemy of the text. In Genesis 38 Tamar adorned herself to look like a prostitute; but in reality, says the text, she was a righteous woman and was recognized as such by Judah himself (Gen 38:26).

Ruth is not a loose woman. Boaz recognizes this right away and calls her an אשת חיל (3:11); it is necessary to translate this phrase here with "an honest woman," as she well showed when she gleaned among the harvesters. Besides, had she not begun by ignoring young Moabite men and attaching herself to her mother-in-law? One act of goodness follows another and then surpasses it.

---

[9] The parallel with Tamar asserts itself here again in that Tamar also placed her fortune completely in Judah's hands. He could have denied the incriminating objects she sent and put her to death as he had intended. Cf. Tamar Frankiel, "Ruth and the Messiah," in *Reading Ruth*, ed. Kates and Reimer, 331.

[10] Danna Nolan Fewell and David Gunn, "'A Son Born to Naomi': Literary Allusions and Interpretation in the Book of Ruth," *JSOT* 40 (1988) 99–108. Jon Levenson has written concerning another exegete: "This implication puts the commentator in the unusual situation of having to argue against the sacred text he has chosen to expound" ("Liberation Theology and Exodus," *Reflections* 86.1 [1991] 2–12).

[11] Sasson, *Ruth,* 83.

[12] For the most recent example see Dan Brown, *The DaVinci Code* (New York: St. Martin's, 2003).

### Naomi's Strategy (3:1-5)

3:1 Naomi her mother-in-law said to her, "My daughter, I need to seek some security for you, so that it may be well with you. 2 Now here is our kinsman Boaz, with whose young women you have been working. See, he is winnowing barley tonight at the threshing floor. 3 Now wash and anoint yourself, and put on your best clothes and go down to the threshing floor; but do not make yourself known to the man until he has finished eating and drinking. 4 When he lies down, observe the place where he lies; then, go and uncover his feet and lie down; and he will tell you what to do." 5 She said to her, "All that you tell me I will do."

### *Notes on 3:1-5*

Naomi's plan is detailed and there is nothing hasty about it. She deliberately develops a course of action to unblock a narrative in danger of getting itself stuck in the mud in a case of social assistance on the part of Boaz. Or even worse, the two women risk being simply forgotten, because the harvests are now finished, and Boaz could disappear after his generous intervention in chapter 2. The winnowing is the last act, after which what was begun will be aborted. This is not what Naomi intended to furnish as security (מנוח) for Ruth. Ruth became Naomi's "daughter" (בתי), whether or not this term makes modern commentators uncomfortable. But the issue is not Naomi asserting her authority over her, but her affectionate protection. She understands that they have come to their last chance.

Regarding Boaz, it is a matter of putting him in a *test* situation. Behind him stands the profile of the temple party at the time of the restoration. As such, Boaz is conservative, right-thinking and pious, socially comfortable and biologically aged, and a pillar (בעז) of the Bethlehem community. On all these levels, Boaz will be put to the test, according to a "plot"[13] appropriate to force an existential decision. This is the reason Naomi finishes her speech with the words: "and he will tell you what to do." The final decision will come from Boaz, according to which he will pass the test or not.

Hence Naomi's meticulous plan includes a great unknown: Will this be sufficient to bring the "bourgeois gentleman" out of his sociojudicial shell?[14]

The parallel with the story of Tamar in Genesis 38 is obvious. Like Tamar the Canaanite, Ruth will put herself in a compromising situation in order to induce the one who hides himself behind custom and the good form of not getting involved. In the two cases, if there was a "plot," it would be costly for the women who set it in motion. And what is true for Tamar and Ruth is also true for Naomi. She seems to remain in

---

[13] Linafelt, "Ruth," 48.

[14] Linafelt correctly states that Ruth wants to "push him past his moral and theological platitudes" (ibid., 55).

the background and send her daughter-in-law to the front line, but her own "security" depends on that of Ruth. If, as it is unfortunately logical to think, Boaz keeps his dignity and is offended by Ruth, or if he cynically takes advantage of the dark to do with her what he would not do in broad daylight, Naomi would be the first to lose.

Everything effectively depends on Boaz: "he will tell you what to do"—in other words, in which direction the events will develop. But, faithful to her impetuous temperament (cf. above on 2:21-23), Ruth (contrary to Tamar) will not await a problematic decision by Boaz; rather she will dictate for him what he must do (3:9) with success (3:11).

It is part of the artistic skill of the author to make Naomi a strong presence in the remainder of the chapter—even though she is absent. She remains in the background and is not mentioned by Ruth or by Boaz in their conversation. Nevertheless, the whole scene finds its full significance with her and for her.

**[3:1]** Naomi, for the first time, takes the initiative: she is watching out for Ruth's welfare. Until now, it was Ruth who protected and nourished her mother-in-law. But Naomi's initiative will be of short duration, for, in the continuation of the chapter, Ruth will not follow her orders to the letter (despite 3:6). She will put Boaz on the spot (3:9; see below). According to the constant literary structure in the book, Naomi's dynamic pace will ricochet at the end of the narrative in 4:16.

Referring to 1:9 (מנוחה, "security"), here one has מנוח, from the same root. Note again in Naomi's mouth the affectionate "my daughter," "that it may be well with you," couched in an interrogative form of speech.

"That it may be well with you." This phrase implies that Ruth will be happy in marriage (Jer 42:6), will have a long life (Deut 4:40, etc.), will be prosperous (Jer 40:6), and will have many children (Deut 6:3).[15] The parallel with the vocabulary of Ruth 1:8-9 is evident, but one has passed from the expression of a theological vow to its accomplishment by human initiative. Thus it is verified once more that the action of God, according to the book of Ruth, is "incarnate" in human action. The verse corresponds to 2:8-9, where Boaz also put two negative rhetorical questions and called Ruth "my daughter." Boaz and Naomi are from the same generation. The use of the particle אשר ("that") here instead of למען ("in order") is found again in Deut 4:40 and 6:3.

**[3:2]** This verse recalls 2:1 and 20 (note the use again of the possessive "our," as in 2:20). Boaz is not their nearest kinsman, but in the second tier after another, about whom we shall hear in chapter 4 (see 4:4). The choice of Boaz by "chance," then by Naomi and Ruth, therefore becomes *preference*. In keeping with her desire to substitute herself for her mother-in-law, Ruth indicates that Naomi's preference is also her own.

---

[15] Hubbard, *Ruth,* 198.

"Winnowing barley at the threshing floor." The Hebrew could be vocalized differently to read "the threshing floor near the gates," as an allusion to the gates of the city as the location of the threshing floor (see 1 Kgs 22:10; Jer 15:7). Boaz threshes his barley at the time of the wheat harvest? Perhaps farmers kept their barley to thresh at the same time as their wheat, about seven weeks later.[16]

**[3:3-4]** The threshing floor was a socially important place in ancient agrarian societies, on an equal level to the water source in daily life. Hosea 9:1 denounces the fertility rites that Israel practiced on the threshing floor in imitation of other Near Eastern peoples. Even if the same rites are not acted out in Ruth 3, it is clear that Boaz would have celebrated a fruitful harvest with food and drink. The scene evoked recalls the one in the cave outside Sodom, where the incest between Lot and his daughters occurred (and the births of Moab and Ammon, Gen 19:30-38). As opposed to Lot though, Boaz will be conscious and the master of his decisions. This is in part what Naomi foresees and says to her daughter-in-law before sending her to the threshing floor: "he will tell you what to do" (v. 4).

The directions Naomi gives to Ruth are, following the precedent in the speeches of Boaz, in an "unusual" style, as Campbell states.[17] It is necessary to make an important remark on the language of the book of Ruth. Here and elsewhere one finds linguistic ambiguities, especially in the personal pronouns. Now, this happens each time in the speech of a third person filled with explosive passion because the issue is so decisive for the speaker, whether it is Naomi addressing herself to Ruth, or of Boaz to So-and-so. I think that the rabbis and medieval Jewish commentators were not mistaken when suggesting that these texts betray the nervousness of the speakers. Here Naomi says, "[you] put on your best clothes/I will get dressed." Then, at the crucial moment in her instructions to her daughter-in-law, she adds, "you will go to bed/I will go to bed." From the same perspective, in 4:5 Boaz comes with the ambiguous "you bought/I bought," which introduces a psychological element of feverish expectation in his speech.[18]

It is true that, according to Zakovitch (who refers back to Kutscher), these grammatical abnormalities are not necessarily forms of the first person singular, for one rediscovers them as second person imperative in the Isaiah scroll from Qumran (1QIs[a]) with a reflexive sense. The form is influenced by Aramaic.[19]

---

[16] Sakenfeld, *Ruth,* 52. On threshing see B. S. J. Isserlin, *The Israelites* (Minneapolis: Fortress Press, 2001), 155.

[17] Campbell, *Ruth,* 120.

[18] Samuel b. Naḥman (Amora, third–fourth century) prefers the K (first person) to the Q (second person) and explains that Boaz, knowing that So-and-so would refuse the complete redemption, purchased the field in advance, indicating as well that he would marry Ruth—another example of the abundance of love, we might add. Among modern exegetes, the K is also preferred by D. R. G. Beattie, "*Kethibh* and *Qere* in Ruth iv.5," *VT* 21 (1971) 490–94.

[19] Zakovitch (*Ruth,* 136) refers to Yehezkel Kutscher, *The Language and Linguistic Background of the Isaiah Scroll (1QIsa),* ed. Elisha Qimron, STDJ 6A (Leiden: Brill, 1974).

In conclusion, it is not, of course, impossible that the present literary composition of Ruth was preceded by popular stories with a comparable motif (for example, according to Gunkel, an elderly widow miraculously bringing a child into the world), whether in prose or poetry. This may be where certain archaic forms (?) of the present text of Ruth find their origin. After all, several major classical musicians were also inspired by popular songs. But the distance between Brahms or Schubert and the street song is immense. The error of Jacob Myers, to my way of thinking, is Gunkel's error—that, a priori, what is chronologically earlier is better, more poetic, purer, more artistic, and deeper.

On the contrary, I would say that the author of Ruth made use of the ancient forms of narrative language with brio in order to give a greater density to her discourse, and I would credit the postexilic author with the genius that Myers would look for in an elusive antecedent. I would find proof in 3:12, which Myers contends is "corrupt" and "dittographic." Boaz is again the speaker here. He was just startled on discovering the presence of a woman in his bed. And his confusion is of course not appeased by the strange comments that she makes to him: "You are my *gōʾēl,* marry me!" One imagines Boaz's mixed feelings; but, as we noticed above, the biblical narrative does not express emotional states other than by indirection—in other words, by what is displayed externally. Boaz "is startled" (v. 8). Now he stammers ועתה כי אמנם כי אם, something like, "uh . . . , now if it is true that maybe. . . ." If this is a sign of "corruption" in the text, then the famous exclamation applies: *felix culpa!* ("O fortunate sin!"). Fortunately, the poets do not have the same criteria for their inventions as the critics have for their analyses.

Regarding Ruth's preparations, Salmon bar Yeroḥam says that Ruth got dressed befitting the situation, that is, not in her work dress. This compares to Tamar, who "put on a veil" (Gen 38:14). Ruth must anoint herself (cf. Song 1:3, 13; 3:6; 4:14; 5:1, 5, 13). She adorns herself as a bride (cf. Est 2:12; Ezek 16:8-9; Jdt 10:3; see also the parallel text of "Inana and Dumuzi"[20]). Sasson takes great pains to quote the text of Ezek 16:8-12 extensively in order to show the numerous parallels with our text.[21] The book of Ruth's borrowing from the book of Ezekiel is an additional factor in favor of a late date. One will note that Naomi evidently transforms the narrative past tense of Ezekiel (*waw* + imperfect) into a near future form, all the while keeping the Ezekielian form, but with *waw* + perfect.

These preparations by Ruth, clearly intending to seduce Boaz on the threshing floor, serve equally pivotal roles in the narrative: the time of mourning is finished (cf. David in 2 Sam 12:20).[22]

One finds the term מרגלתיו here and in Dan 10:6. מרגלת are the parts of the body covered both day and night; literally, the feet, a metaphor for a man's genitals

---

[20] *ANET,* 639.
[21] Sasson, *Ruth,* 66.
[22] Ostriker, "Redeeming of Ruth," 61.

(see Isa 7:20; for the image see Exod 4:25; Ezek 16:25). In the exposition of the "feet" of Boaz, the Midrash sees a parallel with the חליצה (the taking of the shoes from the one who refuses the *yibbûm*) in Deut 25:5-10. The trait is interesting when one contrasts it with the opinion expressed by some, concerning Ruth 4, that the taking off of the shoes in question there would not be the חליצה. On the contrary, Naomi discreetly recalls to Boaz the חליצה imposed on the recalcitrant one. (The whole chapter applies the legal adage: *res ipsae loquitur*, "the thing speaks for itself.") If it is a question of a circumstantial complement of place after the verb "to lay bare," it is necessary then to understand that Ruth will lay herself bare at Boaz's "feet" (see v. 8),[23] but then one hardly understands why Ruth got dressed with so much care in the first place.

The word גלית is never employed in the case of a woman undressing a man, but for a man with respect to a woman (as direct complement, see Lev 18:6ff.; Deut 22:30 [MT 23:1]). In certain cases, a man or a woman gets undressed (for a woman, see Lev 20:18; Ezek 23:18; and especially Isa 57:8). The parallel with Genesis 38 is evident. Note that Tamar and Ruth "choose clothes as a code for their sexuality," as Nielsen says.[24] Ruth nevertheless does not disguise her identity as Tamar does, but reveals it totally to Boaz.

"He will tell you what to do" means something like, "It is in God's hands!" and has the same uncertainty regarding the following sequence of events.

Trible says justly that the two meetings between Ruth and Boaz hardly resemble one another. "The first meeting was by chance; the second is by choice. The first was in the fields; the second at the threshing floor. The first was public; the second private. The first was work; the second play. The first was by day; the second by night. Yet both of them hold the potential for life and death."[25]

**[3:5]** "All that you tell me I will do." A chain reaction is set in motion, for in v. 11 it is Boaz who will say to Ruth, "I will do for you all that you ask." This last declaration marks the triumph of Naomi and her plan.

One will note the alternation of the points of view in this chapter, which passes from Naomi to Ruth, then to Boaz, then goes back to Ruth. Boaz, says Naomi, will tell Ruth what to do; Ruth will do what her mother-in-law tells her; Boaz "surrenders his weapons" and will adjust himself to Ruth's decision. In short, Ruth is now the central agent of the events. The older generation relies on the younger, the one of higher social status on the lower, the stronger of the world on the weaker (1 Cor 1:27), masculine authority on female wisdom. In Ruth 2:1 Boaz was "man of substance"; now he recognizes in Ruth a "woman of substance" (3:11). Such a reversal of values is at the very least subversive.

---

[23] Sasson, *Ruth*, 69–71; Campbell, *Ruth*, 121; Nielsen, *Ruth*, 68–69. Thus the versions.
[24] Nielsen, *Ruth*, 70.
[25] Trible, *God and Rhetoric*, 183.

The instruments of this revolution are themselves extraordinary: they consist of offering oneself, which logically would have meant defeat and surrender. Boaz could inflate his own importance and perhaps treat it as natural that this "servant" (2:13; 3:9) bows to him (cf. 2:10) and gives him whatever he wants. Naomi's intuition would then be completely ruined; Ruth would be violated (despite the fact that it would technically have been consensual sexual relations); and Boaz would remain the petty bourgeois, satisfied and triumphant as he was in chapter 2.

None of that happens; but Ruth will stake everything on this matter. The unforeseeable happens. The one who has represented from the beginning the extravagant choice wins Boaz, the right-thinking one, to her cause. Of course, in the universe of Boaz, there were no shortage of pious formulas (2:4); but the story had gotten stuck in the status quo. The Moabite will unblock the story with her incarnate vision. It is her person, her flesh, that she will use as a lever. To see in her offer that of a "feminine" submission is highly regrettable. The redemptive passion does not belong to any slave mentality (cf. Gal 5:13).

## The Seduction Scene (3:6-15)

6 So she went down to the threshing floor and did just as her mother-in-law had instructed her. 7 When Boaz had eaten and drunk, and he was in a contented mood, he went to lie down at the end of the heap of grain. Then she came stealthily and uncovered his feet, and lay down. 8 At midnight the man was startled, and turned over, and there, lying at his feet, was a woman! 9 He said, "Who are you?" And she answered, "I am Ruth, your servant; spread your wing[a] over your servant, for you are the redeemer."[b] 10 He said, "May you be blessed by Yhwh,[a] my daughter; this last instance of your goodness[b] is better than the first; you have not gone after young men, whether poor or rich. 11 And now, my daughter, do not be afraid, I will do for you all that you ask, for all the assembly of my people know that you are an honest woman.[a] 12 But now, though it is true that I am a redeemer,[a] there is another redeemer[b] more closely related than I. 13 Remain this night, and in the morning, if he will act as redeemer for you, good; let him do it. If he is not willing to act as redeemer for you, then as Yhwh lives, I will act as redeemer for you. Lie down until the morning."

14 So she lay at his feet until morning, but got up before one person could recognize another; for he said, "It must not be known that the woman came to the threshing floor." 15 Then he said, "Bring the cloak you are wearing and hold it out." So she held it, and he measured out six measures of barley,[a] and put it on her back; then he went into the city.[b]

**9**[a] NRSV: "your cloak"; K: כנפיך ("your wings"); Q, LXX, Syr: כנפך ("your wing").
**9**[b] NRSV: "next-of-kin"; MT: גאל (throughout, unless otherwise noted).
**10**[a] NRSV: "LORD" (throughout).

**10**[b] NRSV: "loyalty"; MT: חסד.
**11**[a] "worthy woman"; MT: אשת חיל.
**12**[a] NRSV: "near kinsman"; MT: גאל.
**12**[b] NRSV: "kinsman"; MT: גאל.
**15**[a] Literally "six barleys."
**15**[b] Heb. MSS, Syr, Vg: ותבא העיר ("then she went into the city").

### Notes on 3:6-15

**[3:6]** Not a word is said concerning the emotional state of Ruth, going alone squarely into harm's way on the threshing floor, with the plan to lay down at the side of a sleeping man. This strongly resembles the narrative in Genesis 22 (the sacrifice of Isaac), which is emotionally charged, but in which the emotions are only suggested by the text.

**[3:7]** Why Boaz slept on the threshing floor has given rise to various theories. It may simply have been that the man was able to go no further than the threshing floor and had to sleep there. The Midrash, for its part, finds it unworthy for Boaz to sleep at the foot of the barley pile; but the reason was "to watch the grain." *Ruth Rabbah*, however, finds a nobler reason; it is signified by the text mentioned above, Hos 9:1: Boaz wanted to avoid having his threshing floor used for immoral ends. Hosea 9:1 does mention the threshing floor as a place of fornication. It is understandable that, at the time of the harvest, some found an occasion for license there. A certain element of imitative magic with the fertility of the fields may also play a role. Boaz "gladdened his heart" (NRSV "was in a contented mood") for, as the psalm says, "May those who sow in tears reap with shouts of joy!" (Ps 126:5).

Significantly, our text says, "he gladdened his heart"; see, among others, Judg 16:25; 2 Sam 13:28; and Est 1:10. About the last parallel cited, the ancient rabbis contrast the attitude of Boaz, who respected Ruth's offer to his wishes, with Ahasuerus, who, on the contrary, ordered his wife Vashti to present herself naked in public (as understood by the Midrash).

"Stealthily" (בלט). In Judg 4:21 בלאט, which our text may echo,[26] means "undercover" (TOB *furtivement*, "furtively").

"Uncovered his feet." "The 'traditional' roles of pursuer and pursued are reversed," says Ilona Rashkow.[27] Symbolism transcends the reality. Adele Berlin and Mieke Bal have correctly noticed that there is a contrast between the audacious dynamism of Ruth in quest of the *gōʾēl* and Boaz going to sleep. I am reminded of a poem by Victor Hugo called "Booz endormi" (Boaz Slept), in which sleep is a transparent metaphor for his sexual impotence. Without necessarily accepting Hugo's con-

---

[26] Linafelt, "Ruth," 52.
[27] Ilona Rashkow, "Ruth: The Discourse of Power and the Power of Discourse," in *Feminist Companion to Ruth*, ed. Brenner, 38.

clusion on this point, the immobility of Boaz certainly expresses the indecision in which he left Ruth and that Naomi now wants to break through.

**[3:8]** The middle of the night is the critical moment when past and future meet and anything can happen, for better or worse (cf. Genesis 32; Exodus 11–12). As Paul Humbert says, this is "the hour of change . . . the hour of pathos par excellence."[28] See Judg 16:3; Job 34:20; Matt 25:1-13.

The scene recalls Gen 19:30-38 (the incestuous birth of Moab and Ammon), and both narratives use a similar vocabulary: בלט in Ruth, and לט (the same verbal root) in Genesis; "night," "lay down," "know," "go into."

The meaning of the verse is clear, but there are some difficulties with the philology. Boaz is said to be "startled" or "frightened," which perhaps should be understood in this context as "trembled." Then the next verb וילפת is a problem. Ibn Ezra relates it to Job 6:18 (while the Midrash and Rashi rather think about Judg 16:29). Job 6 and Judges 16 are the only two other literal witnesses of לפת. An anonymous rabbi in *Ruth Rabbah* says *estorst* ("twist"); (Pseudo) David Qimḥi: "to seize," "to muster its members" (?). Beattie agrees with the meaning of "to twist" on the basis of the Arabic *lafata*.[29] The critical consensus is that it is necessary to understand that Boaz "turned over." (But *b. Sanh.* 19b thinks that the word comes from לפת ["turnip"]: his skin turned livid like a turnip from fear; it froze.) I think that it is necessary to understand that Boaz awakens with a start, like after a nightmare perhaps caused by the semiconscious discomfort of an unexpected presence in his bed; he then recoils (וילפת). The author communicates that Ruth's presence in his bed is the last thing Boaz expected.

**[3:9]** "Who are you?" Usually the questions "Who?" and "What?" in Biblical Hebrew are less innocent than they appear. With Honig, one may wonder if Boaz is not suddenly hesitant about the identity of this Ruth the Moabite whom he thought he knew.[30]

"I am Ruth." Hubbard points out that this is the first time that Ruth identifies herself with her name, now having attained the level of an independent personality in the eyes of Boaz. She is no longer "the Moabite" (cf. 2:6) or a servant (2:13).[31]

"Your servant" (אמתך). This word is different from the one in 2:13, and one could see here a progression in the sense that the new term employed by Ruth would indicate a servant apt to become a concubine. But Zakovitch (on the basis of Gen 16:1; 21:10, 13, regarding Hagar) sees no difference between the terms, employing

[28] "l'heure de la péripétie . . . l'heure pathétique par excellence" (Humbert, "Art et leçon," in *Opuscules*, 101).

[29] Beattie, *Jewish Exegesis,* 229.

[30] Honig, "Ruth the Model Emigrée," 61.

[31] Hubbard, *Ruth,* 229.

one and then the other for the same person.[32] One could respond that Hagar was a שִׁפְחָה *before* becoming Abraham's concubine and afterward became an אָמָה.

"Your wing." The Ketib reads singular; the Qere reads plural (in reference to 2:12 on the subject of the divine protection ["his wings"] of which Boaz spoke and which Ruth nicely recalls by use of the same vocabulary). The singular relates back to part of Boaz's clothing, and the gesture of covering (the nakedness of) a woman is a symbol of marriage (cf. Ezek 16:8; Deut 22:30 [MT 23:1]; 27:20).[33] The contrast to Hos 2:3 (MT 5) is blatant. What Boaz said in the preceding chapter becomes prophetic here. The French expression that suits this situation in chapter 2 is: "il ne croyait pas si bien dire . . ." ("The result went beyond what he thought he said"). Rauber writes:

> In a moment, the process of understanding is completed. Everything culminates and merges in this image of ingathering: the wings of the Lord sweeping in to himself the people, the arms of Boaz gathering to himself the maiden Ruth, the arms of the young men drawing into the barns the grain. It is a moment of imaginative splendor and depth.[34]

Ruth "literalizes the metaphor."[35] Yhwh's protective wing is, concretely, Boaz's wing/cloak. This is the same phenomenon that the text alludes to when Ruth says, "you are a *gōʾēl*." As protector, Boaz is invited to take her, metaphorically, under his wing and, concretely, to become a *gōʾēl* of Naomi's/Ruth's clan.[36] This process of de- metaphorization finds a pronounced parallel in another feminine work from about the same era, the Song of Songs.[37]

Contrary to what Naomi (naively) thought, assuming that the man would take the initiative of action, it is Ruth that dictates what to do. The whole book portrays men as inferior to their tasks and women as having to take their places with authority. This feminine initiative finds evident parallels in Genesis 19 and 38 (Lot's daughters and Tamar). This is no literary coincidence. The reader is referred back to the linguistic and ideological parallels between Ruth and Genesis 19 above (see the introduction, p. 30). The parallels with Genesis 38 are detailed in the commentary on Ruth 4:12.

The text says nothing about the possible sexual relations between Boaz and Ruth on the threshing floor. One can imagine, as I do, that Boaz respected this woman

---

[32] Zakovitch, *Ruth,* 141.

[33] Compare W. Robertson Smith, *Kinship and Marriage in Early Arabia* (repr., Boston: Beacon, 1963), 105; and Paul A. Kruger, "The Hem of the Garment in Marriage: The Meaning of the Symbolic Gesture in Ruth 3:9 and Ezek. 16:8," *JNSL* 12 (1984) 79–86.

[34] Rauber, "Literary Values in the Bible," 171.

[35] Francis Landy, "Ruth and Romance of Realism," 298.

[36] Cf. ibid., 300.

[37] Cf. my *Romance, She Wrote.*

offered to him and thus confirmed the intuition of Naomi, who sent him her daughter-in-law. Phillips, on the contrary, maintains that they had sexual relations, and even, since Boaz was drunk like Lot in the sordid story of Genesis 19, "sleeping Boaz" does not know if they had had sexual relations, like Lot not remembering anything after waking up. In any case, Boaz was then placed in a compromising position, especially if the woman became pregnant from his act. He consequently had to act swiftly and officially marry Ruth.[38]

One must then, with Phillips, regard the question of property sold by Naomi a trick of Boaz, concealing the true problem: his union with a foreign and poor woman. After this deception, Boaz draws undeserved honor at the expense of So-and-so, who is fooled in the matter (and with him the "elders," "the whole people," and the choir of the women, as well as naive readers, a group among whose number I gladly choose to be).

The least one can say then is that all the characters of the story are, somehow or other, devious and that Boaz had the unbelievable luck in playing his cards close to his vest that Naomi just happened to have a piece of property to sell. Such a cynical reading of Ruth is not very attractive, all the more so as it completely ignores the principal motif of the story, *ḥesed* (see among others Ruth 3:10).

According to the Midrash—where the interpretation is exactly the opposite of Phillips's—Boaz showed himself even superior to Joseph's restraint in front of Potiphar's wife.

"You are *gōʾēl*." On the notion of *gōʾēl* see below on chapter 4. But the absence here of the definite article is important. It indicates that Ruth is not ignorant of the existence of others (or of another) near kin of Elimelek's clan.[39] Besides, in 2:20 Naomi had warned Ruth that Boaz was only one *gōʾēl* among others.

I must, with Landy, parallel Ruth's declaration in this verse with Boaz's earlier question: "Who are you?" Boaz asks who she is; she replies to him saying who *he* is.[40]

**[3:10]** In 3:10-11 one finds the fourth blessing of the book and a reminder of 2:11-12. Boaz tells Ruth that this new demonstration of *ḥesed* is even greater than the earlier one that Boaz had praised her for: Ruth's care of her mother-in-law.

One saw in the preceding—and one will see it in the continuation—that the narrative unfolds on two planes: narrative and legal. On the narrative plane, Boaz is offered a pretty young woman who comes to him to propose marriage because he is legally a *gōʾēl*. Boaz's reaction also has to be considered on two levels. He says that this act of *ḥesed* by the young woman surpasses the earlier one. For, on the legal plane (see what follows), Boaz had no obligation with respect to Ruth (strictly

---

[38] Anthony Phillips, "The Book of Ruth—Deception and Shame," *JJS* 37 (1986) 14.
[39] Cf. Sasson, *Ruth,* 82.
[40] Landy, "Ruth and Romance of Realism," 301

speaking, only with respect to Naomi), and he recognizes right away that Ruth has no more obligation with respect to him (as *yābām* or as *gōʾēl*). She could simply have gone after younger men. That she places herself, through a broad interpretation of the law, under a constraining dictum so as to redeem her in-laws is a superior *ḥesed* to everything that preceded it.

On the narrative plane, her offer is an act of charity to which Boaz does not remain insensitive. The Midrash talks about Ruth's self-sacrifice in choosing the older Boaz, for she did that לשם השמים ("for the love of God," which is also an expression used by martyrs). We do not know how old Boaz was; according to the Jewish tradition, he was eighty years old at this time. It was evidently not the habit of young people to call a girl of their age בתי, "my daughter" (cf. also 2:8). Boaz's age in the Midrash is certainly exaggerated; he still works on the threshing floor and personally oversees his harvesters. But the story of Ruth parallels Naomi's age (1:12; 4:15) with that of Boaz (3:10). Not only does Ruth substitute herself for her mother-in-law by marrying a Judean, but he belongs to her mother-in-law's generation, not to hers (to the happy astonishment of Boaz).

Boaz, in any case, is not a fool and understands that the young woman intensifies her self-sacrifice by her advances toward him. She chooses to be with a man older than herself, and, evidently, shuns a better party for a woman as attractive as she is. This moves Boaz more than if she had fallen in love with him. For, here again, Ruth shows her *ḥesed*, not blind romance. Her choice is motivated by other criteria that will become clearer in the ensuing story, knowing Boaz's noble character, his fidelity toward the Law, his devotedness to the customs of his people, and his compassion for the widow and the poor. Ruth considers these qualities of the man, which she recognizes by intuition and by experience (see chap. 2), as more important than being physically attracted and than being well matched with regard to age.

Ruth's goodness toward Boaz (repaid one day by Boaz toward Ruth) provokes the gratitude of a man concerned about his sexuality, as Bal emphasizes: "he is most grateful to her for she will help him out of *his* misery."[41] From this perspective, the blessing of the elders in 4:11: "May you produce children [or: act with חיל] in Ephrathah" = "may you be potent," takes on a more direct meaning, pointedly adding, "through the young woman who is coming into your house." Isn't Boaz, as his name reflects, "strong, the powerful one"?

Sasson translates here, "There will henceforth be no need to seek men, whether poor or rich."[42] But the meaning is more probably in the sense that Ruth had not gone to look for another man. Be that as it may, Boaz uses an expression with double meaning: "to go after [young men]" can refer to fornication (cf. Prov 7:22; Hos 2:5

---

[41] Mieke Bal, *Lethal Love: Feminist Literary Readings of Biblical Love Stories,* ISBL (Bloomington: Indiana Univ. Press, 1987), 71.

[42] Sasson, *Ruth,* 72.

[MT 7]). This explains the version adopted by Tg with the explicit, "to commit fornication with them." In short, the ambiguous atmosphere of the chapter is not abated.

"My daughter." Throughout the narrative, Ruth's femininity and her life as a woman are characterized in various ways: wife (of Mahlon), widow, daughter-in-law (of Naomi), foreigner, servant, confidant, daughter (of Naomi, of Boaz), remarried, mother. Such a list clearly shows the number of changes in her story until it is "fulfilled" in her maternity. Already, when she is loaded down with food by Boaz, "she symbolically carries what Naomi wants most: Boaz's seed."[43]

Retrospectively, one might wonder why the author decided to present an older character as Ruth's partner and future husband. But, if one supposes replacing him with a younger man, the story would proceed at an altogether different pace. Ruth is young, beautiful, and desirable; the "young Boaz" is impetuous and is quickly obsessed by the beautiful woman. The recourse to the popular court in chapter 4 becomes pure manipulation by Boaz to arrive at his own ends. Then there is no true respect of the Law on his part, and the court case is only a disguised ploy. Then it is not a question of going beyond the letter of the Torah, but of shamelessly using it. In short, the "old Boaz" is not a secondary element in the narrative, but an essential ingredient to its message.

[3:11] "Do not be afraid." Boaz awakened with a start in v. 8, and the Hebrew verb indicated fear (as after a nightmare); now Ruth must not be afraid! Of course, the formula is traditional (Gen 35:17; 1 Sam 4:20; 2 Kgs 6:16). But what would Ruth be afraid of? Of Boaz's refusal, evidently, but perhaps also of an indiscreet act on his part. She is "an honorable woman" and exposed to the loss of her reputation. Boaz reassures her: he will not act toward her like an irresponsible lover without scruples, but as a *gōʾēl*.

"Honest woman" (אשת חיל) is an expression that one finds in Prov 12:4 and 31:10 (see above on 2:1, regarding Boaz).[44] Boaz tells Ruth that everyone knows that she is an אשת חיל, and the context clearly shows that Boaz is thinking, not about her social and economic status, but about her *ḥesed*. An anonymous rabbi in *Ruth Rabbah* says that a man may sometimes be ashamed of his wife's family; but Boaz says here that everyone knows the value of Ruth (cf. Prov 12:4). Here again, therefore, the element of *ḥesed* transcends all others. This is the supreme principle before which everything else pales (as love [אהבה] is in the Song of Songs).

"The assembly of my people" (the population of my town) is in contrast to the oft-repeated motif of "the Moabite" or "the foreigner." This is a synecdoche for

---

[43] Étan Levine, *The Aramaic Version of Ruth,* AnBib 58 (Rome: Pontifical Biblical Institute Press, 1973), 83.

[44] Trible keenly recalls the parallel mention of Boaz in 2:1 and says, "Female and male; foreigner and native; youth and age; poor and wealthy—all these opposites are mediated by human worth" (*God and Rhetoric,* 184). On this phrase see also Christine Roy Yoder, "The Woman of Substance (אשת חיל): A Socioeconomic Reading of Proverbs 31:10-31," *JBL* 122 (2003) 427–47.

"town council," in other words the judicial body of the elders that, effectively, met at the gate of the city.[45] In Deuteronomy the numerous mentions of "the gate" are placed in the context of social justice toward foreigners, Levites, widows and orphans, and the disinherited.

[3:12] With "though it is true that . . ." (כי אמנם כי אם), the language becomes rocky. I mentioned this above regarding 3:3-4. It is unclear whether Boaz is stammering in his confusion and, probably, his hesitation at accepting Ruth's challenge, on one hand, or this is a flowery and pompous style to which he was accustomed, on the other hand. The accumulation of useless words—up to five—is difficult to communicate in English. Boaz says something like, "and now, if it is of course true that if [I am a redeemer]." He is obviously searching for his words and speaks more to himself than to Ruth, wondering how to proceed in this confused situation since he cannot claim the right and duty of the *gōʾēl* but would nevertheless like to marry Ruth. Ruth, in fact, gives him hope—unexpectedly. The continuation of his speech corresponds to this. In v. 13 he invites Ruth to spend the rest of the night with him—as he had insisted that she remain in his field in chapter 2—without, however, taking advantage of her. Thus he voluntarily keeps all his options open. For the moment he wants her but cannot have her. In the next chapter of the book, he will arrange things to combine what he wants and what he can have.

As for the confused speech, one finds a similar idea in 4:5, where Boaz says קנתי ("I buy") instead of קנתה ("you buy"); see the commentary on 4:5, p. 130).

"Another kinsman more closely related." The author is fond of these delayed revelations, a literary device of slowing down the narrative. In the following chapter, for example, one will learn that Naomi sells a field that had not even been mentioned before. Earlier Naomi waited a considerable time before divulging to Ruth that Boaz "is one of our *gōʾēl*s" (2:20).

This new information serves not only to advance the story, but it necessitates a readjustment of the reader's comprehension. Since Boaz is not the first *gōʾēl,* why was he chosen by Naomi instead of So-and-so? The only pertinent reason is the sensitivity of Boaz and the nonaptitude of So-and-so to interpret the Law generously. Naomi's wager is successful as early as chapter 3; it is triumphant in chapter 4.

Ruth is the only text that combines the levirate law and the law of redemption. Strictly speaking, these are two different laws and without internal relation. It is only by interpretive amplification of the two that their semantic fields eventually meet and blend. Then the duty of the levirate is no longer imposed only on "brothers living together" (Deut 25:5; in other words, on the brothers that have not divided the paternal inherited property between them), for the spirit of the law, as opposed to the letter,

---

[45] Obad 13; Mic 1:9. See Code of Hammurabi §126, *ANET,* 171a, for the term *bàbtum* as "a feminine formation for *bàbum,* 'gate.'" See *ANET,* 171 n. 96.

is limitless. Similarly, the redemption of Elimelek's field is no longer the duty only of the nearest kinsman, and the redemption in question is no longer limited to an impersonal commercial transaction, for it implies the recourse to every means so that an heir of the deceased may someday have full possession of the family property. The discrepancy between the book of Ruth and the Deuteronomic stipulations cannot be explained by the fact that Ruth is an earlier document than Deuteronomy, but quite the opposite by an interpretation of the text of the Law that is almost "evangelical."[46]

That Boaz does not have the status of a primary "redeemer" evidently emphasizes the intentionality of Ruth's action and the providential character of Boaz's intervention.[47] Boaz is certainly a kinsman of Elimelek's family (cf. Ruth 2:1; 3:2); but he is not the nearest one. He is, however, the one that Naomi chooses, and she was preceded by chance (2:3). The links of blood pass, therefore, to the second line by virtue of some other criterion, to which I will return later. The parallel of the election of a younger one, frequent in the Bible, is striking. The principle of the covenant transcends that of kinship proximity.

Now, in the context of the book of Ruth, this does not lack irony, since the unique goal of the whole adventure is to assure the continuation of Elimelek's line. This will be realized through a double paradox: Obed will have a Moabite as his mother and he will have Elimelek's distant kinsman for his father—someone who could have been forgotten. In the story of David, a descendant of Boaz, the prophet Samuel is obliged to inquire of Jesse about the "youngest" of his sons, who is David, whom the father did not even mention (1 Sam 16:11). By a reversal in the order of things—and one must appreciate this point—Boaz is not "the youngest one," but the oldest one.

Moreover, the author of Ruth produced one of the more paradoxical documents in the Bible. Ruth, the central heroine, is not an Israelite; Naomi is a widow without descendants; Boaz is an elderly man without offspring; and God remains hidden. Even the reported events are more clandestine than public. This is true of the scene in chapter 3 on the threshing floor during the night, after Boaz was lying at the edge (a liminal place!) of the grain pile.

**[3:13]** The language continues to indicate hesitation and difficulties by its redundancies, in particular the root גאל ("redeem"). Boaz is in the uncomfortable situation of sitting between two chairs, one might say. On one hand, he is not first on the list of "redeemers"; but on the other hand, he intends to marry Ruth.

---

[46] *Pace* Campbell, *Ruth,* 133. But Campbell judiciously cites 2 Samuel 14, where one sees King David give priority to the principle of justice over the letter of the law during the audience granted to the wise woman of Tekoa.

[47] Salmon bar Yeroḥam says that Boaz (in v. 14) wanted to keep Ruth's visit a secret from "Tob" (Mr. Good [see n. 48 below] = So-and-so) so that he would have no pretext to refuse the redemption because Ruth had not come to him but to Boaz.

The verb גאל appears three times in this verse with, as object complement, the second person singular feminine pronoun. Anticipating the development one will see in chapter 4, Boaz speaks here of a גאלה of Ruth. This is a giant step toward the substitution of Naomi by Ruth; for, lawfully, the one that is the potential object of the גאלה is Naomi, the Judean widow of Elimelek. Ruth, in all, is nonexistent before Judean law. It is in quality like being a "double" of Naomi that Boaz recognizes her rights (in chap. 4 Boaz at first talks exclusively about Naomi's business).

לני הלילה ("Remain this night"). This is the same word used in 1:16, when Ruth swore to stay where Naomi would stay (cf. also 2:23). Now Boaz invites her to stay with him this night. This is the second time that Boaz invites Ruth to remain with him (see 2:8). Obviously, Boaz likes the company of Ruth. But the link to 2:23 also indicates that Ruth's devotion to Boaz is part of her devotion to Naomi. Later, the fruit of the relation with Boaz, Obed, will be greeted as "the son of Naomi."

One may wonder why Boaz wants Ruth to spend the night with him when he just recognized that the relation could have no future. The stammering in v. 12 could convey the expression of Boaz's desire in v. 13. Boaz faces a dilemma. On one hand, he is an honorable man, as Ruth is an honorable woman; and he has no intention of taking advantage of Ruth's offer. If it was otherwise, he would not evoke the obstacle of a closer redeemer and would not bind himself to the young woman by oath. He could well send Ruth back to her home in the middle of the night. On the other hand, the offer is made, so it would be cavalier not to recognize it as such. Sending back the young woman without further ado would expose her to humiliation, which Boaz had no intention to cause, and would acknowledge his defeat in advance, while he desires the young woman. Furthermore, one must not underestimate the risk run by a young single woman wandering in the night, as illustrated in Song 5:7.

Boaz says, "Good; let him do it [redeem you]!" and suddenly his style becomes "loose," a sign of his vexation in thinking that the first *gōʾēl* could well make use of his prerogative.[48] The verse is an assembly of words composed with the root גאל (no less than four words out of fifteen). Boaz becomes almost comical; he cannot prevent himself from talking about "desire" (חפץ). It is true that the term is already present in the law on the levirate in Deut 25:7-8. One will appreciate Boaz's Freudian slip by which, instead of quoting the text of Deuteronomy literally ("desire to take [a woman]"), he hides his feelings by saying, "desire to redeem."

**[3:14]** In the image of Boaz's confusion—betrayed by his stammering—the situation on the threshing floor is particularly confused. All the more so since a deep obscurity runs through the whole chapter. The characters recognize one another gingerly (v. 8), and their relative anonymity is finely emphasized by the employment of "the man" and "the woman" instead of Boaz and Ruth (3:8, 14, 16, 18). The atmosphere is

---

48 The Midrash understands "good" as the name of the primary redeemer. He is therefore called "Mr. Good."

highly sexual. The verb שכב, "lie (with)," appears eight times in vv. 4-14, and the verbal root ידע, "to know," is frequent here. Ruth passes the night at Boaz's "feet," like a spouse in reality before being a legal spouse. But it is rather as a "mistress" that she leaves the bed at dawn, before the light of day. The text maintains the suspense as a backdrop of secrecy and danger. If there was an oral tradition preceding the written composition, it is in details such as these that it is manifested. From now on, Ruth is no longer alone in risking her reputation; Boaz is also implicated.

"It must not be known." אל-יודע is another uncommon verbal form for Hebrew (the only other example is Gen 41:21).

Pierre Crapon de Caprona designates the gift of oneself by Tamar in Genesis 38 and of Ruth in this chapter as *sacred.* Tamar disguised herself as a sacred prostitute; Ruth comes to a place taboo for women, the threshing floor, which is forbidden to them, probably because the seed is a symbol of sperm (Latin *semen*). This symbolic association explains why Boaz takes care that Ruth is not seen. One also understands why he donates grain for her mother-in-law.[49]

**[3:15]** It is unnecessary to see a compensation for sexual favors in Boaz's gift of grain to Ruth for Naomi. Boaz's gift is a new sign of his respectful interaction with these two women. As the scene of chapter 3 happens on the threshing floor, the least that one can expect from Boaz, owner of the harvest and willing to marry Ruth, is that he shows himself generous with respect to her and to the one that she protects and represents.

A number of commentators have raised the ambivalence of the grain given by Boaz: edible seed for the seed to come. In a poetic vein, Nehama Aschkenasy writes, "her bulging apron serves as evidence and promise of things to come."[50] But it is necessary to extend the line and notice that Ruth carries this grain to Naomi (here and at the end of the preceding chapter). This is renewed testimony to the self-assigned goal of Ruth: to provide an heir to Naomi.

Moreover, in the remainder of the story, Ruth will no longer speak. From here until the end of the story, she will be referred to in the third person. The same thing happens to Naomi. Her speech ends on a note of expectation (3:18). Thus the supposed "manipulation" of Boaz in chapter 3 becomes in chapter 4 Boaz's own manipulation through his lawful shrewdness. The gender balance is reestablished.

The difficulty in this verse comes up regarding the quantity of barley that Ruth is given. The six measures (ephahs?) of barley already embarrass the Midrash because it is too heavy for a woman: Boaz really gave her six symbolic grains! It is followed by *Ruth Rab.* 7.2; *b. Sanh.* 93ab; Rashi, and so on. The Tg rather thinks that

---

[49] Pierre Crapon de Caprona, *Ruth la Moabite: Essai,* Essais bibliques 3 (Geneva: Labor et Fides, 1982), 88.

[50] Nehama Aschkenasy, "Language as Female Empowerment in Ruth," in *Reading Ruth,* ed. Kates and Reimer, 111.

God gave Ruth the strength to carry such a weight (approx. 120 liters, which might weigh 200-300 pounds!). Here we are in the realm of legend. We find the same difficulty again with Salmon bar Yeroḥam; it was necessary not only for Ruth to be able to carry this burden, but that her shawl contains this quantity. (As a reminder, Ruth, at the end of the day in 2:17, has an ephah of grain—approx. 20 liters [according to the minimalist interpretation]). An anonymous rabbi, more prudently, says than Boaz gave her six measures according to the standard adopted in the city (of Bethlehem). Among modern commentators, Bertholet and Nowack think it was six omers. But since the term "omer" is a masculine noun in Hebrew, it would be necessary to read שׁשׁה ("six") in the text. What is more, the quantity is now too small (sixty percent of an ephah). One returns therefore to six seahs that apparently a strong peasant is able to carry (cf. Tg).

But what about the "shawl"? This one is called in the text המטפחת, which one finds only here and in Isa 3:22 (where it is listed among party clothes, etc.). The term is different from the one in Ruth 3:3. Commentators have suggested that Ruth's load is meant to mislead those who would see her leaving the threshing floor in the morning.[51]

Later, in her report to Naomi (v. 17), Ruth specifies that the grain is not for herself, for fear (says Rabbi Albabetz) that one will think that this is the price of her misconduct on the threshing floor.[52]

"He went into the city." This remark is to be understood as a parenthesis focusing upon what the women do in the meantime (vv. 16-18).[53] One could also follow the lead of several Hebrew manuscripts and ancient versions and read, "she returned to the city," which would connect back to 2:18.

### Ruth Reports to Naomi (3:16-18)

16 She came to her mother-in-law, who said, "How did things go with you, my daughter?" Then she told her all that the man had done for her, 17 saying, "He gave me these six measures of barley,[a] for he said, 'Do not go back to your mother-in-law empty-handed.'" 18 She replied, "Wait, my daughter, until you learn how the matter turns out, for the man will not rest unless he settles[a] the matter today."

17[a] Literally "six barleys."
18[a] NRSV: "but will settle."

---

[51] Zlotowitz, *Ruth,* 118.
[52] In *Shoresh Yishay* (on Ruth), 16e and following.
[53] In addition, Sasson (*Ruth,* 217) considers 2:18-22 and 3:16-18 as "connectives."

## Notes on 3:16-18

**[3:16]** Each of the first three chapters of the book concludes with a "return," a motif of singular importance. It is unnecessary to insist here on the centrality of the concept to the fifth century B.C.E. in Judah.

This verse uses popular language that is unusual in biblical literature. The idea is clear, nevertheless, and we must understand it as follows: "What about you [מִי־אַתְּ, = מַה־אַתְּ; cf. Judg 13:17; Gen 33:8; or even מִי = אֵיךְ, "how"; cf. Amos 7:2, 5], my daughter?" This is the same question that Boaz put in 3:9. But while in the earlier context Boaz inquired about the identity of the young woman on his "bed," here that translation would not mean anything. "My daughter" prevents all confusion. Naomi's question, literally "Who are you?" means something like, "How did things go for you?" Salmon ben Yeroham paraphrases, "Are you a widow again, or did he do what you desired?" The rabbi is intentionally ambiguous here. He also comments on "all that the man had done for her" (אֲשֶׁר עָשָׂה לָהּ), taking it as "all that he said," for his promise is as good as done. Boaz, he says again, was not pushed by his desire for marriage, for he could have allied himself to a more powerful family than to a foreigner. And neither was Ruth, for all she wanted was to remain with her mother-in-law in all circumstances.

On the threshing floor, the characters of the three principal actors of the book are transformed. Boaz is no longer the petit bourgeois that he was and the two women are no longer the underprivileged widows in quest of security. The events are able to follow their course only now that the decisive turn is taken.[54]

**[3:17]** "Do not go back to your mother-in-law empty-handed." Ruth seems to add something to the speech of Boaz. The same situation already prevailed in 2:21 (see that discussion). If Boaz did not explicitly mention Naomi, one has in any case an interpretation of his intention (and attentions).

It is not appropriate that Ruth be deprived, as is Naomi. She is the fullness of Naomi, not the mirror of her despoiling. See 1:21: the "emptiness" of Naomi is responded to by the "nonemptiness" of Ruth. This motif is central to the book. The author emphasizes it while making these words of Ruth the last ones coming from her in the story; in the following verse, it is Naomi who pronounces her last words.[55] The two women have made the initial foray, and it is now necessary to see "how the matter will turn out" (3:18).

In the exchange between Naomi and Boaz through an intervening person (a structure present in the entire story), the food goes from Boaz to Naomi by the

---

[54] Cf. the discussion of the novella in the introduction and Lawrence M. Wills, *The Jewish Novel in the Ancient World* (Ithaca, N.Y.: Cornell Univ. Press, 1995), 185–245.

[55] A similar trait is emphasized by Trible, *God and Rhetoric,* 187. The same phenomenon regarding Boaz appears in Ruth 4:9.

intermediation of Ruth, and the instructions concerning the seduction scene go from Naomi to Boaz through the same channel.

**[3:18]** The language continues to be vernacular in Naomi's mouth. She recommends that Ruth wait quietly. There is an *inclusio* here with the invitation for Ruth to sit that recalls the end of chapter 2 (2:23), where the same verb is used. Naomi has thrown the ball into the air; we must now see where it will fall, "how the matter turns out," an expression lacking in the Syr and that does not occur anywhere but here in Hebrew (but in Aramaic see Ezra 7:20; ‫די יפל לך ל-‬). The expression ‫נפל דבר‬ is rare and is never used in the sense of "a matter that results." On the contrary, the sense is generally "to remain without effect, not to succeed" (cf. Josh 21:45; 23:14; 1 Kgs 8:56; 2 Kgs 10:10). In order to arrive at the obvious meaning of the expression in Ruth 3:18: "[how] the matter will finish," a theological development, in my opinion, is to be subsumed under the sense illustrated in Ruth 2:3, where chance becomes opportunity (see again below on 4:1). In any case, Naomi remains confident. Boaz will not delay completing this matter (‫דבר‬) once begun. We must translate ‫כי אם‬ here with "unless." Any delay would indicate that the scene on the threshing floor was devoid of meaning.

# Chapter Four

## Reference Passages

The reference passages dealing with the *gōʾēl* and the *levir* in the epigraph to chapter 2 apply here as well.

### Family Property

- "Why should the name of our father be taken away from his clan because he had no son? Give to us a possession among our father's brothers." (Num 27:4)
- "Yhwh forbid that I should give you my ancestral inheritance." (1 Kgs 21:3)
- "Then his brother's wife shall go up to him in the presence of the elders, pull his sandal off his foot, spit in his face, and declare, 'This is what is done to the man who does not build up his brother's house.' Throughout Israel his family shall be known as, 'the house of him whose sandal was pulled off.'" (Deut 25:9-10)

### Adoption Procedure

- "Joseph removed them [his sons] from his [Jacob's] knees." (Gen 48:12; cf. 50:23)

## Overview

In chapter 4 of the book of Ruth, we arrive at the conclusion of the narrative. This chapter is even denser with regard to the practice of the law, and Boaz plays the role of interpreter well-versed in arcane legalities. If he is not a scribe and cannot be compared to Ezra, he is in any case well prepared for the session at the gates of the town of Bethlehem.

The text is generally well preserved; but it is necessary to employ textual criticism regarding vv. 4 and 5.

The story ends on a harmonious note. A new era begins. At any rate, such is the imagination of the author. Her thesis is that only love (חסד) triumphs, so only the generous interpretation of the Torah prevails over meticulous but narrow observation; then all hope is allowed. Even a member of a cursed people could become the mother of a messianic king. The society is transfigured. It welcomes the renewal of her history with gladness and words of blessing. That which the sometimes harsh and violent politics of governors Ezra and Nehemiah (cf. Neh 13:21, 25) has been incapable of realizing, the restoration promised by the prophets of the exile, love would accomplish.

Love is *ḥesed*, a generous act that goes beyond any legal formulation, because it surpasses legalism. Now it is remarkable that the narrative in chapter 4 brings us into the arcane territory of a legal procedure. The Law must be accomplished, for that, in the end, will be the instrument of reconciliation and restoration. Its arbitration is the only alternative to the arbitrary. The Law prevents *ḥesed* from becoming vague and without real substance. The conjunction of love and justice is the factor of redemption (גאלה). The accomplishment of the Law is the surpassing of the Law.

As I have mentioned at different points of this study, the book of Ruth is "gospel-like." Jesus will resume its message and say "Love your enemies" (Matt 5:44; Luke 6:27, 35), love the Moabite, instead of rendering her anonymous in the rigidity of a stereotype. She is called "Ruth"; her name is a promise of plenitude, of quenching thirst. Missing this full potential would have incalculable consequences. In fact, history would be aborted, without King David, without the Messiah. At most what would remain would be a closed-off community (cf. Ezra 9:9; Neh 2:17, etc.) walled in its virtuous solipsism. This is not Israel's vocation. To the call of the nations, in the person of Ruth, the *true Israel*, in the person of Naomi and of Boaz, offers its welcome. *Ḥesed* produces *shalom*.

In the legal sphere, it is necessary to reflect on what the term *gōʾēl* implies here.[1] The law/right of "redemption" with respect to a property let go for financial reasons is the duty of the "redeemer" (Lev 25:24-34; Jer 32:7-15). The meaning of the word *gōʾēl* is "savior, redeemer": the one who redeems relatives from economic slavery (Lev 25:47-49) and who avenges shed blood (Num 35:19; cf. 2 Sam 3:27,

---

[1] On this notion see D. R. G. Beattie "The Book of Ruth as Evidence for Israelite Legal Practice," *VT* 24 (1974) 251–67; Millar Burrows, "The Marriage of Boaz and Ruth," *JBL* 59 (1940) 445–54; Eryl W. Davies, "Ruth IV 5 and the Duties of the *Goʾel*," *VT* 33 (1983) 231–34; Robert Gordis, "Love, Marriage, and Business in the Book of Ruth: A Chapter in Hebrew Customary Law," in *A Light unto My Path: Old Testament Studies in Honor of Jacob M. Myers,* edited by H. N. Bream et al. (Philadelphia: Temple Univ. Press, 1974), 241–64; A. R. Johnson, "The Primary Meaning of the Root *gʾl*," in *Congress Volume: Copenhagen, 1953,* VTSup 1 (Leiden: Brill, 1953), 67–77; D. A. Leggett, *The Levirate and Goʾel Institutions in the Old Testament, with Special Attention to the Book of Ruth* (Cherry Hill, N.J.: Mack, 1974); Jack M. Sasson, "The Issue of *Geʾullāh* in *Ruth,*" *JSOT* 5 (1978) 52–64; and Thomas Thompson and Dorothy Thompson, "Some Legal Problems in the Book of Ruth," *VT* 18 (1968) 79–99.

30). On the model of God, who is the *gōʾēl* of his people (Isa 43:1; cf. Job 19:26), he is protective, avenging, victorious, redemptive of his clan, and in particular of the poor and disinherited. God, as *gōʾēl*, is also the advocate of his people (Ps 119:153-54; Lam 3:52, 57-58) and rescues from death (Psalms 69; 103; 104; cf. Isa 43:1; 44:22; Ruth 2:20).

Many point out that the "redeemer" does not have the duty to marry a widow without child, which duty belongs to another jurisdiction: the levirate. The request of Ruth in 3:9 is therefore improper, according to many. They forget, however, that the "redeemer" redeems property that he himself will not possess, but rather the poor kin that had lost the property. In the case of Naomi, the matter gets complicated. There is no longer any living person in Elimelek's line. For whose profit, therefore, should the "redeemer" redeem the land? This will be the question debated in chapter 4 of the book. In a striking shortcut, Ruth volunteers to extend Elimelek's line by proxy, which would make Boaz the redeemer of the ancestral land (as *gōʾēl*) and the begetter of the one who will eventually inherit it (as *levir*). This is what Boaz understands when he explains the issue, in Ruth 4, to So-and-so—who withdraws as soon as it is clear that his descendants will not inherit the field.[2]

One is to conclude that Boaz does not give priority to his proper eventual descendants from a previous marriage, which is confirmed by his place in the final genealogy. He does not redeem the field to the benefit of a line that would be completely secondary in comparison with that of Elimelek (what So-and-so almost did) but, by supererogation, to the direct benefit of Naomi. By virtue of this act of pure altruism, the neighbors shout, "a son has been born to Naomi!' (4:17).

It is evident from all this that the action of the "liberator" joins that of the *levir* in the story of Ruth.[3] The two legislations, originally independent of each other, are here overlapping through a series of extraordinary circumstances. Indeed, a whole group of laws find a potential application in the case of Ruth, *on the condition that hesed presides over all judgments in the matter*. Without *hesed*, no Mosaic law is applicable here, beginning with the proselytism of Ruth the Moabite, her gleaning, her appeal for a "liberation" to which she has no right, the redemption of Elimelek's ancestral land, the levirate marriage, the adoption of Obed by his grandmother, and so on.

The entire story of Ruth depends on an all-inclusive interpretation of the Torah. It is evident that a restrictive interpretation of the Law would render the narrative null and void. A Moabite has no place in Israel; she is nothing more than an intruder.

Boaz recognizes in Ruth an אשת חיל. However one translates that expression (which we also find in Prov 12:4; 31:10), she is established as a moral equal with Boaz, who was called גבור חיל in 2:1.

---

[2] Eryl W. Davies understands the problem in the same way; see "Ruth IV 5," 231–34.

[3] Cf. Campbell, *Ruth,* 132–37.

The biblical preoccupation with religious questions sometimes obscures social relationships, to which the religious decisions are nevertheless supposed to respond. On the social level, nothing is evidently more important than the question of marriage and descent. This question is absolutely basic in the books of Ruth and Song of Songs, for example, and it is far from absent in many other texts, such as Genesis, Ezra, Nehemiah, Chronicles, and Proverbs.

Marriage in the ancient Near East, as in most ancient and modern agrarian societies, is considered the most effective means of preserving the inheritance of land within the familial domain. Marriage is therefore strictly endogamous. When, following extraordinary historical circumstances, Judean males entered into exogamous marriages with foreigners (the inverse position is not mentioned in the texts), a "purist" reaction did not look favorably on it, as attested in Ezra 10 and Nehemiah 10. From this perspective, Ruth is the expression of a counterreaction. For one to understand the whole scope, it is necessary to take into consideration what the critics too often forget yet what is capable of shedding light on the problematic issues in Ruth 4.

From the social standpoint, it was theoretically possible for So-and-so to resolve the difficulty presented by the embarrassing introduction of Ruth into the transaction about Naomi's property. Since the self-appointed redeemer—represented here by a sort of notary or lawyer in the person of Boaz—insisted on the inseparability of the field and the Moabite, So-and-so could have taken her as his concubine. He nevertheless even rejects this option because it would provoke, in the case of primogeniture, conflicts between the children of his first marriage and children of the second.[4] So-and-so expresses this in other terms in Ruth 4.

But if So-and-so shows reluctance before running the risk, Ruth herself (and especially she) follows her commitments to the end. This is the reason, legally, the "lawyer" Boaz had to play the game of "double or nothing" in this matter before taking Ruth himself—not as his concubine, but as his legitimate (and not secondary) wife. The scene represented in Ruth 4 is a suspense story of the first order. So-and-so would have well been able to wreck everything, a possibility that he makes real, to the dread of the reader, in his first move to redeem Naomi's property. It is true that to make Ruth a concubine would have moved us considerably away from the levirate, and this is what gives authority to the argument of Boaz when he invokes a stronger law, a more sacred duty, and presents himself as *yābām-gōʾēl*.

---

[4] This conflictual position is illustrated by the jealousy of Sarah, who has a son, Isaac, vis-à-vis Ishmael and his mother Hagar (Genesis 21). The conjunction of the *gĕʾullāh* and levirate (for the protection of the "name" implies heritage) complicates the transaction in Ruth 4. On the subject of So-and-so's options, Davies says, "he would clearly be acting contrary to his own interests, for he would have forfeited the inheritance of his deceased brother (here Elimelek not Mahlon) to the son born of the levirate union. . . . To undertake the obligation, therefore, would generally have been regarded as an act of great benevolence, for the levir would have assumed certain obligations without necessarily deriving any corresponding benefits" (Davies, "Inheritance Rights and the Hebrew Levirate Marriage [Part 2]," *VT* 31 [1981] 268).

The deceased Elimelek and Naomi (because of her age) depend on a substitute to perpetuate their line. Elimelek has no brother and Naomi does not fill the essential condition of being a young widow who was able to give her husband children after his death. The situation is thus far from bringing together the elements of a "normal" levirate marriage. The story of Ruth takes us into abnormality; the peak point was attained by the Moabite origin of the one who substitutes herself for the Judean widow without heir, for the levirate marriage is strictly an internal custom. Clearly, if Ruth does not fill the legal conditions, she will not have to accomplish the legal duty either; this is, on her part, the result of an extraordinary *ḥesed*.

Now Ruth's option does not remain a private matter, for she sets the tone for all the important characters in the story. Boaz, the "second" *gōʾēl,* has no obligation to marry Naomi, a widowed relative who had children—and who, in any case, is no longer in a position of giving birth—or especially her Moabite substitute. One can say the same thing regarding the redemption of Elimelek's property. Boaz is not obligated to redeem it since, on one hand, Elimelek's line is practically nonexistent—and, consequently, the property would not be redeemed for the profit of anyone. On the other hand, Boaz is not the *gōʾēl*, but a more or less vague "acquaintance" (cf. Ruth 2:20). By contrast, the one called So-and-so here has this responsibility with respect to his impoverished kin, according to Lev 25:25. But being a pale version of Boaz, he evades this duty. The text suggests that Boaz offers him a sort of loophole through a maximalist interpretation of the letter of the law: So-and-so should marry Ruth, a substitute for Naomi. From one end of the story to the other we sail in extravagance.

Mieke Bal has perceptively seen that So-and-so is implicated in the same legal and moral dilemma as Boaz.[5] But, as opposed to Boaz, So-and-so feels secure only in the letter of the law. Boaz chooses life for the living; the anonymous *gōʾēl* chooses letter "that kills."

### A Parcel of Land Belonging to Elimelek?

Boaz challenges So-and-so on the subject of a property that is suddenly mentioned for the first time (4:3). One can subscribe to the thesis of Salmon ben Yeroḥam that Naomi had inherited her husband's field at the death of her two sons (for the story must remain plausible for readers and such an inheritance is not unbelievable, at least during a particular era, see Numbers 27 and 36; cf. below). But this resolves only part of the problem.

Most critics cannot hide their difficulty or their disappointment in the face of an element of a beautiful story that appears to them as a weakness. They want to know: Why complicate a story at the last minute that was so well crafted and that draws no additional merit from it? Where does this property come from that, retrospectively,

---

[5] Bal, *Lethal Love*, 75.

casts doubt on Naomi's poverty and vulnerability? This is evidently a problem, and even a well-known insoluble problem. If, on the one hand, Naomi can sell a field that belongs to her, how did she come to inherit from her husband while the legal texts do not foresee such a transfer from the deceased husband to his widow? On the other hand, why did Ruth go to glean in a stranger's field instead of on the family parcel?

To all these questions it is necessary to reply that, besides the fact that the narrative is a story and not a historical report, one can imagine that Naomi received this field in dowry for her marriage and that it reverted to her in her widowhood. She puts a field up for sale now that, in her present position, does not gain her anything because she is not able to cultivate it. During the years of exile in Moab (cf. the mention of the "fields of Moab"), the property may have been used in usufruct by others (cf. 2 Kgs 8:6), which would explain why Naomi delayed the sale: she had to wait for the tenants to leave. Reduced to the last extremity, after consuming the fruit of Ruth's gleaning, she goes "to release" the last trace of the existence of the Elimelek clan.

Be that as it may, the sale of the field must be situated in its legal perspective; it is constituted by Lev 25:23-25, interpreted broadly. The law establishes the following points:

1. The land belongs to Yhwh; no portion can be sold definitively, for the land was distributed once and for all to Israelite families.
2. The possibility must remain open to redeem what was sold—by the former owner or by his kin with capacity of *gōʾēl*.
3. If the redemption does not take place, the new owner keeps the property until the next Jubilee Year, and then the parcel of land returns to the original owners or to one of their heirs.

One can conclude from this that whatever Naomi had to sell, she hopes now to recover it by the intermediary of a *gōʾēl*. When did this happen? As I said at the conclusion of the commentary on chapter 1, Malbim notices that Naomi and Ruth return to the country at the time of the barley harvest (Passover) and concludes that it is too late to sow Elimelek's field.[6] That would explain why Naomi had to sell the field; it was necessary for their survival, which was more pressing.

Why wait, then, to attempt to redeem it? Simply because Naomi's position demanded that she fulfill the conditions of redemption by a *gōʾēl*. As for Naomi's perseverance in this matter, it is due to the necessity to keep the property in the family, just as Naboth was concerned about this in 1 Kings 21. Whoever obtains the field also obtains Naomi/Ruth (Ruth 4:5), precisely because the inalienability of the land is linked to the perpetuation of the family line. Legally, the parcel belongs to Elimelek's descendants. Now Naomi was past the age of childbearing, during which she would

---

[6] See on Ruth 1:22 above.

have been able, theoretically, to produce a candidate for inheritance (cf. Ruth 1:12 in an ironic fashion). The only resource is Ruth as her substitute. Whoever redeems the land redeems by the same token Elimelek's descent, a forthcoming descent, through the intermediary of Ruth. Ruth 4:5 is an understatement. The buyer of the parcel will not possess it; he buys it for someone else, in this case the future Obed, "son of Naomi," so-called because Boaz, in the legal sense, is only an adoptive father, or in any case a substitute father.[7] The situation is complex. The adoptive father is also the fathering parent, and this is confirmed by Ruth 4:21 ("Boaz fathered Obed"). This issue is important, for it establishes a distinction between the legal and the existential. In daily practice, Boaz is the husband of Ruth and the owner or, at least, the one who has usufruct of the obtained field. Obed is his son. But supposing that Boaz had other children from a previous marriage, these will not inherit the field, which comes back to Elimelek in the person of his "descendant," Obed.

But if one stops here, the problem is insoluble by self-suffocation, so to speak. Indeed, if Naomi had a legal right to the property of her deceased husband, she was therefore not so destitute as we were led to believe. Why would Ruth go to glean in the field of a neighbor? Why, on the other hand, is it necessary to redeem the property in question? And from whom?

The Jewish tradition says that the field had fallen into disuse and that there was no one to redeem it. No one offered assistance, because Naomi had brought with her a Moabite, in spite of Deut 23:6 (MT 7) (the Moabite has no access to the community of Israel). Boaz also abstained.[8] Malbim also worries about the discrepancy with Naomi's initial poverty.[9] She could have addressed herself directly to So-and-so or to Boaz and attempted to persuade either one of his legal duty toward her; but she chooses rather to depend on Ruth—which seems like another way of saying that Naomi voluntarily renounces the strict application of the Law. Ruth the Moabite is an "outlaw"; nothing legal can be constructed on such a basis.

Most surprising is that no one has wondered if, effectively, the question of the property could be raised only *once the strict legality was overcome*. For the text clearly shows that the problem exposed by Boaz in Naomi's name is not a problem of subsistence, of גאלה in the strict sense of the term, but of perpetuation of the family and of its establishment—which is a problem within the jurisdiction of the levirate (but expanded to the extreme). For Elimelek's line to continue, it is necessary for the property to remain in the family's possession. But the economic question passes to the second level here. If one is anxiously keeping within the limits foreseen by the Law, there is no ground for Naomi to claim the redemption of the field of her

---

[7] This is the key to understanding the role assigned to Joseph in the Gospel birth narratives: although the biological father of Jesus, he is considered the adoptive father in comparison with the "legal father," namely God. Cf. Cyrus H. Gordon, "Paternity at Two Levels," *JBL* 96 (1977) 101.

[8] Thus Bachrach, *Mother of Royalty,* on Ruth 1:22.

[9] Malbim, *Megillat Rut,* ad loc.

deceased husband and the continuation of his line. Elimelek's property will be bought by someone else (anonymous in the story), and furthermore, the Jubilee Year did not arrive—the story would not fail to say it if it was otherwise. As for continuing the line, Naomi is too elderly to hope that she could bring another son into the world. It is לפנים משורת הדין, ("beyond the letter of the Law") that the matter is reopened and calls for a new judgment.

Now, if one objects to this reading of the texts that the buyer of the field, to whom one will necessarily have to pay the price of the "ransom," is not even present at the time of the deliberations at the gate of the town, the response is very simple. This person has no role to play in the story; he can remain on the sidelines and be even more anonymous than So-and-so. He is only a potential buyer of the field. He has nothing to contribute in terms of speech or solution to the story.[10]

Once this possibility is pushed aside, So-and-so still remains. He is ready to pay Naomi and become the buyer (or "redeemer"). Once in his possession, though, the field passes finally to another branch of Elimelek's clan and, in the absence of an heir of the deceased Ephrathites, remains the property of So-and-so and his descendants.

Boaz cuts this machination off by marrying Ruth, a substitute for Naomi, with the intention and hope of producing an heir for Elimelek's clan. No sum of money is implied in this transaction. Naomi no longer has to sell her field, thanks to the גאלה of Boaz. What Boaz "acquires" is Ruth, who brings the price of real estate with her.

The marriage of Boaz to Ruth depends on the levirate, which could not apply to Naomi, but Ruth has done everything to make it possible. The passage from negative to positive is transacted by the intermediary of real estate, the destination of which will be debated, but which will finally bring about a discussion of the real subject. First, it is necessary to settle the problem of the field, for this field "belonged to Elimelek" (4:3); and with a single exception, no legal text in the Hebrew Bible mentions a widow alone inheriting from her deceased husband. This is even the opposite of what is suggested in Num 27:9-11.

If one reviews the better attempts at explanation by modern critics, one obtains the following result: Campbell, for example, invokes 2 Kgs 8:1-6.[11] But the Shunammite widow had a living son. One can apply the term of "testamentary executrix" ("trustee") to her that Neufeld uses (we will return to this), but not to Naomi.[12] In the absence of a son, Naomi has no one to whose benefit she could be proxy while exploiting the field of her deceased husband. This is the reason I would see in the

---

[10] Judiciously, Myers remarks on "the completeness" of the story of Ruth (*Linguistic and Literary Form*). The narrative avoids telling anything that is not indispensible to the plot. This is a characteristic trait of biblical narration in general; cf. Erich Auerbach, *Mimesis: The Representation of Reality in Western Literature,* trans. W. A. Trask (1953; repr., Princeton: Princeton Univ. Press, 1974), 3–23.

[11] Campbell, *Ruth,* 157–58.

[12] E. Neufeld, *Ancient Hebrew Marriage Laws* (London: Longmans, 1944), 240–41.

practical account of the book of Ruth, which speaks of Elimelek's field inherited and sold by Naomi, a reference to a late era when women enjoyed a sort of emancipation.[13] But the redemption of Naomi's field by her near kinsman remains highly improbable. How does one explain the fact that the buyer would pay for land that at the death of the widow would revert in any case to him, since she leaves no direct heir? It is only in the case where "a son is born to Naomi" (4:17) that the field would legally return to the widow until her son was able to inherit and to use it himself. The anonymous buyer (and absent from the whole scene) has therefore to have been an outsider to the family.

In all this, a basic detail is not yet sufficiently emphasized. One finds it nevertheless in the background of the first example of women becoming owners of the family land. In Numbers 27 the daughters of Zelophehad inherit from their deceased father in the absence of male heirs (Num 27:5-8; cf. Josh 17:3-6), with an important provision in Num 36:6-7. It is clear according to these (postexilic) texts that the real estate belongs to the family, to the clan. This is the ownership that is important to safeguard, even if women have to assume this responsibility in the absence of men, but always in the name of the whole family, which remains the true owner.

The problem is that when women assume this responsibility, they can remarry and, consequently, pass the property to another family. This is the case discussed in Numbers 36. With regard to Naomi, she does not present such a difficulty, thanks to her age, except that she sees herself obliged by her economic situation to sell the field. So-and-so could redeem it, but Boaz objects that Ruth is left out of the transaction. She also belongs to the Elimelek clan by her marriage with Mahlon, and she is consequently coproprietor with Naomi. Hence an exogamous remarriage of Ruth could alienate the family property, which will not happen, says Boaz, for he will marry the Moabite as a "second" *gŏʾēl*.[14]

In this whole affair, legally speaking, the weak point is evidently the pleading in favor of Ruth. This is not, as many believe, that a widow is said to be owner, for there are other comparable cases in the Bible (cf. Josh 2:1-14 [Rahab]; Judg 17:1-13 [the mother of Micah]; and Job 42:13-15 [the daughters of Job]). But Boaz cannot present his arguments on the subject of Ruth except by virtue of a broadened interpretation of the Law and while committing himself personally to his interpretation.

The transaction at the gate of the town, therefore, caused by the intervention of Boaz, invites the one who could redeem the field to help the widow to reintegrate the field into the family inheritance. If So-and-so does not buy the field, Boaz will do so

---

[13] In the Jewish colony of Elephantine, in the fifth century B.C.E., widows inherited from their spouses, but it took a long time before this right was recognized for them in Palestine, and even then it remained controversial. It is probable that only the progressive inhabitants of Judah, in the Second Temple period, approved this aspect of women's emancipation (cf. Jdt 8:7).

[14] Cf. Davies, "Inheritance," 142: "The 'name' was clearly associated in some way with inheritance, and the purpose of the levirate marriage was . . . to prevent the alienation of the ancestral estate."

himself. Boaz forces the decision: he obliges So-and-so to uncover himself, whether through buying the field that he hopes eventually to appropriate for himself, or renouncing his rights. The first move of So-and-so is to redeem for Naomi the field that belongs to Elimelek's clan, of which he himself is a member. This is, in a way, a generous gesture, but this is also, and in first place, an act of obedience to the Law. In Lev 25:25-28 one finds the following clause concerning the redemption of property: "If anyone of your kin falls into difficulty and sells a piece of property, then the next of kin shall come and redeem (וְגָאַל) what the relative has sold" (v. 25). Beattie probably has it right when he suggests that the redemption of the property of a kinsman did not mean that the one who redeemed it had access to all the rights to this property.[15]

The text invoked by Campbell (2 Kgs 8:1-6, the property returned to the son of the Shunammite that Elisha had revived) is useful if it is not limited in the way Campbell does. The Shunammite widow is the "testamentary executrix" of a property that legally belongs to her son. This would effectively be the case of Naomi if she had a son. Boaz anticipates this in his challenge to the legal *gōʾēl*. According to the hard-line interpretation of Boaz, redeeming the field—which is envisioned by So-and-so in the name of Lev 25:25—involves generating a son for Naomi, so that before the maturity of the child she will be the trustee and beneficiary. This is the reason there is a link, which many exegetes find enigmatic, between the redemption of property and the levirate marriage presented by Boaz. The two come together because the one remains incomplete and sterile without the other.

So-and-so would also go as far as possible in obedience to the moral law concerning the land. He would redeem the field in respect of the law's exhortation. But when Boaz shows him where even that could take him, he desists. In other words, So-and-so's performance of the Law is so literal that it does not accomplish anything at all. The widow remains without offspring and the redemption of the property constitutes a momentary assistance and moral support that does not affect Naomi's permanent condition. Such is not the spirit of the Law, according to Boaz, for it is evident that the problem put by Boaz supposes the abandonment of the letter of the Law. He invites So-and-so to go beyond his moral obligations and to become the levir of Naomi, that is, by substitution, of Ruth,[16] who fills the physiological conditions that allow her to provide the birth of a direct heir, thus perpetuating Elimelek's line. So-

---

[15] Beattie, "Book of Ruth," 251–67.

[16] Hubbard attempts to escape the dilemma by distancing himself from the texts of Genesis 38 and Deut 25:5-10 on the levirate. The book of Ruth would invoke only the *gĕʾullāh* duty, not the levirate. But even at the level of vocabulary, there are similarities between Ruth 4:5 and Deut 25:5 (אֵשֶׁת הַמֵּת, for example), or between Ruth 4:4, 10 and Deut 25:7. It takes a lot of effort, on the other hand, not to see in the story of Ruth the problem of the levir. Leggett is closer to the truth when he sees in the suggestion of Boaz to So-and-so the application of the *gĕʾullah* in its spirit as an exemplary *goʾel* (*Levirate and Goʾel Institutions,* 289–91). Hubbard himself is obliged to conclude, "love decreed duties more stringent than law" (*Ruth,* 60).

and-so then declares himself incapable of supporting at once the redemption of the property and the maintenance of a completely impoverished foreign woman. This would, he says, "damage my own inheritance," since the benefit would return in any case to Ruth's child or, more precisely, to Naomi's child whom she would legally "adopt"—which she does with Obed at the end of the story (4:16).

The rhetorical hypothesis imagined in 1:12-13 is suddenly actualized. The decision justified by So-and-so to buy the field—Naomi is too elderly to conceive a child and is not therefore part of the transaction—is in an unexpected way again wholly placed in question as soon as the issue is raised of simultaneously becoming the *gōʾēl* of Naomi's property—a rather good transaction—and Ruth's levir—which could be revealed as a very bad business.

One understands so much better that So-and-so needs to look more than once before purchasing, when one remembers the implications of a classical levirate marriage in which the principal goal is to furnish the deceased with a male heir. This is not, in most cases, a true marriage, since the levir does not have to continue to have sexual relations with the widow, his sister-in-law (or, here, his kinswoman). In the Sanskrit *Laws of Manu* §62, one reads, "When the purpose of the appointment to cohabit with the widow has been attained in accordance with the law, these two [the brother-in-law and his former sister-in-law, who has become his spouse] shall behave toward each other like a father and daughter-in-law."[17]

It is clear that levirate marriage is not far removed from incest. This is what incites Judah to renounce living with Tamar after they conceived a child. But in the case of So-and-so, this risk does not exist, and the levirate can therefore be transformed into a durable union. Consequently, the son born of this marriage would be, at once and legally, Elimelek's child (the child of Naomi, his widow) and the child of his true father, in short, a double heir—the heir of two different heritages. The story shows that Obed is at once "the son of Naomi" and "the son of Boaz," which is attested by the genealogy that is the coda to the narrative. Hence the refusal of So-and-so, when he notices that the arrangement would endanger the inheritance that he wishes to bequeath to his own children after his death.

Boaz, for his part, accepts the "danger." Obed will not only inherit "Elimelek's field," but everything that belongs to Boaz (if he did not previously have children), that is, a considerable fortune. The "son of Naomi" (4:17) can legitimately be called her *gōʾēl* (4:15), for, thanks to him (and to the wonderful woman who is his mother), Naomi passes from bitterness (1:20) to joy, from emptiness (1:21) to fullness, from death (2:20) to life (4:15).

From this perspective beyond the Law, it is significant that the narrator induces us, as I noted above, so frequently to imagine the "patriarchal era," that is, the era

---

[17] Cited by Thompson and Thompson, "Some Legal Problems," 95. Levirate marriage was employed in a comparatively vast geographic area. It is mentioned in the Sanskrit, Assyrian, Hittite, Hurrian, Elamite, and Ugaritic laws.

preceding the revelation at Sinai. This is also the tactic Paul will employ in his insistence on God reckoning Abraham righteous before the gift of the Law (Rom 4:1-5; Gen 15:6). The whole book of Ruth is also centered on the perpetuation of the generations in Israel and, by extension, on the indispensable culmination of salvation history (*Heilsgeschichte*)—here in the person of David, then in the Messiah. It is not simply out of an antiquarian concern that the author has Naomi call God "Shadday" (1:20-21), a divine name that insists on his promise of offspring to the founding fathers (and mothers). Naomi's problem (which also becomes Ruth's and Boaz's problem) is the same as that of the ancient patriarchs, beginning with Abraham. God reveals himself to them as Shadday (cf. Exod 6:3), as he also does to Job, whose children are dead (cf. Job 8:2-7, etc.). The promised births will then invariably be extraordinary ("not of blood," as John 1:13 says).

Obed is twice a miracle child. First, he is born of an unexpected union between a young Moabite and an aged Israelite. Second, the text that relates his birth—"Yhwh made her conceive, and she bore a son" (Ruth 4:13b)—marks the fulfillment of the vows addressed to Ruth by Boaz in 2:12 and 3:10. Yhwh at last broke the circle of death, famine, and emptiness that embraced Naomi at the beginning of the story (1:20-21).

More than that, the formula of 4:13b echoes a frequent biblical declaration relating to the birth of children of promise. In the first century of our era, Philo already drew attention to this characteristic of the text. Children of the divine promise are miraculous children.[18] Their line begins with Isaac, who is born to parents who were too elderly to conceive. Jacob, who is the fruit of the infertile Rebekah, is the second illustration. The text becomes then more insistent. Rachel implores her husband: "Give me children, or I shall die" (Gen 30:1), to which Jacob replies in a prophetic manner: "Am I in the place of God?" (30:2). She then gives birth to Joseph while recognizing that "God has taken away my reproach" (30:23). Next come Moses, Samuel, David, Solomon, and then Immanuel. The gospel finally insists on the miraculous birth of the Messiah, the last descendant of a line that dates back to Israel's origins.

Obed, quite obviously, has his place there. He is born of the union of an Israelite holy man and an exemplary Moabite widow, although these parents are not the "true" begetters, since he is a son of God. In the human genealogical line, he also enjoys a rather paradoxical status. He is "the son of Naomi," who conveys the tragic image of an Israelite widow without child.[19] She is "restored" so that a patronymic is not obliterated from Israel. It is therefore fallacious to say, as Trible does, that the women of Bethlehem "perceive this infant as restoring life to the living rather than

---

[18] See Philo, *On the Cherubim* 12-14.

[19] This is again pure fiction to have Naomi play the role of the woman without children when she has, indeed, given birth to two sons, even though dead. See E. Lipiński, "Le mariage de Ruth," *VT* 26 (1976) 124–27.

restoring a name to the dead. They speak of Ruth the bearer and not of Boaz the begetter. And they themselves name the baby. Repeatedly, these women stand as opposites to the elders."[20]

For Obed's birth to occur, a succession of unforeseeable and even improbable events had to take place. It was necessary, for example, that a foreigner—as were all the matriarchs (cf. Ruth 4:11-12)—become a mother in Israel. It was even necessary for her to take the place of her mother-in-law, as the ancient servant-concubines (Hagar, Bilhah, Zilpah) substituted themselves for the legitimate but infertile wives (cf. Gen 16:1-3; 30:1-6, 9-13), so that their children legally belonged to their mistresses.[21] Now, if this practice is ratified by certain codes of laws in the ancient Near East, it is certainly not by the letter of Israelite law (cf. Lev 18:3). Retrospectively, these sagas, including the one of Tamar in Genesis 38, are viewed as exceptions, as cases "beyond the law" with a positive value, while Lot's incest is judged negatively (Gen 19:30-38).[22]

With Ruth, the situation strangely recalls this era before the Mosaic laws. If one had doubts on this subject, they are disallowed after the elders of Bethlehem mention Rachel, Leah, and Tamar in Ruth 4:11-12 (with this coherence between them that "the power of the male is overruled by the female subject").[23] Now in the case of the ancient matriarchs, the result obtained by the substitution of mothers/bearers is often sordid (cf. Gen 29:31—30:24).[24] With Tamar, the narrative becomes absolutely scandalous, and things cannot get any more despicable, it seems.[25] No less than the sublimity of Ruth is necessary to redeem the past and indeed transform these episodes into examples of the extraordinary and the numinous. In the same way, Genesis 19 receives a new light through intertextuality with Ruth. Without the double incest of Lot there would have been no Moab, Ruth, David, or Messiah; the *Heilsgeschichte* would exhaust itself in failure like a wadi in the sands of the desert.[26]

In the economy of the Law, the adultery-incest-prostitution of Tamar remains what it is. Similarly, the enticement of Boaz by Ruth (chap. 3) is an illustration of the feminine traps that the wisdom literature recommends running from (cf. Prov 5:1-20;

---

[20] Trible, *God and Rhetoric,* 194.

[21] Regarding Ruth 4:11, the Midrash notes that Rachel and Leah were infertile during the first years of marriage. They were ⁽iloniot, which the Tg translates as "made to look masculine" (cited by Broch, *Ruth,* 100). The Midrash also compares Ruth the Moabite with the matriarchs of foreign origin.

[22] The marriage of Abraham and Sarah is a type expressly prohibited as incestuous by the Law (Gen 12:13; 20:12; Lev 18:9).

[23] Bal, *Lethal Love,* 78.

[24] Cf. André LaCocque, "Une descendance manipulée et ambiguë (Genèse 29,31—30,24)," in *Jacob: Commentaire à plusieurs voix de Gen. 25–36. Mélanges offerts à Albert de Pury,* ed. Jean-Daniel Macchi and Thomas Römer, MB 44 (Geneva: Labor et Fides, 2001), 109–27.

[25] It is remarkable that the only competition with this scene in Genesis 38 is the deadly adultery of David (the descendant of Tamar and of Ruth) with Bathsheba.

[26] The Midrash on Ruth 1:9 contrasts the people of Moab and the Moabite as an individual.

6:20—7:37).[27] In the economy of *ḥesed*, on the other hand, these same acts are transformed, because they are acts of love and sacrifice. Mary the Egyptian prostituted herself at the harbor of Marseilles to pay her transportation to Jerusalem in order to weep at the grave of the Christ; the Catholic Church rightly canonized her. Dietrich Bonhoeffer plotted against Hitler's life, and no one would be so hypocritical as to cast a stone at him. Moses killed the Egyptian persecutor and is praised by Stephen (Acts 7:24-25).

This is the lesson of Ruth, a lesson received by Boaz and rejected by So-and-so. The latter condemned himself to remain forever without genealogy. Who could ever descend from So-and-so? So-and-so, this is Nemo! Boaz builds a durable house and makes a name in Israel by his descent (4:14). Of course, So-and-so is, after the events, just as he was beforehand. He did not jeopardize the talent that he had received; he only buried it like a corpse. His respect of the prescription maintained the status quo. He draws neither honor nor shame from it (the abandoned woman in the matter does not spit in his face, as an Israelite girl would have had the right to do). So-and-so earned his living (also, by an uncanny irony in the material sense of the word, for, by his refusal to get involved, he could entertain the hope anyway to inherit the property of his deceased kinsman himself, after the Jubilee Year, for example). He is a perverse example of the preaching of Ezekiel 18: the righteous saves himself to the exclusion of any other. His gain is also his loss.

The contrast to Boaz, who chooses extravagance, is blatant. The Midrash says that he died on his wedding night.[28] One can interpret this view in various ways. That can be, on the part of the Midrash, erecting a hedge around the levirate marriage with Ruth: as soon as he impregnated Ruth, he dies. This would also be belated revenge of the oral tradition against a man that dared to cross legal limits.[29] Boaz crossed the line and died.

Or better, in the more favorable interpretation, Boaz completely accomplished his vocation; he was born for that night. What would come after this apogee could only be ridiculous. Boaz lost his life, but his loss is also his gain.[30]

---

[27] As Brenner comments: "the original sin of incest appears that much more base and preposterous by its attribution to resourceful females who dupe a weakling father. . . . We might interpret Ruth 3 as if Ruth the Moabite uses sex in order to seduce Boaz. . . . In short, the socio-sexual humour deployed for depicting the foreign group Moab is well-established" (Athalya Brenner, "Who's Afraid of Feminist Criticism?" *JSOT* 63 [1994] 44).

[28] *Ruth Zuta* 55; *Leqaḥ Ruth* 4.17; *Yalkut Shimeoni* on Ruth 4:13. The Midrash has great difficulties fully admitting Ruth into Israel. After his marriage, Boaz is identified with Shaharaim from 1 Chron 8:8-9 who was "from the children in the fields of Moab" (*Ruth Rab.* 4.1).

[29] Hence the Midrash, suddenly, as we saw above, gives a name to So-and-so; he is called *Ṭôb*, "Mr. Good." Cf. Ruth 3:13, where the term טוב can be understood as being the name of the initial redeemer. The Midrash adds (on 4:1) that Boaz did not call him by his name because he did not deserve it.

[30] On this subject, the Midrash also notices that with 4:13 the name of Ruth disappears. As soon as she is pregnant, everything is accomplished concerning her.

Nevertheless, the little relief of the figure of Boaz is verified up to the end. When his son is born, it is not he that gets to name the child, but the neighbors. After that (or before?), he disappears from the story. The neighbors also invoke the names of Rachel and Leah, whose mention here has a major importance and requires development. But it is remarkable that the thirteen children of Jacob are not named by their father either but by their respective mothers.[31] As for Boaz, the text does not credit him with the birth of Obed. He is "the son of Naomi." On this subject it is necessary to emphasize once more that the book of Ruth is not a romance, but a commentary on the Torah. Ruth followed Naomi and became the voluntary substitute for her mother-in-law. Ruth's God and people are those of Naomi. The story carries the name of Ruth because the spotlight is on her. But in a sense the traditional title of the book is misleading, for the magnitude of Ruth is precisely to efface herself before Naomi. It is for her that she marries a man from her mother-in-law's generation. It is for her also that she has a child. Designating Obed as Naomi's son is, against all Cartesian logic, the triumph of Ruth.

Imagining another text in which Ruth's child "would return" to her would transform the story into a romantic idyll, a good subject for a Hollywood film. Ruth's devotion to Naomi would then be purely sentimental and the levirate marriage with Boaz a simple means to bring about a "happy ending." Ruth's staggering conversion to Judean religion then also becomes a means for a romantic ending. Another attribution, such as "the son of Ruth," would have made her the reference point and transform Naomi into a satellite. Finally, it is Naomi that would have placed herself "under the wings" of Ruth and not the opposite, as the story insists.

In its actual form, the denouement of the story certainly does not make Ruth disappear, as some commentators claim. At the moment Naomi is declared "full" and no longer "empty" as at the beginning, the one who filled her is not forgotten. Her name is pronounced as the one that "bore a son [Obed]" and surpasses in value seven sons in the eyes of Naomi. A passage such as 1 Sam 1:8 comes to mind. Elkanah sadly asks Hannah, "Am I not more to you than ten sons?" In an intimate relation such as that between a husband and wife, it can happen that they are "more than ten sons" for each other. Perhaps it is rare, but it happens. What is extraordinary in the declaration of Ruth 4:15 is that a daughter-in-law would become this much for her mother-in-law. It would be necessary to remain quite insensitive to skip over this detail in the biblical text without emotion.

No, Ruth does not disappear from the text. She, the foreigner from Moab, is worth more than seven Obeds to Naomi. We have to await Jesus of Nazareth to rediscover a comparable praise of a gentile. All that the text could add on the subject of Ruth would only be anticlimactic, a fall into the trivial.

---

[31] Cf. Francine Klagsbrun, "Ruth and Naomi, Rachel and Leah: Sisters under the Skin," in *Reading Ruth,* ed. Kates and Reimer, 270.

A similar lack of understanding often accompanies the conclusion of the book. The final genealogy indeed returns to a masculine lineage, which is surprising in a book "about women." It relates to Obed, but also to Perez, to David and, by implication, to the Messiah to come. Here also, however, Naomi and Ruth are far from absent. Throughout the book they fought for a cause: the genealogy is their announcement of victory.

Perhaps today we are not able to understand very well the importance of this cause. In the West, individualism has become so excessive, so egocentric, that all devotedness to a future generation appears obsolete and even ridiculous in the eyes of some. Family links have become so relaxed to the point of being considered handicaps to individual autonomy. What one gains by this is nevertheless extremely doubtful. Worldwide galloping demography, it is true, is not an encouragement to return to healthier conceptions of the family and its continuity. But the facts of history do teach us that we cannot take the survival of the group for granted. After Auschwitz, the people of Naomi—who are also Ruth's people—know that they are vulnerable. It was already so in ancient Israel. The discontinuation of the name— that is, of the family, the clan—meant annihilation. A whole history remained without culmination, all a development without a future. The expression in Biblical Hebrew is "to cut off the name" (כרת שם; cf. Josh 7:9; Isa 14:22; Zeph 1:4), the same term used in Ruth 4:10.

This is the reason the two women devoted themselves to assure the future of a family in Israel. If one thinks that, by so doing, they voluntarily reduced themselves to be instruments of reproduction, one misunderstands the issue. For it is not a matter of any "demographic" reproduction, such as the Nazis advocated for Germany under the Third Reich. Ruth adopts Naomi's people because those people are devoted to God. "Your God [shall be] my God" (1:16). What has to be assured is not the number but history, the promise, the hope. The typical modern individual does not have any history, only episodes, like the soap operas on television. But Israel has a history, a history oriented toward the coming of the kingdom of God and its regent, the Messiah. To the extent that a Christian confesses that the Messiah came, one reads the book of Ruth as the very condition of the existence of the Nazarene, descending from David, who descended from Obed, who descended from Ruth the Moabite. The genealogy of Ruth 4 concludes with points of suspension, one might say. The rabbis have rightly extended the line that is sketched. "Jesse was the father of David. . . ." From the line of David, they say, will come the Messiah. The New Testament book of Revelation says *Maranatha*—"'Surely I am coming soon.' Amen. Come, Lord Jesus!" (Rev 22:20).

In the New Testament proclamation, women that humbly stayed in the background now step forward squarely in the light. The evangelist Matthew resumes the Obed genealogy:

Judah [was] the father of Perez and of Zarah *by Tamar* . . . and Salmon [was] the father of Boaz *by Rahab*, and Boaz [was] the father of Obed *by Ruth* . . . and David was the father of Solomon *by the wife of Uriah.* (Matt 1:3-6)

Here are four women whose origins and sometimes reputations remain doubtful—nothing of the sparkle of the legendary hero's ancestry. It was thus necessary that the one greeted as the Messiah have ancestors such as Tamar the Canaanite, Rahab the prostitute, Ruth the Moabite, and Bathsheba the adulteress! That is quite a surprise. Matthew nevertheless does nothing but emphasize the paradox and ancient scandal. The book of Ruth gives the great King David an awkward grandmother: a native of Moab, a convert to Judah's religion.[32] Her husband, a Judean, is the child of a Canaanite prostitute, Rahab. As for the son and heir of David, the glorious King Solomon, he is born of "Uriah's wife," that is, of an adulteress and a murderer. One will note that in 1 Chron 3:5 the mother of Solomon is the Canaanite Bathshua (1 Chron 2:3). She shares the same name with Judah's wife (Gen 38:2, 12). The Messiah would have a loaded ancestry! One can understand why David's legitimacy was contested. This is what brings the Yahwist (J), for example, to develop a theology of God's gracious gifts and choices. God gives power to the younger—or less qualified—if that pleases him:

- Isaac—Gen 4:1-16; 21:1-7
- Rachel—Gen 25:21-28
- Ephraim—Genesis 48
- Gideon—Judges 6
- Samson—Judges 13
- Saul—1 Sam 9:1—10:16
- David—1 Sam 16:1-13

The succession following David is no less rocky. In 2 Samuel 13–20 + 1 Kings 1–2, Amnon, the elder son, violates his half-sister Tamar; the line of succession is completely disrupted. Then Solomon, a younger son, usurps the throne, supplanting his elder brother, Adonijah, and executing him. Thus the Davidic dynasty is established by acts of incest, murders, rebellions, and usurpations. The genealogies of David (especially those in the NT) emphasize the scandal of this succession.

It is from this perspective that it is necessary to read the book of Ruth generally and its concluding genealogy in particular. The "femininity" of the book is not stifled at all. Put simply, the story of Ruth is pulled from the episodic and placed,

---

[32] The book of Ruth is subversive in this sense as well since it substitutes another type of kinship for biological descent without a genetic break—what Klingenstein calls "lineage of Idea" (Susanne Klingenstein, "Circles of Kinship: Samuel's Family Romance," in *Reading Ruth,* ed. Kates and Reimer, 201).

from the perspective of Israel's history, into salvation history (*Heilsgeschichte*), which is only really of interest, not of course to Hollywood, but to "the cloud of witnesses."

### The Court Session (4:1-4)

4:1 No sooner had Boaz gone up to the gate and sat down there than the redeemer,[a] of whom Boaz had spoken, came passing by. So Boaz said, "Come over, So-and-so;[b] sit down here." And he went over and sat down. 2 Then Boaz took ten men of the elders of the city, and said, "Sit down here"; so they sat down. 3 He then said to the redeemer,[a] "Naomi, who has come back from the field[b] of Moab,[c] is selling the parcel of land that belonged to our kinsman Elimelek. 4 So I thought I would tell you of it, and say: Buy it in the presence of those sitting here, and in the presence of the elders of my people. If you will redeem it, redeem it; but if you will not, tell me, so that I may know; for there is no one prior to you to redeem it, and I come after you." So he said, "I will redeem it."

1[a] MT: הגאל; NRSV: "next-of-kin."
1[b] MT: פלני עלמני; NRSV: "friend."
3[a] MT: הגאל; NRSV: "next-of-kin."
3[b] NRSV: "country."
3[c] The phrase "who has come back from the field of Moab" is lacking in Syr.

### Notes on 4:1-4

[4:1-2] The narrative continues without interruption and without delay: the first sentence is introduced in Hebrew by the conjunction "and," followed by the subject, Boaz, preceding the verb "to go" (instead of the verb followed by the subject according to the usual Hebrew style). In fact, the movement is a continuation of what had been said about Boaz in 3:15, "and he went [into] the city." The form of the verb in 4:1 is Qal perfect (עלה), meaning something like "Thus Boaz had left. . . ." One will note the nuance of "gone up [to the gate]" counterbalancing Ruth's "descent" to the threshing floor in 3:3, 6. Ruth 3:16-18 could therefore be a section that one could put in parentheses.

The meetings at the gate of a city (or town) are well known. From the outset, it is undoubtedly the wealthy who can pass time at the place where there is the most traffic, where there is a constant wave of going and coming (probably between the exterior door and the internal door, when there are walls).[33] Thus the elders are the

---

[33] "That even small cities were surrounded by a wall with a gate was an achievement of the monarchic period" (Frank Crüsemann, *The Torah: Theology and Social History of Old Testament Law*, trans. Allan Mahnke [Minneapolis: Fortress Press, 1996], 82).

first ones to hear the news and to make political and judicial decisions. Knowledge is an important ingredient of power.

With the advent of kingship, the elders became one of the arms of the monarchic system of justice. Institutionalized by the kings, justice in Israel was carried out at the local level by the intermediary of elders and of freemen. Frank Crüsemann writes, "In nearly all cases, the initial reaction on the injured party is to organize their own group . . . the negotiations involve more or less extensive debate. . . . It is remarkable that the texts lack a mediation figure . . . a third party."[34] On the question of the law practiced at the gate of a town, see Deut 21:19, 15; Lam 5:14; 2 Kgs 23:8; 1 Sam 8:4-5; and Amos 5:12. This was also where wisdom was taught according to Prov 1:21; 8:3; 22:22 (cf. Gen 23:17-18; Deut 22:15; Amos 5:10, 12-15; Deut 19:12; 21:2-4; 25:7-9; 1 Kgs 21:8-14).

The postexilic dating of the composition of the book allows looking at these "elders at the gate of the town" as a nostalgic motif in Ruth. The rule of Ezra and Nehemiah left little room for popular courts "at the gate of the town." Evoking this is already subversive in itself; it questions the legitimacy of the institutions during the Persian era. Moreover, a late date places Ruth among those books in which the setting in life (*Sitz im Leben*) is doubled—the one real, the other alleged. Similarly, a book written in the second century presents Daniel as an exile of the sixth century; Esther is queen of Persia in the fifth century in a story composed much later; Ruth, written in the Second Temple period, presents characters from the time of the judges.

Feminist scholars—in particular Trible—are indignant at the (passive) roles played by the women in Ruth 4. Ruth, in particular, seems to be treated there as an object of inheritance and apathetically consents to this imposition. Recall nevertheless that the social and theological problem of the time was determining if it was necessary for Judean men to send back their foreign wives and children according to the directives of Ezra and Nehemiah. It is logical for that era that the women in the book of Ruth are animated by contemporary preoccupations and presented with the sole concern of offspring (therefore of marriage) and of inheritance (therefore of integration). It is not at all justified today to criticize Naomi or Ruth as if their horizon was uniquely narrow and without breadth regarding the liberation of women.

One will poorly understand the "implosive" revolution of the book if one sees here a disguised enslavement of women. The narrative's insistence on the Moabite origins of Ruth was not designed to sterilize in advance all credit that would be granted to her only in bad faith. Granted by the author in one hand, it would be destroyed on the other. If this was really the case, one would be dealing with the cynical product of a morbid spirit. One also wonders for what purpose such a composition would be written and made public. To excuse the mixed marriages of Solomon? Strange plea that would imagine a Moabite ancestor for his father. To denounce the

---

[34] Ibid., 73. But regarding Ruth 4, he thinks that "The ten men function only as *witnesses* not as arbitrators or even as those who render judgment."

sexual license of foreign women in Israel (such as Rahab and Tamar)? But quite the opposite is true—these women are commended for their courageous initiative; and in chapter 4 Ruth is placed on the same plane as the exemplary matriarchs of the people.

In contrast to the scene in chapter 3—a night that happened without witnesses and outside all legal bounds—Boaz acts here in full daylight, surrounded by witnesses and in the role of a lawyer. As Nielsen says, "In contrast to the world of women, we are now entering the world of men."[35] Boaz surrounds himself with ten elders; this is the figure of the minyan, the minimum number of persons needed to permit a synagogue service.[36]

Boaz presents himself in front of the community that has the sole authority to decide civil matters. Boaz is, in fact, ready to interpret the Law so liberally that it makes it essential that this interpretation be officially ratified and rendered viable. Boaz therefore submits to the judgment of a *moral* community recognized as such because of its intrinsic qualities (and, probably, of the royal Persian authority in the background). The interpretation of the Law depends essentially on the integrity of the interpreter. Several laws will be put in question, such as the ostracism with regard to Moab, the law of redemption (*gĕʾullāh*), and the levirate (*yibbûm*). Beyond the purely legal questions that Boaz raises, the problem for the community will be to know whether it will fill its vocation as "support group" for Boaz, Naomi, and Ruth. A strict application of the Law, in fact, would exclude these three persons instead of including them. The temptation in this sense is all the stronger since Ruth is a Moabite, Naomi is a widow without male support and therefore without civil strength, and Boaz is not the (first) *gōʾēl* in this matter.

According to the *inclusio* structure of the book of Ruth, So-and-so the Judean in chapter 4 corresponds to Orpah the Moabite in chapter 1, which does not lack irony. Both characters receive the privilege of the "vision," but they are not able or do not want to believe it. Only exceptional personalities dare the extravagance of faith or of *ḥesed*. Centuries after Ruth, Jesus of Nazareth would center his preaching on the extravagance of losing everything in order to gain everything. He would also relate a story about a hero who was a despised foreigner, a Samaritan. By this example, he would teach to a priest, a Levite, a specialist of the Law, the true reading of the Torah. Ruth, one might say, is the "Samaritan" of the book that carries her name. And Boaz is the "doctor of the Law" who understands the message—as in the gospel—and is transformed by it.

**[4:1]** As in 2:4, the construction וְהִנֵּה (lit. "and behold [that]") indicates a change: "Now, it happened that . . ." emphasizes the chance effect in the sequence of the nar-

---

[35] Nielsen, *Ruth*, 82.

[36] One remembers previously, in chap. 1, that the triple refusal before Naomi yielded to the insistence of Ruth was interpreted by the rabbis as confirming a rule for "discouraging" the proselyte candidate.

rative. As I have said, 4:1 is a continuation of 3:15 rather than of 3:16-18; the latter verses were a sort of parenthesis.

"The *gōʾēl* . . . came passing by." One will note this new coincidence in the narrative (cf. 2:3, 20; 3:2). Later, a story such as Esther will proceed from one coincidence to another. This is a distinctive sign of a late narrative and particularly of the novella. The miracle in the ancient stories has now been replaced by opportune events.

פלני עלמני ("Someplace," "So-and-so"): as in 1 Sam 21:2 (MT 3); 2 Kgs 6:8. The formula does not apply to persons except in very late texts (cf. Dan 8:13; Matt 26:18).[37] Trible says in a pithy formula: "Anonymity implies judgment."[38]

**[4:2]** The Jewish tradition continued to be astonished by the welcome Ruth the Moabite received in Israel. According to the Talmud, the presence of ten elders was necessary to decide the acceptability of a Moabite in Israel (*b. Ketub.* 7b).

The intervention of elders is not necessarily a sign of antiquity, as noted above. Their functions, according to the Deuteronomist, implied the protection of the social order. They oversee levirate marriages (Deut 25:8); they investigate the question of a fiancée's virginity (22:13-19); they judge the renegade son (21:18-21); and so on.

**[4:3]** Naomi returned "from the field of Moab." The verse clearly shows the intention of the author to use this motif as an *inclusio* with the "field of Moab" at the beginning of the story (1:2).

"Parcel of land" (חלקת השדה). The expression is a little surprising; Ibn Ezra thinks that perhaps Elimelek had a small piece of property on a part of the field. But one finds the same wording in 2:3, where it is a question of Boaz's field. It seems, therefore, that the author envisions שדה as an inclusive term, whether in Moab or in Judah. Hence a particular field is designated חלקת השדה.

The term "field" appears sixteen times in the book:

- "the fields of Moab"—1:1, 2, 6, 22; 2:6
- "the field of Moab"—1:6 and 4:3
- "the field" or "the portion of the field"—2:2, 3a, 3b, 8, 9, 17, 22; 4:3, 5.

The texts that seem to go against my explanation are those where one finds the singular form, "the field of Moab." But in 1:6 the expression that appears twice there is in mutual asymmetry, "the fields of Moab" being followed by "the field of Moab" (unless we understand with the Jewish tradition that Naomi learned of the news at the end of the famine in Judah in a particular field of Moab). In 4:3 the phenomenon is

---

[37] See Sasson's discussion in *Ruth,* 105–7; he wrongly calls the formula a "farrago."

[38] Trible, *God and Rhetoric,* 190. Phillips succinctly says, "Because . . . [he] would deny Elimelech's name in Israel, the author ironically denies him a name" ("Book of Ruth," 10).

inverted. By asymmetry with the first occurrence of הַשָּׂדֶה in the verse, one also has the singular, "the field of Moab," for it is a matter of contrast with each other. One leaves the first one empty (the one in Moab; see 1:5) and arrives at the other "filled" (this is the root meaning of the name "Ruth").

It is necessary to understand that Naomi is selling the field (the perfect form in legal language has a participial sense). Some Jewish sources say that the past tense of the verb indicates Naomi's determination. One finds the same situation, adds Zakovitch, in Gen 23:11.[39]

"Our brother" (לְאָחִינוּ) should be understood in the widest sense of the term— despite the efforts of the ancient rabbis to consider the two men and Elimelek as the sons of the same father, Nahshon (cf. *b. B. Bat.* 91a). It was necessary to stick as closely as possible to the letter of the law in Deut 25:5; this is accomplished by the broadest interpretation of the word "brother." The procedure is not extreme, as various passages demonstrate, such as Lev 25:25, 35, 39; 2 Sam 1:26; Amos 1:9. In these texts as well, the word "brother" has a broad sense.

**[4:4]** The usage of the independent personal pronoun in this verse reinforces the passage to another actor: "as for me. . ."; "I said" = "I thought (or) I have determined." As we also saw in v. 3, the perfect tense has participial value in legal language. Sasson translates, "I declare." Similarly, in this context, the Hebrew expression גָּלָה אֶת־אֹזֶן, "to open the ear (of someone)" (translated by TOB: "to inform") means "to enjoin (someone)" (we find the expression again in 1 Sam 9:15 [NRSV "revealed"]; Job 33:16; 36:10, 15). And "I may know" is understood to imply "whether I am to continue with my pleading."

In what follows, it is definitely a matter, in the first place, of a commercial transaction. It is marked by terms such as "to buy" and "to sell" (cf. v. 3). This is, as we saw above, an indispensable turn to introduce the crucial problem of the levirate. In any case, the whole judicial-commercial tone continues until the end of the hearing, and Boaz will speak of "acquiring" Ruth in marriage (4:5, 10), while, as we shall see, the expression suits only because Boaz presents the whole matter as a transaction between So-and-so and himself. The redemption of Ruth, which was the question in 3:13, passes, in chapter 4, by way of the redemption of Naomi's property.

"Those sitting here." Campbell points out the frequency of the verb "to sit/be seated" from Ruth 3:18 on: Ruth sits in the house; Boaz sits at the gate of the town; then So-and-so, the ten elders, and the other numerous witnesses sit.[40] The narrative becomes solemn: it is a matter of legal jousting in order to arrive at what meaning to give to the Law. The seriousness of the business demands the meeting of the court, with the presence of the opposing parties, witnesses (that the text designates as those

---

[39] Zakovitch, *Ruth,* 155.
[40] Campbell, *Ruth,* 145.

"sitting"), and the ten judges (or jurors). The object of the debate is stipulated by the fivefold repetition of the root גאל ("redeem") in this verse.

The first anomaly is in Boaz's use of personal pronouns: ואם־לא יגאל ("and if *he* does not redeem"). The Qere, multiple manuscripts, and the versions have "if *you* do not redeem," which is evidently the easier reading. If one maintains the MT, it is necessary to imagine that at this point in time Boaz turns toward the elders of the town. One finds the same consonantal formation in Lev 25:54, which means that Boaz may well be quoting the Torah here, or, according to Zakovitch, the text of Ruth 3:13 thus creates a perfect parallel with the Leviticus passage.

"I [myself] will redeem it," says So-and-so. One finds the same emphasis again on the subject of the verb as in 4:1 (Boaz). The narrative maintains the suspense. At first, Boaz is undone by his opponent. So-and-so decides to assume his responsibilities according to the law. In that respect, the text echoes the initial good intentions of Orpah (cf. 1:10). But Boaz still has another arrow in his quiver, as the following verse demonstrates, and—again like Orpah—So-and-so does not register himself in salvation history and remains anonymous.

### Boaz's Dangerous Gambit (4:5-12)

5 Then Boaz said, "The day you acquire the field from the hand of Naomi, I am also acquiring[a] Ruth the Moabite, the wife[b] of the dead man, to maintain the dead man's name on his inheritance." 6 At this, the redeemer[a] said, "I cannot redeem it for myself without damaging my own inheritance. Take my right of redemption yourself, for I cannot redeem it."

7 Now this was the custom in former times in Israel concerning redeeming and exchanging: to confirm a transaction, the one took off a sandal and gave it to the other; this was the manner of attesting in Israel. 8 So when the redeemer said to Boaz, "Acquire it for yourself," he took off his sandal. 9 Then Boaz said to the elders and all the people, "Today you are witnesses that I have acquired from the hand of Naomi all that belonged to Elimelek and all that belonged to Chilion and Mahlon. 10 I have also acquired Ruth the Moabite, the wife of Mahlon, to be my wife, to maintain the dead man's name on his inheritance, in order that the name of the dead may not be cut off from his kindred and from the gate of his native place; today you are witnesses." 11 Then all the people who were at the gate, along with the elders, said, "We are witnesses. May Yhwh[a] make the woman who is coming into your house like Rachel and Leah, who together built up the house of Israel. May you produce children in Ephrathah and bestow a name in Bethlehem; 12 and, through the seed[a] that Yhwh will give you by this young woman, may your house be like the house of Perez, whom Tamar bore to Judah."

5[a] K: קניתי ("I am acquiring"); Q: קניתה ("you are acquiring").
5[b] MT: אשת; NRSV: "widow."

**6ª** MT: הגאל; NRSV: "next-of-kin" (throughout).
**11ª** NRSV: "LORD" (throughout).
**12ª** MT: זרע; NRSV: "children."


### Notes on 4:5-12

[4:5]The style in v. 5 is hurried. Boaz must immediately neutralize So-and-so's deci-sion. At this point, Boaz again mixes the chain of personal pronouns (see above). He comes with an argument that is a continuation of the suggestion to redeem the field "from the hand of Naomi" (the one who sold it): the redemption also implicates the widow of Elimelek's son, Ruth the Moabite. She also has a right to the field in ques-tion, according to Boaz; for it is basically a matter of more than a purely commercial transaction. The goal is "to maintain the dead man's name on his inheritance."

One feels that Boaz has just played the trump card. He anticipates his victory so much at this point that he says, "I am acquiring" instead of "you are acquiring." No Freudian slip could better indicate Boaz's nervousness and also his feeling to have stymied his opponent. Redeeming "from the hand of Naomi" (the owner) implies that the field will remain at her disposal throughout her life. Redeeming from the hand of Ruth changes the transaction completely. It is no longer a question of lifelong rev-enue but of redeeming the field in favor of a third person (Ruth), who will survive through her potential descendant.

One must emphasize that the formal object of the debate remains from one end to the other the *field* and what it represents for the continuation of the family. Ruth comes after, as future mother of the one who continues Elimelek's line.

As I said above, there is confusion in the personal pronouns employed by Boaz. He says, "I am acquiring" (thus K), which is read by the Masoretes (Q): "you are acquiring [at the same time]." One can keep the Ketib here as Sasson does, fol-lowed by Nielsen, without short-circuiting the surprise effect that makes So-and-so stumble. "If you redeem the field, I shall redeem the wife of the deceased," this despite the fact, it is to be added here, that she is a Moabite and is not protected by the Law, strictly understood. The text of v. 5 emphasizes once again that Ruth is a Moabite.

But in this case, the גאלה action is split and the future of the field is seriously put in question. Moreover, one will notice in the speech of Boaz the accumulation of phrases to discourage So-and-so ("the Moabite," "the spouse of the dead man," "the name of the dead man on his inheritance"). Placing Ruth together with Naomi pre-pares one for the end of the sentence. The property is redeemed in favor not only of Naomi, which would render the transaction without danger of alienation in the future, but also of Ruth, which changes everything.[41] It is necessary to divide the verse in the

---

[41] See Code of Hammurabi §§171, 177 (*ANET,* 173–74). Boaz will lose the money he has spent for the purchase of the field and the son of Ruth/Naomi becomes the heir. Consistent with themselves,

following manner: "The day you redeem the field from the hand of Naomi and from Ruth the Moabite, the wife of the deceased, I will surely redeem [her] in order to restore the name of the dead man on his property." In fact, Ruth knocked down the wall of separation between an Israelite and a Moabite by claiming for her mother-in-law, through herself, the גאלה of Boaz. At that point, he represents his marriage to Ruth as a levirate union.[42]

The prepositions "from the hand of" and "of [Ruth]" are problematic, since the field was sold by Naomi and, commercially speaking, does not belong to her or will no longer belong to her, and still less evidently to Ruth. But in a legal sense (according to the Mosaic law), the field is again understood as belonging to Elimelek's family and his sons. Legally or ideally, the field belongs to Naomi and to Ruth, her substitute.

"And from the hand of Ruth" should be understood elliptically. Strictly speaking, the formula is legally inexact. But, according to the logic of the story, Ruth became "one flesh" with her mother-in-law (cf. 1:14: דבק; and 1:17: only death can separate them).

The "name of the dead man" is mentioned three times in this chapter (vv. 5, 10 twice). Johanna Bos is justified in contrasting this repetition, as well as the vow that Boaz "bestow a name" (4:11), with the fake and anonymous redeemer.[43] Suddenly the chapter swarms with names of ancestors and concludes with a genealogy of descendants. Ruth is completely surrounded, and all the people who have become her people embrace her.[44]

The levirate marriage with Ruth—to which there is at least an allusion in this verse—completes the redemption *according to Ruth's interpretation* in 3:9. If So-and-so redeems Naomi's field, this must be with the intention of bequeathing it to the heir (so far nonexistent) of Elimelek's line. Naomi is no longer of childbearing age; but Ruth will substitute herself for her, says Boaz.

The socio-legal context of this masterstroke from Boaz is probably the following: according to the development of the levirate in the biblical texts (and beyond), the dangerous proximity of this custom to incest drives priestly authorities of the Second Temple period to condemn it—pure and simple. Leviticus 18:16 and 20:21 forbid sexual relations between brother-in-law and sister-in-law. One can see here the

---

Fewell and Gunn see Boaz's pleading as manipulative of the patriarchal system and even conclude that he mocks the system (*Compromising Redemption,* 93); but such an interpretation is wrong. The issue in Ruth is much deeper than a mockery, and its hermeneutical bearing is much more important.

[42] *Pace* Salmon ben Yeroḥam, et al.

[43] Johanna W. H. Bos, "Out of the Shadows: Genesis 38; Judges 4:17–22; Ruth 3," *Semeia* 42 (1988) 37–67.

[44] Trible writes that Ruth finally will not have been but a means in the hands of men and "to ends of men" (*God and Rhetoric,* 192). But is bearing children and perpetuating a family a uniquely male ideal? The feminine dimension in chap. 4 and in the whole story is far from absent; on the other hand, Boaz's silence in the section of 4:14-17 is, if one may dare to say, eloquent.

opposition of Ezra and Nehemiah to the levirate about 445 B.C.E. (later, the custom is recalled in the Gospels about a purely theoretical question from the Sadducees, who were opposed to the doctrine of the resurrection of the dead; Matt 22:27-28; Mark 12:18-27; Luke 20:37-38). The rabbis of the tannaitic era later considered the levirate as aberrant.[45]

Thus to take up the question in the book of Ruth is already in itself a polemic, in any case, against the grain of fundamentalist teaching during the Second Temple period. Furthermore, Boaz's argument becomes seriously deviant when he intervenes for a young foreign woman. It is true that she is a widow without child, and with that the danger of incest is nonexistent, since neither So-and-so nor Boaz is brother of Mahlon, and their degree of kinship, whatever it is, is with Naomi, not with the Moabite.

As a result, Boaz appears stricter in his observance of the Law than the partisans of Ezra and Nehemiah are claiming to be. But in order to accomplish the Law, one should precisely not send back the foreign wives, as the governors of Judah wanted to do. The argument appears faultless to the elders and to the assembly of people at the gates of Bethlehem, who applaud Boaz's achievement and shower him with blessings.

**[4:6]** For the Midrash, So-and-so's refusal is motivated by the fact that Ruth is a Moabite and he is afraid of dying like Mahlon and Chilion. Rashi himself interprets So-and-so's refusal as an exegetical and moral misunderstanding of Deut 23:3 (MT 4), for the text concerns the men and not the women, a differentiating principle we saw formulated in the Talmud (*b. Yeb.* 76b). But one might rather compare So-and-so's reluctance to Onan's reluctance in Genesis 38.[46]

"Take my right of redemption [for] yourself" is ambiguous. One can hear, "in regard to you." But the reader also knows that Boaz considers his redemption of the field for Naomi and Ruth as a personal deed of kindness.

**[4:7]** In the background of this new development, there is once again a legal custom that is important to evoke here. It is a matter of the custom called הגאולה והתמורה ("redemption and exchange"). The latter term indicates an exchange, a substitution. In Hebrew, "substitution" is תחלף or תמורה, used almost synonymously in Leviticus 27. Leviticus 27 forbids the exchange of animals offered to Yhwh, even for a superior-quality beast (cf. 27:33).[47] By extension, here So-and-so will make an exchange

---

[45] Cf. J. Jacobs, "Levirate Marriage," *JE* 8:45–46.

[46] Some interpreters see this verse of Ruth 4 as an interpolation, but I cannot find any plausible reason for setting it aside.

[47] Leviticus 27 concludes the book of Leviticus and seems to have very little to do with the rest of the book. But such a unique text may represent an old tradition (cf. Carol Meyers, *Discovering Eve: Ancient Israelite Women in Context* [New York: Oxford Univ. Press, 1988], 170–71). Sasson explains the

(תמורה) of rights and duties (גאלה) while burdening Boaz with his own responsibility in this matter. As a sign of what he undergoes, he removes his shoe *in the manner of the levir renouncing his sister-in-law* according to Deut 25:9-10! Even though the term is not used here, one nevertheless thinks of the חלצה (from a verbal root meaning "to release"), allowing the widow to return to her family and eventually to remarry outside of the clan of her deceased husband (*m. Yeb.* 2:5; *b. Yeb.* 24a; 39b; *Ber.* 13a). In Ruth the term is חלף, which applies rather to a purely commercial operation. Ibn Ezra points out that, consequently, this is not the rite of the חלצה. That may technically be the case, but it is necessary to add that there is at least an allusion to this last custom here, and that this allusion must be sensed by the reader if she wants to understand the text.

The custom in question is made solemn by the double mention of "in Israel" in this verse and by the accent placed on its antiquity (לפנים, which indicates that the procedure had become obsolete [cf. 1 Sam 9:9] at the time of the book's composition [sixth-fifth century]; see again below). The custom consists in an attestation by exchanging a sandal between the two parties (לרעהו. . . איש, "one . . . to the other"; cf. Gen 11:3, 7; Ruth 3:14; etc.).[48] Since it is a matter of a contract, it is normal that the buyer receives a token. What is important is that Boaz holds lawful confirmation (תעודה) of his full right to the field and to the levirate marriage with Ruth.

The sudden mention of "Israel" (four times in the chapter) is remarkable. Evidently, the author intends on widening the reach of a story that could seem purely local and anecdotal to national dimensions. With Boaz bringing the matter before the court of Bethlehem (cf. also "all the assembly of my people" in 3:11), one had already turned a corner toward the generalization of the case. Now, "Israel" transcends "Bethlehem" on the spatial plane and "In the days when the judges ruled" on the temporal plane. Effectively, between 1:1 and 4:22, one passes from an obscure Ephrathite family to the great King David.

The "sandal" (נעל, *naʿal*) in question here derives from the Hebrew root נעל, which means "locked" (closed with a strap), as in Song 4:12. Here, and there, one can see an erotic allusion, which is also not absent from Deut 25:5-10.

On the symbolism attached to the shoe, Rowley judiciously refers to an article by Isidor Scheftelowitz. "The shoe is namely a symbol of the law, of judicial process. Already in ancient Egypt, the sandal was the symbol of power, authority."[49] In

---

difference between social גאלה and commercial תמורה (*Ruth,* 141–42). Ruth's author stresses that in all social and commercial dealings, the handing over of a shoe made them official.

[48] Phillips is probably right when he explains Deut 25:9-10 and the removal of the delinquent brother's shoe as signifying that he has illegally acquired his dead brother's property. Instead of receiving a sandal as a token of legal acquisition (cf. Ruth 4:7), his own shoe is removed and his family is called "the house of him whose sandal was pulled off" (Deut 25:10) (Phillips, "Book of Ruth," 4). Note that in Ruth 4:8 So-and-so prevents Naomi's or Ruth's intervention by removing his own shoe, even if, perhaps, he will be called "he whose sandal was pulled off" anyway.

[49] Scheftelowitz, "Die Levirats-ehe," *AR* 18 (1915) 255: "Der Schuh gilt nähmlich als Symbol des

addition, there are parallels in India and in the texts from Nuzi, in Mesopotamia. In reality, it is the possession of the shoe that is the sign of domination. The shoe universally symbolizes the woman. Speaking of a divorced spouse, the former husband says, "She was my slipper, I have cast her off" (an Arabian form of divorce).[50] The removal of the sandal "signifies humiliating submission to another authority (cf. Isa 20:2-4)."[51] It is probable that in Deut 25:5-10 the sandal is removed from the foot of the one who refuses the levirate as a sign of his dispossession.[52] Rashi says that it remains uncertain who gives the sandal to whom. For Ibn Ezra, it is Boaz's sandal in exchange for the property, or, on the contrary, the sandal represents the right of redemption.

The mention of the shoe is incidental and refers to an ancient custom no longer in use at the time of the composition of Ruth. At the time of Jeremiah (sixth century), it was already no longer practiced (Jer 32:10-15). This is an imprecise chronological indication, but valuable.

The parallel with the story of Judah and Tamar in Genesis 38 has imposed itself throughout the book of Ruth. Here again one will think of the pledges given by Judah to Tamar, whom he takes for a prostitute on the way of Timnah. The sandal (of So-and-so) plays a somewhat different role but remains a pledge in a particular transaction (cf. Ps 60:8 [MT 10] = 108:9 [MT 10]). The textual reference this is based on is nevertheless Deut 25:9, in which one sees the sister-in-law, frustrated by the nonperformance of the levirate, spitting in the face of the defaulting *levir* and removing his sandal.[53]

Here also one could understand that Boaz removes the sandal of So-and-so, as the widow does in Deuteronomy 25. This reading takes into account Ruth 4:6, "take my right of redemption for yourself" (גְּאַל לְךָ אַתָּה גְאֻלָּתִי). This is understood well in the ancient Jewish sources. According to the Targum, Boaz removes the sandal (of So-and-so); this is therefore a חֲלִיצָה. Josephus interprets it in the same way (see below). Salmon bar Yeroham says that So-and-so gave his sandal to Boaz.[54] Rowley is probably too persnickety when he says, "The taking off of the sandal here does not mean that there was purchase or sale of a property, for the kinsman [So-and-so] neither bought nor sold anything."[55] Ibn Ezra, for his part, says that the sandal represents

---

Rechts, des Besitzes. Schon bei den alten Ägyptern ist die Sandale das Symbol der Macht, der Herrschaft."

[50] Cf. Calum M. Carmichael, "A Ceremonial Crux: Removing a Man's Sandal as a Female Gesture of Contempt," *JBL* 96 (1977) 321–36; idem, *Women, Law, and the Genesis Traditions* (Edinburgh: Edinburgh Univ. Press, 1979); idem, "Treading in the Book of Ruth," *ZAW* 92 (1980) 248–66. Julius Morgenstern says that in Deuteronomy 25 the sandal signifies the female's restoration of her liberty vis-à-vis her brother-in-law's authority ("The Book of the Covenant [Part 2]," *HUCA* 7 [1930] 169).

[51] Carmichael, "Ceremonial Crux," 332 n. 2.

[52] Phillips, "Book of Ruth."

[53] One will note that Salmon ben Yeroham discusses the levirate at length, which he says applies here.

[54] Beattie agrees, for, he says, "Boaz bought nothing from the *goʾel*" (and consequently owed him nothing) (*Jewish Exegesis,* 183).

[55] H. H. Rowley, "The Marriage of Ruth," in *The Servant of the Lord and Other Essays on the Old Testament* (London: Lutterworth, 1965), 174.

the right of redemption from which So-and-so releases himself. One inevitably thinks of Esau selling his birthright. Except that what sells stealthily in Genesis 25 (cf. v. 31) here is accomplished officially and before witnesses. The oath demanded by Jacob (25:33) is replaced here by an object acting as a seal (as in Genesis 38). Strouse and Porten keenly notice that Naomi's words in Ruth 3 ("uncover his feet," 3:4) now retrospectively have prophetic meaning.[56]

For the parallel to Deut 25:9 to be perfect, Ruth would have had to remove the sandal from So-and-so's foot and spit in his face for abandoning her.[57] But, as liberal as the author of the book may be, she could not allow a Moabite to humiliate to this point a member of her adopted people in this way. It is therefore Boaz who performs the rite (without any further humiliation—that remains implicit), and the explanation of his gesture is changed into a simple commercial custom.[58]

One will note on this subject that there is no overt question of shame with regard to So-and-so here, just as there was no question of shame in the case of Orpah in chapter 1.[59] The book of Ruth remains irenic to the end, while it is, subtly, a critique of the priestly society of the Second Temple. Its goal is not to heap shame on the conservative fundamentalists of the time, but to bring them to a generous comprehension of the Torah.

"This was the manner of attesting." The term "attestation" (תעודה) does not appear again except in Isa 8:16, 20, where the sense is close to "Torah" (NRSV "testimony" and "instruction"). Here the word has become more general in its use, thus following a semantic development of vocabulary toward secularization.

**[4:9-10]** The process of generalization continues (see 4:7 above): "the whole people" are witnesses. The scene recalls Josh 24:22 and 1 Sam 12:5. In these two passages, as here in Ruth 4:9, the mention of "today" is remarkable. In Joshua 24 the term is strongly emphasized in v. 25, "that same day." The intention is obviously to mark the beginning of a new era. "Today" is the first day of the future. In a sense, what comes after in the story traces the outline of "another story," as Dostoevsky says when Sonia rejoined Raskolnikov in Siberia.

Boaz makes the transaction official, but the enthusiastic agreement of the

---

[56] Strouse and Porten, "A Reading of Ruth," 67.

[57] Josephus effectively paraphrases our text while having Ruth spit in the face of So-and-so, according to the law (*Ant.* 5.9.4). Of course, Naomi could have played this role assigned by Deuteronomy 25 to the widow neglected by the defaulting levir. But the text in Ruth 4 places Ruth in the spotlight, who substituted herself for Naomi; Naomi was previously mentioned only as the seller of the field; she cannot, of course, reproach So-and-so for not impregnating her.

[58] Some have argued that So-and-so is claiming to be incapable of assuming his responsibilities rather than stubborn. But the difference between the two options is tenuous. When a "brother" refused the levirate, without a doubt he would have alleged all sorts of excuses.

[59] Regarding shame, Lyn Bechtel says, "Both formal and informal sanctions were used to control undesirable or aggressive behavior, to manipulate status, and to dominate others" ("Shame as a Sanction of Social Control in Biblical Israel: Judicial, Political, and Social Shaming," *JSOT* 49 [1991] 75).

elders is more than a certification. Through Boaz's "conversion" to a liberal interpretation of the Law, it is the whole institution that is transformed (meaning the Second Temple). The elders lift Ruth the Moabite to the same level as the matriarchs Rachel and Leah, "who together built up the house of Israel." The obvious parallelism between Ruth and Tamar is thus emphasized. Tamar erected the house of Judah by Perez, that is, the messianic dynasty. For Ruth, this is spiritually "to pass from misery to wealth," and for Naomi, from deprivation to fullness. The integration of the Moabite into the people of her choice carries her to the pinnacle of glory and makes her a paradigm on a par with the ancestresses of Israel. The vocabulary and the solemnity of the speech are closely reminiscent of the conclusion of the covenant with God in Josh 24:22.

In the sequence of Boaz's speech, the reader is not surprised to see repetition. עדים אתם היום ("today, you are witnesses") introduces (v. 9a) and concludes the speech (v. 10b). קניתי ("I obtained"), again announced by the stammering in 4:5, appears twice (vv. 9a, 10a), as does שם המת ("the name of the dead man," v. 10aα, 10aβ). On the subject of this last expression, Sasson understands the sentence as being a quotation of a recognized formula. These are the last words of Boaz in the story, as the end of the speech of Ruth and of Naomi had been signaled in 3:16-17.

Boaz buys or redeems the field "from the hand of Naomi," for Naomi is the original owner. Instead of the buyer being a stranger, it is now a kinsman, Boaz, who makes himself proprietor of what used *to belong to* Naomi; and, implicitly, he acts *for* Naomi. Indeed, not only So-and-so is left anonymous in the narrative, but also the one that had or would have bought the field if it had not been redeemed by a *gōʾēl*.

The expression "all that belonged to Elimelek, . . . to Chilion and to Mahlon" (v. 9) means, "all the succession rights of Elimelek's line without restriction," as well as its perpetuation (mentioning Chilion and Mahlon is normal in a judicial procedure). Apart from the field that was in question all along, "all that belongs to Elimelek" and his sons doubtless represents few things. The two women were reduced to gleaning for their food. But, in a legal declaration, it is important to foresee every contingency. Boaz's rights effectively extended to Elimelek's whole family, which Boaz was part of. He is the *gōʾēl*, the head of the clan—before passing this right to the son that he hopes Ruth will bear.

"I have also obtained Ruth . . . to be my wife." The commercial transaction of the redemption of the field implies equally, according to Boaz, the future mother of the heir. These are two sides of the same coin. It is going too far to construct a modern protest against the purchase and sale of women in ancient Israel on the basis of this verse. This practice is open to condemnation, but it must be done on other textual bases.[60]

Besides, Ruth 4 is the only biblical passage in which marriage is called "acquisition." As Sakenfeld says, the verb "to redeem" (גאל) cannot apply to a marriage and,

---

[60] See LaCocque, *Romance, She Wrote,* 179–80.

on the other hand, the usual verbs לקח and נשא (cf. 4:13 and 1:4) do not suit an estate transaction.[61] One will note that for the living to honor the dead does not consist in a veneration of the ancestors, as occurs in many regions of the world, but in the perpetuation of their vital inheritance, their offspring.

**[4:10]** Boaz's mention of "the Moabite" is unexpected and does not add anything, it seems, to the lawful identity of Ruth. But it is Ruth-the-Moabite who merged for the first time the laws on גאלה and the levirate. It is also the Moabite who released the Israelite history from the rut of an unbending and static interpretation of the Law.[62] Finally, it is the Moabite that Boaz, pillar of the Judean community, marries on this day.

Regarding the acquisition of Ruth, the Midrash makes a distinction between the legal act of "taking a wife" (קנה, lit. "to buy") and the reality of the marriage, called קדושין, from the verbal root קדש ("sanctify").[63] The verse repeats v. 5b almost verbatim.

לקים ("to maintain") is an Aramaism found only in late biblical books (cf. Ezra 3:6; Ps 119:26, 36; Est 9:21), just as שלף נעלו ("remove his shoe") in v. 8 is an Aramaism.

ומשער מקומו ("the gate of his place"). We find this phrase again in Deut 21:19 along with the mention of elders. This is an additional verification of the influence of the Deuteronomic literature on Ruth.

**[4:11-12]** Mieke Bal sees in these verses a *mise en abîme*, that is, a microstructure containing in summary form the narrative to which it contributes.[64] The chronology is disturbed (Ruth is compared to Rachel, Leah, and Tamar), the genealogical lineage is broken, the same is confronted by the different, and limits are henceforth no longer stable.

The endorsement given by the elders—followed as a single person by "the whole people"—to the marriage of Boaz and Ruth, and the strong intervention of the "neighbors" in the welcome of the fruit of this union in vv. 14-15, sufficiently demonstrate the public character of marriage in Israel. "Marriages, while intensely personal, private and domestic, also have a critical supra-household dimension and are thus public arrangements with economic if not political implications."[65]

One will note, with Gottwald, the contrast between the masculine world, rejoicing at the good fortune of Boaz to whom Ruth will give children, on one hand,

---

[61] Sakenfeld, *Ruth,* 73. See my development above, p. 112.

[62] One thinks of another non-Israelite with a similar influence on historical Israel: Jethro (Exodus 18).

[63] See Broch, *Ruth,* 99.

[64] Bal, *Lethal Love,* 84–87.

[65] Meyers, "Returning Home," 113.

and, on the other hand, the feminine world, emphasizing the consolation of Naomi by the birth of her (grand-)son.[66] This passes from the legal domain to the more specifically kinship domain. The women eclipse, so to speak, the men and come with decisive declarations. The book of Ruth has, from the beginning, established a distinction between the two universes, the goal being to bring to light the central problem of the story, a problem of women. Thus the narrative proper begins with women and ends with them as well.

כל־העם ("all the people," or "the whole people"). As in 1:19, where the text mentioned "the whole town" (כל־העיר) stirred up because of Naomi's return to the country, thus now כל־העם assembles itself again about her. In 1:19 כל־העיר seemed constituted by women ("and the women said"); here again it is the women that bless Naomi and her (grand-)son (4:14-15). Meanwhile, nevertheless (vv. 11b-12), the elders bless Boaz while mentioning "the woman who comes into your house," as well as "Rachel and Leah," who are followed closely by "Tamar," and finally "this young woman" or "maiden" (נערה; the young woman is like a maiden in this development of her story; see below on 4:13). It thus emphasizes that if Ruth gives birth to a child, this will be a firstborn.[67]

One may compare the blessing formula here to other passages: Gen 24:60 (Rebekah); Tob 7:12-13; and 10:11-12 (Tobias and Sarah).

The reference to Rachel and Leah, the matriarchs of the twelve tribes of Israel, clearly shows that the future of the union of Boaz and Ruth can well be imbued with a comparable importance to the one of engendering the twelve founders of the people of Israel. Now, the text has just recalled that Ruth is a Moabite, which does not lack paradox in the vow of the elders. Furthermore, it is ironic that Rachel and Leah are mentioned here when Jacob had been sent to Laban so that he would not marry a Canaanite (Gen 18:1). Although one must remember, with the anonymous rabbi in *Ruth Rabbah*, that Rachel and Leah were two idolators before being converted by Jacob, after which they "built up the house of Israel." The paradox is again emphasized by the mention of Judah and Tamar and the fruit of their incest, Perez, that the text here associates with his future "dynasty,"[68] as in 2 Sam 7:11 (the "house" of David). Now in 2 Sam 7:27 Nathan promises that God will build David a house. That the author of Ruth refers to this promise of Nathan is again confirmed by both the prophet and the narrator using the term "Ephrathah," as in Ruth 1:2.

"Perez." Besides the mention of Perez in Gen 38:27-30, other texts show the preeminence of this clan in the tribe of Judah, in particular in various genealogies:

---

[66] Norman K. Gottwald, *The Hebrew Bible: A Socio-Literary Introduction* (Philadelphia: Fortress Press, 1985), 557.

[67] In Isaiah 7 the mother of Immanuel is called an עלמה ("young woman"), with the accent placed on the primogeniture of the infant.

[68] The descendants of Perez are celebrated in two postexilic texts: 1 Chron 2:4ff. and Neh 11:4, 6. The last text refers to them as four hundred sixty-eight men of "valor" (חיל, as in Ruth) who returned from exile to Jerusalem. See Sakenfeld, *Ruth,* 78.

Gen 46:12; Num 26:20-21. This preeminence is confirmed by texts that are clearly postexilic (cf. 1 Chron 2:4-5; 4:1; 9:4; 27:3; Neh 11:4-6).

The reference to Tamar is not surprising. She was alluded to indirectly throughout the narrative. The allusion becomes explicit here; see p. 51.

The development of chapter 4 thus drives us toward the peak in the final genealogy with the last word of the book, "David." One notices, with D. F. Rauber, the literary construction "in double cones" joined vertically at their peaks, an hourglass-like figure uniting the expanse of the patriarchal group (Rachel and Leah) to the future collective by the narrow channel of David's kingship. This is what prevents the story of Ruth from being merely anecdotal. The author was careful to widen the horizons of the past and future. On the one hand, 1:1 evoked the era of the judges in a distant past (cf. 4:7, "formerly"); the summoning of Moab, Rachel, Leah, Tamar, Judah, and Perez recovers also the past of the "house of Israel." On the other hand, the final genealogy, and in particular the last word of the book, "David," opens the perspective toward the future (according to the internal temporality of the story).

וַעֲשֵׂה־חַיִל means "and be prosperous." An alternative to the NRSV that I like is, "and empower you to prosper in Ephrathah and that one proclaim your name [that you maintain your reputation] in Bethlehem!" One already finds the term חַיִל in 2:1 and 3:11 with the sense of "substance, value." But in Prov 31:3 חַיִל has the sense of "masculine force" (cf. Job 21:7-8), and in Joel 2:22 the term designates natural forces. One can therefore understand our text as expressing the wish that Boaz be sexually prolific (see NRSV). All the more so since the remainder of the sentence wishes that Boaz "proclaims a name in Bethlehem," as the TOB says, without compromising itself with a clearer translation. We may understand it as "bestow on yourself a name in Bethlehem," or "proclaim the name [of a son] in Bethlehem." Sasson points out that "name" is repeated fourteen times (two times seven) in the book of Ruth. One can also, on the basis of the repetition of this idiom in vv. 14b, 17a, and 17b, conclude with Brichto (who invokes Akkadian parallels) that the formula envisions "the continuation of the family line."[69]

It is, furthermore, a question of "seed" (זֶרַע) in the Hebrew text; but this seed comes from the "young woman" and goes to Boaz. The NRSV's "children" masks the ironic reversal of position when compared with Boaz's gift of seed to Ruth on two preceding occasions (2:16; 3:15). Linafelt, who directs attention to this gender balance,[70] is not, on the other hand, in any sense justified when he says that Ruth is here "reduced to . . . nothing more than a uterus."[71] It is even more surprising to read from the same author that Ruth, who conceived by Yhwh in the following verse (v. 13),

---

[69] H. C. Brichto, "Kin, Cult, Land, and Afterlife—A Biblical Complex," *HUCA* 44 (1973) 21–22.

[70] Linafelt, "Ruth," 75.

[71] Ruth 4:15 would suffice to refute completely such a biased judgment. Besides, Pressler is fairer in noting that in v. 15 Ruth is not praised for her fecundity but for her love (*Joshua, Judges, and Ruth,* 304).

never asked for or desired a child.[72] Linafelt's error is all the more egregious since our text finds its parallel in Gen 24:60, which mentions the seed of Rebekah. Now, this is not the first time that there is implicit reference to Genesis 24. Ruth is a new Rebekah, even though her name is not mentioned in the narrative.[73]

## Marriage and Birth (4:13-17)

13 So Boaz took Ruth and she became his wife. When they came together, Yhwh [a] made her conceive, and she bore a son. 14 Then the women said to Naomi, "Blessed be Yhwh, who has not left you this day without a redeemer;[a] and may his name be renowned in Israel! 15 He shall be to you a restorer of life and a nourisher of your old age; for your daughter-in-law who loves you, who is more to you than seven sons, has borne him." 16 Then Naomi took the child and laid him in her bosom, and became his nurse. 17 The women of the neighborhood gave him a name, saying, "A son has been born to Naomi." They named him Obed; he became the father of Jesse, the father of David.

**13**[a] NRSV: "Lᴏʀᴅ" (throughout).
**14**[a] MT: גאל; NRSV: "next-of-kin."

### Notes on 4:13-17

**[4:13]** "She became his wife (אשה)." Hebrew linguistically distinguishes the different stages of a female's life. From a ילדה ("child"), she becomes a נערה ("girl, adolescent"; cf. Ruth 3:5, a surprising text since it eliminates by this word alone ten years of common life with Mahlon),[74] then, after losing her virginity, an עלמה ("young woman"), and finally, as soon as she is pregnant, an אשה ("married woman"). Thus in 1:5 Naomi is designated simply as "the woman" (האשה) and there is no confusion with her daughters-in-law, because she is the only one of the three with children.[75]

---

[72] Linafelt, "Ruth," 77. The critic thus thinks he is "running to the aid" of Ruth. But he does not consider that he may destroy the whole project. She would have driven the entire matter with the hand of a master, but, in the end, she is no more than a sexual object without constancy, and she is anonymous. Surprised by her pregnancy, she becomes the ancestor not of the great King David but of David the misfit (81)! What became of the beautiful story of Ruth?

[73] Cf. I. Fischer, "Book of Ruth," 44.

[74] The rabbis say that Ruth was forty years old, but that she appeared to be fourteen (*Ruth Rab.* 4.4). The term נערה was already employed to designate Ruth (see 2:5).

[75] Ruth is also called אשה in chap. 3 (cf. 3:8, 11, 14) in the male-female relationship with Boaz. On this basis, the author emphasizes the described situation's ambiguity (cf. Bos, "Out of the Shadows," 59).

In the space of a single verse, Ruth is pregnant and gives birth to a son. The rapidity of the course of the events contrasts retrospectively with the infertility of Ruth and Mahlon's marriage in chapter 1. Yhwh had not granted descent then, doubtless reserving the womb of Ruth for Obed, the firstborn.

In the body of the narrative, Ruth spoke a lot. Now her speech "embodies itself" and, in everything that follows, she is strangely silent.

The child comes from Yhwh and is thus registered in another line, besides that of Elimelek, namely the line of initially barren women who gave birth to children of the promise: Sarah, Rachel, the wife of Manoah (Judges 13), and Hannah.[76] In regards to at least the first two mentioned, Ruth resembles them again from the viewpoint of their foreign origins. As Ostriker says, "the foreign woman builds the house of Israel, once again."[77]

The eventual intervention of Yhwh recalls the book of Job. To minimize it would be equivalent to saying that God did remain blind and deaf to the protest of Job or to the heroic test of Ruth. To the contrary, one is to understand the apparent absence of all divine intervention as communicating not God's indifference but his patience. Even "absent," God is still the Lord of history.

This "theophany," one might say, is in a characteristic context of birth. From one end of the narrative to the other, a certain conception of sexuality is affirmed. In contrast with the fornication in which she could so easily be implicated (cf. 3:10), the one that is idealized here unites the past and the future. She returns life to the dead and assures the future of the familial community. In this sense, the frankly subversive dimension of the story will have finally contributed to familial and social stability. But this stability is opened from every side, allowing a total reinterpretation of the past (Moab, for example) and a decisive thrust toward the future (David). The static stability sustained by Boaz the "pillar" in chapter 2 is replaced by the dynamic stability of Boaz the interpreter and progenitor of chapter 4. The deep paradox is that the

---

[76] In the Yahwist's genealogy in Genesis 29–30, a retrospective reading starting with the birth of Joseph shows that all the preceding names appear as just so many missed attempts at producing the child of promise. Joseph at last is the one, not only born of Jacob's favorite wife (and Jacob's favoritism is suddenly placed in a new light) but effectively born of God, who as the text says, is the one who closes and opens the womb. It is from this perspective that one must read the dialog between Rachel and Jacob in 30:1-6 ("Am I in the place of God?"). Claus Westermann, for example, certainly goes too far when he is content to see there "Jacob's angry retort" (*Genesis 12–36,* trans. J. J. Scullion, CC [Minneapolis: Augsburg, 1985], 473). But pertinently he points to the parallel text of 2 Kgs 5:7, where the king of Israel declares, "Am I God to give death or life?" For the point here, as in Gen 30:1-6, is that only God can do what humans are incapable of. Rachel addresses her petition to someone who cannot respond. It is necessary to note on this subject the inverted order of the terms of Rachel's prayer. The petition is usually addressed to God by the future father (Abraham, Isaac, Manoah). Here it is the spouse that implores and the petition is addressed to Jacob. Jacob's objection is a repairing of order in this disorder. If Rachel has offspring, it will be no thanks to the "performance" of her husband. At the conclusion of the narrative, Rachel gives birth to Joseph, the true child of promise, born "not of blood or the will of the flesh," as John 1:13 says.

[77] Ostriker, "Redeeming of Ruth."

agent of this transformation is a Moabite, the mother of Obed, the great-grandmother of David.

**[4:14]** Sasson emphasizes the absence of parallels to the construction לא השבית ("who has not left [you]"), except perhaps Lev 2:13.[78] The accent is placed on over-coming an obstacle attributed to Yhwh. One notes again the promotion of chance to the status of providence.

**[4:15]** One will note, with Hubbard, that the intervention of Yhwh is *negative:* it is "preventative, heading off the tragedy of bitter old age and familial annihilation that looms so large in the book."[79]

• משיב נפש ("to restore the soul," "rekindle life") = Ps 19:7 (MT 8), on the effect of the Torah. Salmon bar Yeroham refers back, by contrast, to Mic 7:6 ("the daugh-ter-in-law against the mother-in-law") and to the parallel texts of 1 Sam 1:8 ("more than ten sons") and 1 Sam 2:5 ("the barren has borne seven"). As Avivah Zornberg says, this is a return to a previous condition, so that one could say, "the child returned to Naomi."[80]

• More directly, משיב takes the opposite course of 1:21 ("Yhwh brought [השיב] me back empty") and thus announces the change of fortune, the radical change of cir-cumstances. Obed as nourisher of his (grand-)mother makes a parallel with Naomi, the child's "nurse" in the following verse.

The verb translated "restore" or "rekindle" is the same as "return" in chapter 1 but in the factitive mode ("to let return"). Thus the book begins and ends with this motif. What returns, according to the narrative, is the נפש, the "soul, life." The phys-ical return was described in chapter 1. The report then was dark and bitter ("Mara," 1:20). The true return comes only in chapter 4, which is a return of the soul. The restoration is that of the "name," of true identity, when Naomi becomes Naomi, "such as in herself at last eternity transforms her" (Mallarmé).[81]

"Your daughter-in-law" reappears here after having been employed in 1:6-8, 22; 2:20, 22. This is surprising enough here, for Ruth is now remarried. She is at most the former daughter-in-law of Naomi. But, on one hand, the solution of the story comes in accomplishing Ruth's vow to provide her mother-in-law with an heir. Obed was born of Ruth; but even before his birth he had been devoted, in a sense, to Naomi: "a son was born to Naomi!" On the other hand, the parallel with the dramatic episode of Judah and Tamar in Genesis 38 is, once again, lighting up. Tamar, accord-ing to public rumor, is the pregnant "daughter-in-law [who] has played the whore" (Gen 38:24). Obed, as Perez redivivus, cannot be suspected to be the fruit of prosti-

---

[78] Sasson, *Ruth,* 162–63.
[79] Hubbard, *Ruth,* 270.
[80] Zornberg, "The Concealed Alternative," in *Reading Ruth,* ed. Kates and Reimer, 75.
[81] "telle qu'en elle-même enfin l'éternité la change."

tution; but he too is born of a man from the generation that precedes his mother's. Boaz, the new father, is old enough to be his grandfather, for Ruth could be his daughter (cf. Ruth 2:8; 3:10, 11), like Tamar with respect to Judah.

↵"Who loves you." An anonymous rabbi in *Ruth Rabbah* says that this paraphrase for Ruth is employed here in order to avoid saying that Obed is the son of Ruth, for he restores Naomi. Fischer emphasizes that the child is offered by Ruth to her mother-in-law, not to her deceased husband or to Boaz (cf. v. 17).[82]

"She is better to you than seven sons." See above on the parallel with 1 Samuel 1 and 2:5. With this allusion to Hannah, the mother of Samuel, the author evoked four women in succession: Rachel and Leah (v. 11), Tamar (v. 12), and now Hannah. If one adds to this list the constant reminder of Genesis 19 (Lot's daughters)[83] and the allusions to Rebekah (Genesis 24), one has a beautiful series of "matriarchs." Among the "patriarchs," one finds Judah and Perez and allusions to Abraham at the time of his departure from Ur in Chaldea. As a reminder, Naomi represents Israel, her people. If Ruth is more precious in the eyes of Naomi than seven sons, one is also to understand that the Moabite is dearer to the eyes of God than many Israelites.

**[4:16]** Naomi "takes" the child, as Boaz previously "took" Ruth (v. 13). She "adopts" him, as Ruth had previously "adopted" Israel and its God. One remembers that Rachel took the children born of Jacob and Bilhah on her knees to legalize her "maternity" (Gen 30:3).

For Gerleman, Naomi assumes the role of the father who recognizes the child (cf. Gen 48:2; 50:23; and my development above in the overview); and by the same token provides Obed with a purely Judean mother.[84] In any case, the term "nurse" is not limited to suckling (see 2 Sam 4:4): its masculine form goes in the same direction of broadening its meaning (see Est 2:7, Mordecai). The Midrash interprets the word as meaning "adoptive mother."[85] One will be sensitive to the parallel in the construction between "Ruth became his wife" in v. 13 and "Naomi became his nurse." For her also, the thrust of the story makes her a new woman, capable (metaphorically) of nursing a child: "a son was born to Naomi" (v. 17). Note that Num 11:12 presents parallel vocabulary. There Moses ironically asks God if he (Moses) is the parent and nurse of the people in the desert.

Naomi does not speak after the end of chapter 3, which recalls the situation prevailing in 1:18, for example. This provides an occasion to notice that the silences

---

[82] Fischer, "Book of Ruth," 32.

[83] Max Haller parallels Ruth to Lot's daughters and Tamar: "Three times the Old Testament introduces the motif of the woman who knows how to force her contribution to a progeny, at any price, even the abandonment of honor. It is true of Lot's wild daughters (Gen 19:30-38), of Tamar (Genesis 38), and of Ruth the Moabite" (*Die fünf Megillot*, HAT 18 [Tübingen: Mohr/Siebeck, 1940], 1).

[84] Gerleman, *Ruth*, 37–38.

[85] Cf. Broch, *Ruth*, 106.

of Naomi in 1:18 and 4:16 do not necessarily call for a negative interpretation. It is not always a reflection of a bad mood or of ungraciousness.[86]

**[4:17]** "A son has been born to Naomi," because everything that belongs to Elimelek rightfully belongs to Naomi. It is not necessary to see in this choral proclamation a displacement of Ruth.[87] She remains the mother of Obed, as Ephraim and Manasseh remained the sons of Joseph (the Josephites) after their adoption by their grandfather Jacob (Gen 48:12).

To conclude with some scholars that Ruth is despoiled in the matter is poorly to understand that, from the beginning, the central character of the narrative has incessantly related back to another personage, Naomi. "It is necessary for her to increase and that I decrease" (see John 3:30).

Thus Obed has two mothers (a fact that the text puts in parallel with the two mothers of the Israel house, Rachel and Leah), as Perez had two fathers (Judah and the deceased husband of Tamar, in Genesis 38).[88] And if Ruth is then like Tamar, and beyond her, like Rachel and Leah, Naomi is like Sarah and she becomes the "mother" of the child of promise.

The neighbors' naming of the child forms an *inclusio* with 1:20, when they named Naomi. The contrast is great. It is the community that names the child here; and, in the same breath, they name Naomi, while she had prevented them from calling her Naomi in chapter 1.[89]

The term שְׁכֵנוֹת ("neighbors") appears in only one other text, Exod 3:22 (the Egyptian neighbors). Meyers says that there were solidarity groups among women in the same neighborhood (cf. Exod 12:4; Jer 6:24; Prov 27:10, all three despite their masculine forms). In a previous development, we saw that the biblical heroines tend to group themselves into pairs (see the commentary on 1:10, p. 47). In 2 Kgs 4:3 one sees a widow helped by her neighbors.

The neighbors name the child, which is quite unusual (but see Gen 38:29-30, precisely the chapter of Genesis that is pivotal to the narrative of Ruth).[90] The role played by the neighbors here echoes their previous mention in 4:14 and 1:19. The child is named twice (שֵׁם קָרָא), and "Obed" does not correspond to the preceding exclamation as one would expect according to other contexts (cf. Gen 29:31-35;

---

[86] *Pace* Fewell and Gunn, *Compromising Redemption,* 80–82.

[87] The group of women in the book form a choir. As I said in the introduction to the commentary, this is an additional sign of the late date of Ruth. (The same is true for the Song of Songs; see my *Romance, She Wrote*). It is interesting to note on this subject that Gunkel compares the popular blessing in 4:11 (by men) with the choir of the Greek tragedy, spokesmen of public sentiments (Gunkel, "Ruth," 86).

[88] Cf. Klingenstein, "Circles of Kinship," 207.

[89] Cf. Lois Durbin, "Fullness and Emptiness, Fertility and Loss: Meditations on Naomi's Tale in the Book of Ruth," in *Reading Ruth,* ed. Kates and Reimer, 143.

[90] The clearer parallel is to John the Baptist (Luke 1:57-66)

30:6-24; 35:18).[91] Otto Eissfeldt thinks that in v. 17a ("they called [him] a name") there was originally "they named him Ben-Noam."[92] D. R. Ap-Thomas thinks rather of "Obednoam."[93] René Vuilleumier recalls that the tabernacle was at Obed-edom of Gath before David transferred it to Jerusalem (2 Sam 6:10-12; 1 Chron 13:13-14; 15:25). Moreover, Obed-edom is a name that occurs as a servant of the tabernacle at the time of David (1 Chron 15:18, 21; 16:5, 38; 26:4, 8, 15; and perhaps 2 Chron 25:24).[94] But Hubbard proposes a formulaic interpretation of v. 17a; it is something other than a naming. The formula, "a son was born to Naomi," is used as an announcement to the father of the child: the women use a formula as part of the birth announcement to interpret what they are witnessing (cf. Jer 20:14-18; Job 3:3; in Isa 9:6 [MT 5] one finds a public announcement).[95] The strange character of Ruth 4:17a is explained by the fact that the announcement is made not to Boaz but to Naomi, as if she was the "father" of the child; since she is not the one who gave birth, the birth must be announced to her.

One evidently expects a proclamation of a child belonging to Elimelek, certainly not to his widow, for Obed is a future promise for his grandfather's lineage. The attribution of the child to a woman, to a widow that had children, and who is not the real mother of Obed, is a subversive trait, well in line with the narrative.

One has just seen that Naomi assumes the role of the father of the child in the "acknowledgment." One may then follow Hubbard and understand, "they gave him a name" as meaning "they proclaimed his importance" (שֵׁם means "name" and "reputation"). "Name" or "reputation" appears four times in this chapter (4:4, 11, 17a, 17b). It is only now that a name is effectively given to the child: Obed. Thus the suspense was maintained and its relaxation arrives as a (royal?) proclamation.

Obed, as a name, is strongly emphasized here, and it is perilous to try to reconstruct another name "more fitting to the context" and supposedly lost. Indeed, it is clear that the neighbors associate the name Obed ("servant") with his "redemptive" function (גֹּאֵל) with respect to Naomi (v. 15): he will rekindle her life and will be her nourisher. Etymologically, "Obed" has nothing to do with the activities as they are described. Obed means "serving" (the grammatical form is a participle), and I do not think it is necessary to imagine a different speech in the mouths of the neighbors.[96] The date of the book permits us to infer that the prophecy of Second Isaiah concerning the "Servant" was well known and that this figure, as required, was a synonym of redemption and restoration. Besides, the vocabulary of Ruth 4:16-17 is quite close to

---

[91] Cf. LaCocque, "Une descendance manipulée et ambiguë."

[92] Otto Eissfeldt, *The Old Testament: An Introduction,* trans. P. R. Ackroyd (Oxford: Blackwell, 1965), 479–80.

[93] D. R. Ap-Thomas, "The Book of Ruth," *ExpT* 79 (1967–68) 371.

[94] René Vuilleumier, "Stellung und Bedeutung des Buches Ruth im alttestamentlichen Kanon," *TZ* 44 (1988) 193–210.

[95] Hubbard, *Ruth,* 15.

[96] Cf. above, Eissfeldt, Ap-Thomas, et al.

Isaiah, especially Isa 9:6 (MT 5), where one rediscovers the same key terms, like "child," "give birth," "for [us]" (cf. Ruth 4:17: "for Naomi"), "son," "to call his name," and "father of."

Now, what is in question in Isaiah 9? In this same book, the text of Isa 9:6 (MT 5) finds an echo in 22:20-22, on the subject of King Eliakim, a descendant of David,[97] called "my servant" (עבדי) by God "on that day" (cf. Ruth 4:14). "He shall be a father . . . to the house of Judah" (cf. Ruth 4:11-12) / "I will place on his shoulder the key of the house of David" (cf. Ruth 4:17). Moreover, the unique fact that the birth of the child is attributed exclusively to a woman (Naomi) argues in favor of a borrowing from Isaiah (cf. Isaiah 7). This "gynocentric" attribution (as Rutledge rightly calls it) is remarkable and is compatible with the remainder of the book.[98]

With the name of the child, Obed ("servant"), one touches on the central point of the narrative: service to God and to the community.

The role played by the neighbors in the book of Ruth invites deeper reflection. From the beginning of the narrative, they represent the community of Bethlehem (cf. 1:19). In fact, they are the social and psychological community, in contrast to the legal community "at the gates of the town" formed by men.[99] Incidentally, when the two women "returned" in chapter 1, they had to go through this gate, but significantly, the elders played no role. If they had intervened at this stage of the story, it would probably have been to condemn the Moabite and the one who brought her. It is the psychological community, composed of women, that welcomes Naomi and, cautiously, does not mention Ruth. Now, this silence already has positive value since it suspends all judgment on the foreigner. This judgment will come at the end, after the favorable decision of the legal body (4:11-12). They express themselves on the subject of Ruth in 4:15: Ruth is more precious than seven sons to her mother-in-law.

The role of the sociopsychological community culminates in the naming of the child. The very object of the story dictates this unparalleled trait: a member of a loathed people sets in motion the history of the messianic dynasty. The community as such recognizes its providential character and makes official what could have remained in a private sphere (4:16). The supreme sign that the community completely integrates the son of the foreigner (cf. 4:10) is that they give him a name and a reputation of communal and historic order.

"Son of Naomi." This last substitution in the book underscores the importance of the one that preceded it. Obed is the "son of Naomi," and Ruth disappears from the text. Obed is the true *gōʾēl* and Boaz returns to the shadows. But Obed himself is the

---

[97] David himself is called "servant" thirty-three times in the MT (cf. Sasson, *Ruth,* 177). See, in particular, 1 Kgs 11:32; Ps 78:70; and 89:20 (MT 21).

[98] Rutledge, *Reading Marginally,* 25.

[99] The Midrash on Ps 98:3 (and also Rashi on Exod 19:3) says that the expression "house of Israel" designates the women of Israel.

result of a chain of substitutions, not only in the person of his biological mother but also of his father, who took the place of So-and-so and also substituted himself for the deceased Elimelek. Boaz generates a son instead of Mahlon. Naomi is the "mother" of Obed. Ruth is better than ten sons in Naomi's eyes. Obed, rather than his father Boaz, is the *gō'ēl* of his grandmother (4:15).

Even the institutions, as they are reinterpreted in this story, are substituted for one another. The custom of levirate marriage applies now to a widow who had children as well as to a surrogate mother. The law regarding the redemption of the field is applied to a parcel belonging to Elimelek while it was sold by Naomi, and its redemption includes the person of Ruth the Moabite.

In short, the performance of the regulation requires more than obedience to the Law. So Naomi surpasses the terms of the Law and places her daughter-in-law's interests before her own: the story becomes that of Ruth the Moabite and not that of Naomi the Israelite. Ruth goes well beyond what one expects of her and she sacrifices everything in order "to attach herself" to her mother-in-law; she even sacrifices herself for her. Boaz must contravene the ostracism directed at Moabites and marry a foreigner. He redeems a field that will not belong to him and impregnates a woman whose offspring will not be his. For everything to succeed, the Law is necessary; but paradoxically, it must be transcended. For without this transcendence, there is no story of Ruth.

## Genealogy (4:18-22)

18 Now these are the generations[a] of Perez: Perez became the father of Hezron, 19 Hezron of Ram, Ram of Amminadab, 20 Amminadab of Nahshon, Nahshon of Salmah,[a] 21 Salmon of Boaz, Boaz of Obed, 22 Obed of Jesse, and Jesse of David.

18[a] MT: תלדות; NRSV: "descendants"; JPSV: "line"; NIV: "family line."
20[a] MT: שׂלמה; LXX[B]: Σαλμαν; LXX[A]: Σαλμων; NRSV: "Salmon."

### Notes on 4:18-22

[4:18] "These are the generations." This is the same phrase found in Genesis (cf. Gen 2:4; 5:1; 6:1; 11:10, 27; 25:12, 19; 36:1, 9; 37:2; cf. 3:1). The importance of this derivation is that it comes after the narrative has widened the horizon from a family matter to an event affecting the whole people (cf. above). Now the story adopts dimensions appropriate to the covenant between God and his people. That is part of the progressive dynamism of the narrative of Ruth—to widen itself in conical form or, perhaps, in the form of a diamond, for the name of David is the endpoint of its culmination.

The final genealogy is nevertheless considered secondary—indeed "inauthentic"—by almost all commentators. But there are notable exceptions.[100] The genealogy manifests (post-)exilic characteristics (see the Priestly source; cf. 1 Chron 2:5-15 [probably drawing on Ruth 4]). Structurally it corresponds to Ruth 1:1-5, with which it forms an *inclusio*.[101] One will note its unusual placement, at the end of a narrative instead of forming its introduction (cf. Gen 2:4; 6:9; 10:1; Num 3:11; etc.). One will also note the implausibility of Sasson's argument that David was successful thanks to the popular ignorance of his origins.[102]

On the other hand, it is clear that the genealogy comports with the narrative. It begins with Perez, who had just been alluded to in 4:12. It contributes to giving an eminent place to Boaz: his is the seventh name in the list. Similarly, Obed is more significant (cf. v. 17a) than simply being the *gōʾēl* of his legal father Mahlon or of his legal grandfather Elimelek, as well made clear by Ruth 4:11-12 and 14. As I showed in the introduction, 4:18-22 must be considered an integral part of the book. In a literary genre that distances itself from the customary and becomes subversive, the artist does not feel constrained by the conventions. I have discussed this at length in my commentary on Song of Songs.[103]

The genealogy is patrilineal, as required. Of the ten names that comprise the list, only five figured in the preceding narrative (Perez, Boaz, Obed, Jesse, David). But three of these names are set in relief by the place that they occupy: Perez is first; Boaz is seventh; David is tenth.[104] Zakovitch points out that the genealogy emphasizes the passage from a secondary branch of the tribe of Judah by Elimelek, to a primary branch through Boaz, a descendant of Perez.[105]

One may be somewhat astonished that the genealogy is not that of Elimelek by Mahlon and Chilion, since it was their line that was at issue in the core of the book

---

[100] See Leon Morris, "Ruth," in A. E. Cundall and L. Morris, *Judges, Ruth,* TOTC (Chicago: InterVarsity, 1968); Robert Gordis, "Love, Marriage, and Business in the Book of Ruth: A Chapter in Hebrew Customary Law," in *A Light unto My Path*: *Old Testament Studies in Honor of Jacob M. Myers,* edited by H. N. Bream et al. (Philadelphia: Temple Univ. Press, 1974), 241–64; Bezalel Porten, "Theme and Historiographic Background of the Scroll of Ruth," *GCA* 6 (1977) 69–78; Moshe Weinfeld, "Ruth," in *EncJud* 14:518–19; Sasson, *Ruth,* 181–82; Harold Fisch, "Ruth and the Structure of Covenant History," *VT* 32 (1982) 435. On biblical genealogies see Marshall D. Johnson, *The Purpose of the Biblical Genealogies, with Special Reference to the Setting of the Genealogies of Jesus,* 2d ed., SNTSMS 8 (Cambridge: Cambridge Univ. Press, 1988); Robert R. Wilson, "The Old Testament Genealogies in Recent Research," *JBL* 94 (1975) 169–89; Jack Sasson, "A Genealogical 'Convention' in Biblical Chronography," *ZAW* 90 (1978) 171–85; Hanson, "Herodians and Mediterranean Kinship."

[101] Cf. Stephen Bertman, "Symmetrical Design in the Book of Ruth," *ZAW* 84 (1965) 166–67.

[102] Sasson, *Ruth,* 186. See also "Le livre de Ruth," in *La Sainte Bible: Texte latin et traduction française d'après les textes originaux; avec un commentaire exégétique et théologique,* ed. Louis Pirot, vol. 3 (Paris: Letouzey et Ané, 1946); and Rowley, "Marriage of Ruth," 185.

[103] See LaCocque, *Romance, She Wrote,* 1–68.

[104] See Sasson, *Ruth,* 184. Ten generations are also listed in the genealogies of Adam to Noah and Noah to Abraham.

[105] Zakovitch, *Ruth,* 173.

(the parable). But from the standpoint of narrative and history, these characters are altogether secondary. On the occasion of saving their descent and by virtue of the pure altruism of Ruth and Boaz, it so happens that a line much more important, the one of Perez[106]—of which the group Elimelek, Mahlon, and Chilion constituted only a branch—arrives at its apogee in the person of the great King David. This is what the book of Ruth brings as tangible proof of the accuracy of the audacious interpretation of the Law by Boaz following the dazzling intuition of the Moabite. Nielsen is justified in tracing parallels with other texts in which, in similar cases, it is the begetting father that figures in the lists, not the deceased, legal father: see Gen 46:12; 1 Chron 2:3-4 (Judah and not Er). On this subject, the genealogies of Jesus in Matthew and Luke go in the same direction. They include Joseph as the father of Jesus (Matt 1:16; Luke 3:23) and Boaz as the father of Obed (Matt 1:5; Luke 3:32).

Moreover, one should again emphasize that the central thesis of Ruth is as follows: a foreigner, a Moabite, following the example of another foreigner, a Canaanite, proves to be the opportune instrument of salvation history (*Heilsgeschichte*). The narrative repeats, in nobler terms, an older story, the conclusion of which had remained unresolved. Ruth brings Tamar's audacity to fruition while performing an act of similar audacity. Everything should logically (and morally) conclude in infamy; but to the contrary, this accumulation of extravagances is necessary for the birth of David-Messiah.

All the same, one can wonder, with Sakenfeld for example, why the genealogy does not begin with the father of Perez, Judah, ancestor of the tribe of the same name and have him replace Ram or Salmon, two unknown characters.[107] In a way Judah hovers over the whole genealogy that begins with his son Perez, who was already mentioned in v. 12 by the neighbors. One will note nevertheless that in this same verse Perez is, according to the women, the son of Tamar and only secondarily of Judah. The neighbors associate Obed not with Judah but with Perez because of their births in comparable circumstances.

One can also explain the first place granted to Perez and not to Judah by the seventh row that had to be attributed to Boaz and the fifth to Nahshon (see below). As for the similarity of the genealogies in Ruth 4 and in 1 Chron 2:5-15, they probably have a common source and also, as Sasson says, originate with a temple document. The fiction of the book of Ruth is to have provided Boaz with a Moabite spouse named Ruth.

In the genealogical list, the first place is evidently important, just like the seventh, occupied by Boaz. Between the two are a series of insignificant names,[108] sort

---

[106] The book of Ruth gives Perez special importance because of the constant parallels to the story in Genesis 38.

[107] Sakenfeld, *Ruth,* 4.

[108] With the possible exception of Nahshon, who is in the fifth position, that is to say at the hinge between the pre-Mosaic and post-Mosaic ancestors of David. Nahshon the brother-in-law of Aaron, husband of Elisheba (Exod 6.23), is put at the head of Judah to help Moses at the time of the Israel's first census in the desert (Num 1:7; cf. 2:3). His fame is celebrated again during the period of the Second Temple

of stand-ins before a second peak in the person of Boaz. From there, nevertheless, the movement rises: Obed, Jesse, David. The last name, the tenth one, is, as I said, the supreme justification of the generous interpretation of the Law provoked by Ruth. To reject the genealogy of the book with the argument that it comes after instead of before the narration demonstrates a lack of sensitivity with respect to the text. The "suspense" would have lost all charms if it had started out by reassuring the reader of the success of the Moabite's business in Judah. This is as if, at the beginning of chapter 3, the author had said that Boaz was a moral eunuch before telling the risqué scene that follows. What a lot of commentators have a hard time accepting is that Ruth is the triumph of extravagance.

Hezron, son of Perez: see Gen 46:12 and Num 26:21.

Ram is not mentioned in the Torah, and there is a conflict with 1 Chron 2:9.

**[4:21]** Salmon? Several manuscripts have "Salmah," as in the preceding verse. In 1 Chron 2:11 and 51, Salmah is spelled differently: שַׂלְמָא, "Salma." Vuilleumier concludes that 1 Chronicles has smoothed out the readings.[109]

"Boaz became the father of Obed." The biological filiation is equally asserted with regard to Perez and Zerah in Gen 46:12; Num 26:20; and 1 Chron 2:4. As a name, Obed appears again in genealogies depending on Ruth 4: cf. 1 Chron 2:12; Matt 1:5; and Luke 3:22.

**[4:22]** Jesse (the father of David). One will remember Isaiah's prophecy on the subject of Jesse's messianic dynasty: Isa 11:1, 10 (cf. Rom 15:12).

I repeat what I said above: to cut off the genealogy from the book, as recommended by so many commentators, is to sanitize the case advanced by the biblical author. Her demonstration would then remain without proof—and the narrative becomes the kind of romance used by Hollywood.[110]

The central thesis of Ruth clearly finds its anchorage point in an era when the understanding of the Torah had become legalistic and when foreign women were looked upon with suspicion, if not with scorn. We have some information about this era. The books of Ezra and Nehemiah provide us an image with little to rejoice about. One could expect a healthy (and holy?) reaction against such a withdrawal into themselves of the community. The (feminine) author of Ruth came with a fiction of genius, subtly reducing the conservatives of the time to the level of Orpah and of So-and-so. "In jail on account of mediocrity!"[111]

---

(cf. 1 Chron 2:10) and the NT (Matt 1:4; Luke 3:32). In any case, the present genealogy is extremely schematic.

[109] Vuilleumier, "Stellung und Bedeutung," 195.

[110] *Pace* Eissfeldt, *Introduction,* 479–80; Erich Zenger, *Das Buch Ruth,* ZBK 8 (Zurich: Theologischer Verlag, 1992), 11–14.

[111] "En prison pour médiocrité!"; Henry de Montherlant, "La Reine morte" (a play from 1942).

# Conclusion

The preceding analysis strongly emphasizes that the book of Ruth presents a *different* conception of the Torah. Elimelek's family radically distinguishes itself from other Israelite families in that it initially looked for refuge in Moab for its subsistence and its perpetuation. This first movement in the book is essential, for it establishes the background on which the whole story is built right up to the conclusion. In accordance with this position, the principal characters of the book are also marked by their *difference* from those who find shelter in "sameness." Ruth is a Moabite woman, but not like the rest of her people. She becomes Israel's blessing, while her ancestors had paid Balaam to curse Israel![1] Naomi is a widow and "bitter." But unlike so many widows without children in Israel, she will be filled on the levels of affection, succession, and generation. Boaz comes from Bethlehem, but he goes decidedly against the grain. More fundamentally, the *difference* in Ruth is a generous and expansive understanding of the Law. Everything in the story depends on this interpretation. Everything is also re-created by it. Interpretation here is worldview (*Weltanschauung*).

This is the reason why the *difference (différence)* is also *deferment (différance)*, as Derrida says.[2] The full meaning of Ruth is *deferred*; the full interpretation is deferred, though inaugurated in Ruth, until the Nazarene comes; a fullness that itself is deferred until the Parousia. In this new universe that is interpreted differently (and deferringly), there is no longer any Judean or Greek, said Paul (Gal 3:28). Before him, the book of Ruth had proclaimed that there is no longer any Judean or Moabite; there is no longer any enemy—even the difference and the deferred are transcended.   *AT-ONE-MENT*

Another question posed by the deconstructionist, (post-)modern movement would concern what the structure of the book of Ruth excludes from its perspective. What does it suppress? The question is pertinent, but it is singularly minimized by the fact that Ruth is precisely a protest, a subversion of Israel's legal system. An anti-

---

[1] *Ruth Rabbah* concludes: "Moab, whence Ruth came, was not conceived [by God] for the purpose of fornication, but for celestial ends."

[2] Jacques Derrida, *Of Grammatology,* trans. Gayatri Chakravorty Spivak (Baltimore: Johns Hopkins Univ. Press, 1976).

_EXCLUDES_

_IMMIGRATION_

_+ !_

system, of course, can itself become a countersystem; but it seems to me that this is no more the case with Ruth than with the teaching of Jesus going in the same direction. Making dogma from one or the other cannot be done except in bad faith. What the book of Ruth excludes—for all construction is exclusion—is the whole system of meticulous interpretation, fatal to all generosity, by the Second Temple fundamentalists. Excluded also is a certain male fundamentalistic patriarchalism and its paternalistic attitude, of which (the old) Boaz displayed an example in Ruth 2. Also missing is a narrow, self-complacent nationalism prone to create a spirit of harsh judgment on "the others," that is, the Moabites, the foreign women, the barren ones, the "losers." But, all that being said, what the book of Ruth excludes is insignificant in comparison with what it includes.

In the book, one voice nevertheless became inaudible, that of Orpah. Of course, the narrative did not stifle her, for she was able to express herself, and even, in all liberty, give a sudden change of direction to her own speech (1:10, 15). But once she made another choice, in contrast to her alter-ego Ruth, she became "the hollowed side" of Ruth's speech. Orpah becomes (without genetic or sociocultural determinism) what Ruth could have been and refused to be. This is the reason, if the author continued to give free expression to Orpah's speech, she would maintain an ambivalence that Ruth categorically refused (1:16). Similarly, Boaz rejects the bourgeois narrowness personified in So-and-so's choice.

It is therefore verified once again in the instance of the book of Ruth that indeed all construction—even irenic—does violence to what remains unexpressed. But one must immediately add that Orpah is not an outcast or a scapegoat. She leaves and rejoins her natural group as she has been invited to by Naomi/Israel. In this way, she rejoins the ordinary, not the aberrant. Ruth, by contrast, chooses the extraordinary and the extravagant, and this is how her existential choice is immediately interpreted (1:15). If Orpah's voice loses itself in the steppes of Moab, it is because the extraordinary does not suffer being limited by the ordinary. Now this is what the artistic creation of the character of Orpah purported to shed light upon: Orpah is the Sancho Panza side of human choices.

_? ← AFTER MARRYING AN ISRAELITE?_

Once this confrontation is established between the antihero and the hero (cf. 2:1 and 3:11)—Kierkegaard would say, between the husband and the lover, the general and the soldier—the remainder of the story probes ever deeper for the meaning. After the Moabite prelude, we are transported to Bethlehem, where a new pair of differences are brought into play (the word would please Derrida) and become the reason for the story. The confrontation is now transposed to the level of a literal interpretation of the Law—according to which the presence of Ruth in Bethlehem is unbearable—and an expansive reading that recognizes that the Law has an inchoate nature. The Torah is less a dictation than an orientation. Obedience to the Law has to be continually reinvented. I know how to hate evil—murder, theft, adultery, coveting. But the problem always remains of knowing how to love.

How to love—such is the grand question put to all the characters of the story. The key term is *ḥesed*, because the key to the Law is freely given love implying the refusal of "categorizing" others. Even the Moabite is integrated—and more than integrated since she becomes the exemplary model of *ḥesed*, the very basis of God's covenant with his people. *ARGUE THIS TOO*

Thus the narrative and the prescriptive in Israel are in a way rewritten. The ancient rabbis saw this clearly. They concluded from the story of Ruth that the legal ostracism imposed on the Moabites should be interpreted as affecting the men of this people, not their women. This rabbinic readjustment is again insufficient, but the move goes in the right direction. Ruth "rewrites" the Torah. According to this rewriting, Israel's election is inclusive. The laws on inheritance, widowhood, the levirate, the rights of the poor and foreigners, and sexual "promiscuity" are burdened by the notion of "difference." The intertextuality that unites the Torah and Ruth does not allow reading Ruth except through the prism of the Torah; and vice versa it is necessary to read the Torah through the rereading of Ruth. As I said above, the new rewriting, by the "hand" of Jesus, is the prolongation and accomplishment of this one in Ruth (and other writings such as Deutero-Isaiah, Trito-Isaiah, Jonah, Song of Songs).

It would be an error to understand this intertextuality as spreading itself solely on a diachronic axis: the Torah, then its interpretation (by Deuteronomy, by the book of Ruth, etc.). The synchronic axis decidedly precedes the other. The reading (called *l'écriture* by Derrida) of the Torah precedes its having been written (the Torah is pre-existent, say the rabbis). The malediction on Moab is an interpretation of the Torah although paradoxically being part of the Torah. The story of Ruth is a divergent interpretation. It puts anew the question, so dear to Foucault, for example, of deviance: Would "Moab" after all be a mere projection/creation by some for the sole purpose of constructing a normative identity of Israel? Isn't that just what the fifth-century autocratic government of Ezra and Nehemiah proves, that which reiterates the anti-Moabite ostracism? The violence exercised by the governors (cf. Neh 13:25; Ezra 7:26) confirms well the Foucauldian denunciation.

In the narrative, Ruth the Moabite, the deviant par excellence, reverses the norm. She turns things on their head: Ruth herself becomes the prototype of the *ḥasid* (this is an Israelite moved by *ḥesed*). Suddenly, Deut 23:3 (MT 4) (cf. also Neh 13:1) is rewritten while neutralizing its dimension of self-sufficient exclusivism.

The most important aspect of the First Testament is its constant rewriting.

But, whatever its intrinsic importance, one cannot stop investigating the book of Ruth with the simple conclusion that the story proposed to its original readers an expansive understanding of the law of Moses. This conclusion, which takes account of the *Sitz im Leben* of the compilation of the text, must itself be amplified by the *Sitz im Leben* of the modern reader. Every reading takes place in the stream of interpretation of the text—its *Wirkungsgeschichte*. As I have already indicated, this proceeds through the magisterial and existential commentary of Jesus of Nazareth, then of Paul interpreting Jesus, of Augustine and Luther interpreting Paul, of Karl Barth interpreting his predecessors, and so on. On the Jewish side, the line passes through the Masoretes, the talmudic and midrashic sages, Maimonides, Rashi, and so many others since.

The "Law" in its generous reception certainly represents the Torah; it also represents, by semantic extension, the prescription under all its forms, including the modern judicial system. The book of Ruth has something to say on the subject of judicial systems, and it certainly has something to say on the subject of the presence of foreigners among us. It recalls that God himself is on the side of immigrants, widows, orphans, the poor, and the marginal. It is also a reminder that great things can come from the most unexpected quarter. And, because a despised Moabite can generate the Messiah, all "Moabites" and other natives of the "third world" deserve welcome and respect. From this point of view, Ruth results not only in the parable of the Good Samaritan (Luke 10:30-35), but in the staggering declaration of Jesus, "Just as you did it to the least of these . . . you did it to me" (Matt 25:40). Boaz's generosity regarding Ruth rebounds so much on the person of the Messiah that it becomes the very condition of his existence. Boaz begat . . . David, and of David is born the future "Son of David," who is also called "Son of Man."

At the minimum on these two fronts—judicial systems and welcoming the foreigner—the horizons of the text and reader meet (just as Gadamer would wish it).[3] Each of them deserves our deepest respect, the respect for the community's interpretation of the text and of the human condition. The two are in paradoxical relation of mutual transcendence. The text—Ruth—transcends the community, since the former interprets the latter. But the community transcends the text, for it precedes it and succeeds it; it is the collective author and is, at the same time, transformed by it. The text bewilders the readers and reorients them. It is, therefore, vain to wonder (with liberation theology, for example) if life interprets the Bible, or the Bible interprets life. They interpret each other mutually. The book of Ruth is as alive as the reading community. "The text has the capacity to 'answer back,' and in the process of interpretation, the interpreters are themselves interpreted."[4] The earnest desire of the commentator is to have helped the reader of Ruth to be interpreted by the text.

"For what reason—asks the Midrash—was the book of Ruth written? To teach us how great the reward is for those who practice *ḥesed* [goodness, loyalty, love]" (*Ruth Rab.* 2.14).

---

[3] Hans Georg Gadamer, *Truth and Method,* rev. ed., trans. Garrett Barden and John Cumming (New York: Continuum, 1988).

[4] Christopher Rowland and Mark Corner, *Liberating Exegesis: The Challenge of Liberation Theology to Biblical Studies* (Louisville: Westminster John Knox, 1989), 67.

# Bibliography

### 1. Rabbinic Literature

Beattie, D. R. G., editor. *The Targum of Ruth*. Aramaic Bible 19. Collegeville, Minn.: Liturgical, 1994.

Ben Eliezer, Toviyahu. *Midrash Leqaḥ Ṭov*. 5 vols. in 2. Jerusalem: 1959/60.

Börner-Klein, Dagmar. *Der Midrasch Sifre Zuta*. Rabbinische Texte 2/3A. Stuttgart: Kohlhammer, 2002.

Buber, Solomon, editor. *Ruth Zuta*. Vilna: Rom, 1925.

Epstein, Baruch, editor. *The Essential Torah Temimah*. 5 vols. New York: Feldheim, 1989.

Hyman, Naomi M., editor. *Biblical Women in the Midrash: A Sourcebook*. Northvale, N.J.: Aronson, 1997.

Ibn Ezra, Abraham. *Abraham Ibn Esras Kommentare zu den Büchern Kohelet, Ester und Rut*. Introduced, translated, and commented upon by D. U. Rottzoll. Berlin: de Gruyter, 1999.

Levine, Étan. *The Aramaic Version of Ruth*. AnBib 58. Rome: Pontifical Biblical Institute Press, 1973.

Neusner, Jacob. *Ruth Rabbah: An Analytical Translation*. BJS 183. Atlanta: Scholars, 1989.

Rabinowitz, Louis I., translator. *Midrash Rabbah: Ruth*. London: Soncino, 1939.

Saarisalo, Aapeli. "The Targum of the Book of Ruth." In *The Targum of the Five Megilloth*, edited by B. Grossfeld, 1–19. New York: Hermon, 1973.

Scherman, Nossom, and Meir Zlotowitz. *The Book of Ruth/Megillas Ruth*. The ArtScroll Tanach Series. Brooklyn: Mesorah, 1979.

Schwartz, Avraham, and Yisroel Schwartz, editors. *The Megilloth and Rashi's Commentary with Linear Translation: Esther, Song of Songs, Ruth*. New York: Feldheim, 1983.

*Yalkut Perushim: 'Al Megilat Rut*. Brooklyn: Podringel, 1994.

*Yalkut She'elot u-Teshuvot*. Brooklyn: Mekhirah ha-rashit etsel Be. m.s. Bigel'aizen, 1993/94.

## 2. Commentaries

Adutwum, Ofosu. "Ruth." In *International Bible Commentary,* edited by William R. Farmer, Sean McEvenue, A. J. Levoratti, David L. Dungan, and André LaCocque, 566–71. Collegeville, Minn.: Liturgical, 1998.

Auld, A. Graeme. *Joshua, Judges, and Ruth.* DSBS. Philadelphia: Westminster, 1985.

Berlin, Adele. "Ruth." In *Harper's Bible Commentary,* edited by James Luther Mays, 262–67. San Francisco: Harper & Row, 1988.

Bertholet, Alfred. *Das Buch Ruth.* KHCAT 17. Tübingen: Mohr/Siebeck, 1898.

Block, Daniel I. *Judges and Ruth.* NAC 6. Nashville: Broadman & Holman, 1999.

Bos, Johanna W. H. *Ruth, Esther, Jonah.* Knox Preaching Guides. Atlanta: John Knox, 1986.

Breuer, Raphael. *Die fünf Megillot.* 5 vols. in 1. Frankfurt: Hoffmann, 1908–12.

Broch, Yitzhak I. *Ruth: The Book of Ruth in Hebrew and English with a Midrashic Commentary.* 2d ed. New York: Feldheim, 1983.

Bush, Frederic W. *Ruth, Esther.* WBC 9. Waco: Word, 1996.

Campbell, Edward F. Jr. *Ruth.* AB 7. Garden City, N.Y.: Doubleday, 1975.

Cellensis, Petrus. *Commentaria in Ruth.* CCSL 54. Turnhout: Brepol, 1983.

Cleland, James T. "Ruth." In *The Interpreter's Bible,* edited by George Arthur Buttrick, 2:827–52. Nashville: Abingdon, 1953.

Craghan, John. *Esther, Judith, Tobit, Jonah, Ruth.* OTM 16. Wilmington, Del.: Glazier, 1982.

Emmerson, Grace I. "Ruth." In *The Oxford Bible Commentary,* edited by John Rogerson and John Muddiman, 192–95. Oxford: Oxford Univ. Press, 2001.

Farmer, Kathleen. "The Book of Ruth." In *The New Interpreter's Bible,* edited by Leander E. Keck et al., 2:889–946. Nashville: Abingdon, 1998.

Fischer, Irmtraud. *Rut.* HTKAT. Freiburg: Herder, 2001.

Fischer, James A. "Ruth." In *The Collegeville Bible Commentary,* edited by Dianne Bergant and Robert J. Karris, 797–803. Collegeville, Minn.: Liturgical, 1988.

Frevel, Christian. *Das Buch Ruth.* NSKAT 6. Stuttgart: Katholisches Bibelwerk, 1992.

Fuerst, Wesley J. *The Books of Ruth, Esther, Ecclesiastes, the Song of Songs, Lamentations.* CBC. Cambridge: Cambridge Univ. Press, 1975.

Gerleman, Gillis. *Ruth, Das Hohe Lied.* BKAT 18. Neukirchen-Vluyn: Neukirchener, 1965.

Gray, John. *Joshua, Judges, and Ruth.* NCB. Revised edition. Grand Rapids: Eerdmans, 1986.

Gressmann, Hugo. *Die Anfänge Israels (von 2. Mose bis Richter und Ruth).* Schriften des Alten Testaments, part 1: *Die Sagen des Alten Testaments,* 2:263–79. Göttingen: Vandenhoeck & Ruprecht, 1922.

Haller, Max. *Die fünf Megillot.* HAT 18. Tübingen: Mohr/Siebeck, 1940.

Hamlin, John E. *Surely There Is a Future: A Commentary on the Book of Ruth.* ITC. Grand Rapids: Eerdmans, 1996.

Hertzberg, Hans Wilhelm. *Die Bücher Josua, Richter, Ruth.* ATD 9. Göttingen: Vandenhoeck & Ruprecht, 1969.

Hubbard, Robert L. Jr. *The Book of Ruth.* NICOT. Grand Rapids: Eerdmans, 1988.

Jackman, David. *Judges, Ruth.* CComm 7. Dallas: Word, 1986.

Joüon, Paul. *Ruth: Commentaire philologique et exégétique.* 2d ed. SubBib 9. Rome: Pontifical Biblical Institute Press, 1986.

Knight, G. A. *Ruth and Jonah.* TBC. London: SCM, 1966.

Laffey, Alice. "Ruth." In *The New Jerome Biblical Commentary,* edited by Raymond E. Brown et al., 553–57. Englewood Cliffs, N.J.: Prentice-Hall, 1990.

Levine, Amy-Jill. "Ruth." In *The Women's Bible Commentary,* edited by Carol A. Newsom and Sharon H. Ringe, 84–90. 2d ed. Louisville: Westminster John Knox, 1992.

Linafelt, Tod A. "Ruth." In Tod A. Linafelt and Timothy K. Beal, *Ruth, Esther.* BerO. Collegeville, Minn.: Liturgical, 1999.

Lipowitz, Yosef Ze'ev. *Ruth: The Scroll of Kindness.* With the Commentary Nachalas Yosef. Translated by Yaakov Yosef Iskowitz. New York: Feldheim, 2001.

Malbim, M. L. (R. Meir Loeb ben Yehiel Michael). *Megillat Rut.* [In Hebrew.] Reprint, Jerusalem: 'Eṣ ha-ḥayim, 1991.

Matthews, Victor H. *Judges and Ruth.* New Cambridge Bible Commentary. Cambridge: Cambridge Univ. Press, 2004.

Morris, L. "Ruth." In A. E. Cundall and L. Morris, *Judges, Ruth.* TOTC. Chicago: InterVarsity, 1968.

Murphy, Roland E. *Job, Proverbs, Ruth, Canticles, Ecclesiastes, and Esther.* FOTL 13. Grand Rapids: Eerdmans, 1981.

Nielsen, Kirsten. *Ruth: A Commentary.* Translated by Edward Broadbridge. OTL. Louisville: Westminster John Knox, 1997.

Nowack, Wilhelm. *Richter, Ruth und Bücher Samuelis.* HAT 1/4. Göttingen: Vandenhoeck & Ruprecht, 1902.

Rudolph, Wilhelm. *Das Buch Ruth. Das Hohe Lied. Die Klagelieder.* KAT 17. Gütersloh: Mohn, 1962.

Sakenfeld, Katherine Doob. *Ruth.* IBC. Louisville: Westminster John Knox, 1999.

Sasson, Jack M. *Ruth: A New Translation with a Philological Commentary and a Formalist-Folklorist Interpretation.* 2d ed. BibSem 10. Sheffield: Sheffield Academic, 1989.

Scharbert, Josef. "Rut." In idem and Georg Hentschel, *Rut. 1 Samuel.* NEchtB 33. Würzburg: Echter, 1994.

Slotki, Jacob J. "Ruth." In *The Five Megilloth,* edited by A. Cohen, 35–65. London: Soncino, 1946.

**Ruth**

Smelik, Klaas A. D. *Ruth.* Verklaring van de Hebreeuwse Bijbel. Kampen: Kok Pharos, 2000.

Smit, G. *Ruth, Ester en Klaagliederen.* Tekst en Uitleg. Groningen: Wolters, 1930.

Smith, Louise Pettibone. "The Book of Ruth: Introduction and Exposition." In *The Interpreter's Bible,* edited by George Arthur Buttrick, 2:827–52. Nashville: Abingdon, 1953.

Wünch, Hans-Georg. *Das Buch Rut.* Edition C Bibelkommentar, Altes Testament 10. Neuhausen-Stuttgart: Hänssler, 1998.

Würthwein, Ernst. *Die fünf Megilloth.* 2d ed. HAT 18. Tübingen: Mohr/Siebeck, 1969.

Zakovitch, Yair. *Ruth.* [In Hebrew.] Miqra le-Yisrael. Jerusalem: Magnes, 1990. German edition: *Das Buch Rut: Ein jüdischer Kommentar.* Translated by Andreas Lehnardt. SBS 177. Stuttgart: Katholisches Bibelwerk, 1999.

Zenger, Erich. *Das Buch Ruth.* ZBK 8. Zurich: Theologischer Verlag, 1992.

## 3. Studies

Adam, A. K. M., editor. *Postmodern Interpretations of the Bible: A Reader.* New York: Chalice, 2001.

Alter, Robert. *The Art of Biblical Narrative.* New York: Basic Books, 1981.

Anderson, A. A. "The Marriage of Ruth." *JSS* 23 (1978) 171–83.

Andrew, M. E. "Moving from Death to Life: Verbs of Motion in the Story of Judah and Tamar." *ZAW* 105 (1993) 262–69.

Ap-Thomas, D. R. "The Book of Ruth" *ExpT* 79 (1967–68) 369–73.

Archer, Gleason. "Ruth." In *Old Testament Survey,* edited William Sanford LaSor, David Hubbard, and Frederic W. Bush, 520–25. Grand Rapids: Eerdmans, 1982.

Aschkenasy, Nehama. *Eve's Journey: Feminine Images in the Hebraic Literary Tradition.* Philadelphia: Univ. of Pennsylvania Press, 1986.

———. "Language as Female Empowerment in Ruth." In *Reading Ruth: Contemporary Women Reclaim a Sacred Story,* edited by Judith A. Kates and Gail Twersky Reimer, 111–24. New York: Ballantine, 1994.

Astour, Michael. "Tamar the Hierodule: An Essay in the Method of Vestigial Motifs." *JBL* 85 (1966) 185–96.

Atkinson, David. *The Wings of Refuge: The Message of Ruth.* BST. Downers Grove, Ill.: InterVarsity, 1983.

Auerbach, Erich. *Mimesis: The Representation of Reality in Western Literature.* Translated by W. A. Trask. 1953. Reprinted, Princeton: Princeton Univ. Press, 1974.

Bach, Alice, editor. *Women in the Hebrew Bible: A Reader.* London: Routledge, 1999.

Bachrach, Yehoshua. *Mother of Royalty: An Exposition of the Book of Ruth in Light of the Sources.* Translated by Leonard Oschry. New York: Feldheim, 1973.

Bal, Mieke. "Herosim and Proper Names, or the Fruits of Analogy." In *A Feminist Companion to Ruth,* edited by Athalya Brenner, 42–69. FCB 1/3. Sheffield: Sheffield Academic, 1993.

———. *Lethal Love: Feminist Literary Readings of Biblical Love Stories*. ISBL. Bloomington: Indiana Univ. Press, 1987.

Bar–Ephrat, Shimon. "Some Observations on the Analysis of Structure in Biblical Narrative." *VT* 30 (1980) 154–74.

Bauckham, Richard. "The Book of Ruth and the Possibility of a Feminist Canonical Hermeneutic." *BibInt* 5 (1997) 29–45.

Bauer, J. "Das Buch Ruth in der jüdischen und christlichen Überlieferungen." *BK* 18 (1963) 116–19.

Baumgartner, Albert. "A Note on the Book of Ruth." *JANES* 5 (1973) 11–15.

Beattie, D. R. G. "The Book of Ruth as Evidence for Israelite Legal Practice." *VT* 24 (1974) 251–67.

———. *Jewish Exegesis of the Book of Ruth*. JSOTSup 2. Sheffield: JSOT Press, 1977.

———."*Kethibh* and *Qere* in Ruth iv.5." *VT* 21 (1971) 490–94.

———. "A Midrashic Gloss in Rt 2.7." *ZAW* 89 (1977) 122–24.

———. "Redemption in Ruth, and Related Matters: A Response to Jack M. Sasson." *JSOT* 5 (1978) 65–68.

———. "Ruth 2.7 and Midrash." *ZAW* 95 (1983) 422–23.

———. "Ruth III." *JSOT* 5 (1978) 39–48.

———. "Ruth, Book of." In *Dictionary of Biblical Interpretation,* edited by John H. Hayes, 426–28. Nashville: Abingdon, 1999.

Bechtel, Lyn M. "Shame as a Sanction of Social Control in Biblical Israel: Judicial, Political, and Social Shaming." *JSOT* 49 (1991) 47–76.

Belkin, Samuel. "Levirate and Agnate Marriage in Rabbinic Cognate Literature." *JQR* 60 (1969–70) 275–329.

Berlin, Adele. "Poetics in the Book of Ruth." In *Poetics and the Interpretation of Biblical Narrative,* 83–110. BLS 9. Sheffield: Almond, 1983.

———. "Ruth and the Continuity of Israel." In *Reading Ruth: Contemporary Women Reclaim a Sacred Story,* edited by Judith A. Kates and Gail Twersky Reimer, 55–64. New York: Ballantine, 1994.

———. "Ruth: Big Theme, Little Book." *BRev* 12 (1996) 40–43, 47–48.

Bernstein, Moshe J. "Two Multivalent Readings in the Ruth Narrative." *JSOT* 50 (1991) 15–26.

Berquist, Jon L. "Role Differentiation in the Book of Ruth." *JSOT* 57 (1993) 23–37. Reprinted in *The Historical Books: A Sheffield Reader,* edited by J. Cheryl Exum, 83–96. BibSem 40. Sheffield: Sheffield Academic, 1997.

Bertman, Stephen. "Symmetrical Design in the Book of Ruth." *ZAW* 84 (1965) 165–68.

Bewer, Julias A. "The *Ge'ullah* in the Book of Ruth" *AJSL* 19 (1902–3) 143–48.

———. "The *Go'el* in Ruth 4:14, 15." *AJSL* 20 (1903–4) 202–6.

———. "Die Leviratsehe im Buch Rt." *TSK* 76 (1903) 328–32.

Bird, Phyllis. *Missing Persons and Mistaken Identities: Women and Gender in Ancient Israel.* OBT. Minneapolis: Fortress Press, 1997.

———. "The Place of Women in the Israelite Cultus." In *Ancient Israelite Religion: Essays in Honor of Frank Moore Cross,* edited by Patrick D. Miller et al., 41–88. Philadelphia: Fortress Press, 1977. Reprinted in idem, *Missing Persons and Mistaken Identities,* 81–102.

———. "Women (OT)." In *ABD* 6:951–57.

Black, James. "Ruth in the Dark: Folktale, Law and Creative Ambiguity in the Old Testament." *Literature and Theology* 5 (1991) 20–35.

Bledstein, Adrien J. "Female Companionships: If the Book of Ruth Were Written by a Woman." In *A Feminist Companion to Ruth,* edited by Athalya Brenner, 116–33. FCB 1/3. Sheffield: Sheffield Academic, 1993.

Bohlen, Reinhold. "Die Rutrolle." *TTZ* 101 (1992) 1–19.

Bons, Eberhard. "Konnte eine Witwe die *naḥalah* ihres verstorbenen Mannes erben?" *ZAR* 4 (1998) 197–208.

———. "Die Septuaginta-Version des Buches Rut." *BZ* 42 (1998) 202–24.

Bos, Johanna W. H. "Out of the Shadows: Genesis 38; Judges 4:17–22; Ruth 3." *Semeia* 42 (1988) 37–67.

Braulik, Georg. "The Book of Ruth as Intra-Biblical Critique on the Deuteronomic Law." *AcT* 19 (1999) 1–20.

———. "Das Deuteronomium und die Bücher Ijob, Sprichwörter, Rut." In *Die Tora als Kanon für Juden und Christen,* edited by Erich Zenger, 61–138. HBS 10. Freiburg: Herder, 1996.

Brenner, Athalya. "Female Social Behaviour: Two Descriptive Patterns within the 'Birth of the Hero' Paradigm." *VT* 36 (1986) 257–73.

———, editor. *A Feminist Companion to Ruth.* FCB 1/3. Sheffield: Sheffield Academic, 1993.

———. *The Israelite Woman: Social Role and Literary Type in Biblical Narrative.* BibSem 2. Sheffield: JSOT Press, 1985.

———. "Naomi and Ruth." *VT* 33 (1983) 385–97.

———, editor. *Ruth and Esther: A Feminist Companion to the Bible.* FCB 2/3. Sheffield: Sheffield Academic, 1999.

———. *Ruth and Naomi: Literary, Stylistic and Linguistic Studies in the Book of Ruth.* [Hebrew.] Tel Aviv: Sifriat Poalim, 1988.

———. "Who's Afraid of Feminist Criticism? Who's Afraid of Biblical Humour? The Case of the Obtuse Foreign Ruler in the Hebrew Bible." *JSOT* 63 (1994) 38–55.

Brichto, H. C. "Kin, Cult, Land, and Afterlife—A Biblical Complex." *HUCA* 44 (1973) 1–54.

Brin, Gerson. "The Formula 'If He Shall Not (Do)' and the Problem of Sanctions in Biblical Law." In *Pomegranates and Golden Bells: Studies in Biblical, Jewish, and Near Eastern Ritual, Law, and Literature in Honor of Jacob Milgrom,* edited by David P. Wright et al., 341–62. Winona Lake, Ind.: Eisenbrauns, 1995.

Bronner, Leila L. "A Thematic Approach to Ruth in Rabbinic Literature." In *A Feminist Companion to Ruth,* edited by Athalya Brenner, 146–69. FCB 1/3. Sheffield: Sheffield Academic, 1993.

Brueggemann, Walter. *A Social Reading of the Old Testament: Prophetic Approaches to Israel's Communal Life.* Edited by Patrick D. Miller. Minneapolis: Fortress Press, 1994.

Bruppacher, Hans. "Die Bedeutung des Namens Ruth." *TZ* 22 (1966) 12–18.

Bührer, Emil. *Great Women of the Bible, in Art and Literature.* Lucerne: Mercer Univ. Press, 1993.

Burrows, Millar. "The Ancient Oriental Background of Hebrew Levirate Marriage." *BASOR* 77 (1940) 2–15.

———. "Levirate Marriage in Israel." *JBL* 59 (1940) 23–33.

———. "The Marriage of Boaz and Ruth." *JBL* 59 (1940) 445–54.

Bush, Frederic W. "Ruth 4:17: A Semantic Wordplay." In *Go to the Land I Will Show You: Studies in Honor of Dwight Young,* edited by J. E. Coleson and Victor H. Matthews, 3–14. Winona Lake, Ind.: Eisenbrauns, 1996.

Campbell, Edward F. Jr. "The Hebrew Short Story: A Study of Ruth." In *A Light unto My Path*: *Old Testament Studies in Honor of Jacob M. Myers,* edited by H. N. Bream et al. 83–101. Philadelphia: Temple Univ. Press, 1974.

———. "Naomi, Boaz, and Ruth: Ḥesed and Change." *ASB* 105 (1989–90) 64–74.

———. "Ruth Revisited." In *On the Way to Nineveh: Studies in Honor of George M. Landes,* edited by Stephen L. Cook and Sara C. Winter, 54–76. ASOR Books 4. Atlanta: Scholars, 1999.

Carmichael, Calumm. "A Ceremonial Crux: Removing a Man's Sandal as a Female Gesture of Contempt." *JBL* 96 (1977) 321–36.

———. "Treading in the Book of Ruth." *ZAW* 92 (1980) 248–66.

———. *Women, Law, and the Genesis Traditions.* Edinburgh: Edinburgh Univ. Press, 1979.

Caspi, Mishael Maswari. *The Book of Ruth: An Annotated Bibliography.* Books of the Bible 7. New York: Garland, 1994.

———, and Rachel S. Havrelock. *Women on the Biblical Road: Ruth, Naomi, and the Female Journey.* Lanham, Md.: University Press of America, 1996.

Childs, Brevard S. "Ruth." In *Introduction to the Old Testament as Scripture,* 560–68. Philadelphia: Fortress Press, 1979.

Coats, George W. "Widow's Rights: A Crux in the Structure of Genesis 38." *CBQ* 34 (1972) 461–66.

Coxon, Peter W. "Was Naomi a Scold? A Response to Fewell and Gunn." *JSOT* 45 (1989) 25–37.

Craghan, J. F. "Esther, Judith, and Ruth: Paradigms for Human Liberation." *BTB* 12 (1982) 11–19.

Crapon de Caprona, Pierre. *Ruth la Moabite: Essai.* Essais bibliques 3. Geneva: Labor et Fides, 1982.

Cross, Frank Moore. "Kinship and Covenant in Ancient Israel." In *From Epic to Canon: History and Literature in Ancient Israel,* 3–21. Baltimore: Johns Hopkins Univ. Press, 1998.

———. "The Religion of Canaan and the God of Israel." In *Canaanite Myth and Hebrew Epic: Essays in the History and Religion of Israel,* 1–75. Cambridge: Harvard Univ. Press, 1973.

———. "Yhwh and the God of the Patriarchs." *HTR* 55 (1962) 225–59.

Crüsemann, Frank. *The Torah: Theology and Social History of Old Testament Law.* Translated by Allan Mahnke. Minneapolis: Fortress Press, 1996.

David, M. "The Date of the Book of Ruth." *OTS* 1 (1942) 55–63.

Davies, Eryl W. "Inheritance Rights and the Hebrew Levirate Marriage [2 parts]." *VT* 31 (1981) 138–44; 257–68.

———. "Ruth IV 5 and the Duties of the *Go'el.*" *VT* 33 (1983) 231–34.

Davis, Ellen F. *Who Are You, My Daughter? Reading Ruth through Image and Text.* Louisville: Westminster John Knox, 2003.

Day, John. "Asherah in the Hebrew Bible and Northwest Semitic Literature." *JBL* 105 (1986) 385–408.

Day, Linda. "Power, Otherness, and Gender in the Biblical Short Stories." *HBT* 20 (1998) 109–27.

Day, Peggy L., editor. *Gender and Difference in Ancient Israel.* Minneapolis: Fortress Press, 1989.

Derby, Josiah. "The Problem of the Levirate Marriage." *Dor le Dor* 19.1 (1990) 111–17.

Derrida, Jacques. *Of Grammatology.* Translated by Gayatri Chakravorty Spivak. Baltimore: Johns Hopkins Univ. Press, 1976.

Dijk-Hemmes, Fokkelien van. "Ruth: A Product of Women's Culture?" In *A Feminist Companion to Ruth,* edited by Athalya Brenner, 134–39. FCB 1/3. Sheffield: Sheffield Academic, 1993.

———. "Traces of Women's Texts in the Hebrew Bible." In *On Gendering Texts: Female and Male Voices in the Hebrew Bible,* edited by Athalya Brenner and Fokkelien van Dijk-Hemmes, 17–109. BibIntSer 1. Leiden: Brill, 1996.

Dommershausen, Werner. "Leitwortstil in der Ruthrolle." In *Theologie im Wandel: Festschrift zum 150 jährigen Bestehen der Katholisch-Theologischen Fakultät an der Universität Tübingen 1817–1967,* 394–412. Munich: Wewel, 1967.

Dube, Musa W. "Divining Ruth for International Relations." In *Postmodern Interpre-*

*tations of the Bible: A Reader,* edited by A. K. M. Adam, 67–79. St. Louis: Chalice, 2001.

Durbin, Lois. "Fullness and Emptiness, Fertility and Loss: Meditations on Naomi's Tale in the Book of Ruth." In *Reading Ruth: Contemporary Women Reclaim a Sacred Story,* edited by Judith A. Kates and Gail Twersky Reimer, 131–44. New York: Ballantine, 1994.

Ebach, Jürgen. "Fremde in Moab—Fremde aus Moab: Das Buch Ruth als politische Literatur." In *Bibel und Literatur,* edited by Jürgen Ebach and R. Faber, 277–304. Munich: Fink, 1985.

Eissfeldt, Otto. *The Old Testament: An Introduction.* Translated by P. R. Ackroyd. Oxford: Blackwell, 1965.

———. "Wahrheit und Dichtung in der Ruth-Erzählung." *Sitzungsberichte der Sächsischen Akademie der Wissenschaften zu Leipzig* 110.4 (1965) 23–28.

Elliott, John H. *What Is Social-Scientific Criticism?* GBS. Minneapolis: Fortress Press, 1993.

Emerton, J. A. "Judah and Tamar." *VT* 29 (1979) 403–15.

———. "Some Problems in Gen 38." *VT* 25 (1975) 338–61.

Emmerson, Grace I. "Women in Ancient Israel." In *The World of Ancient Israel: Sociological, Anthropological and Political Perspectives,* edited by R. E. Clements, 371–94. Cambridge: Cambridge Univ. Press, 1989.

Eskenazi, Tamara C. "Out of the Shadows: Biblical Women in the Postexilic Era." *JSOT* 54 (1992) 25–43.

Exum, J. Cheryl. *Fragmented Women: Feminist (Sub)versions of Biblical Narratives.* Valley Forge, Pa.: Trinity, 1993.

———. "Is This Naomi?" In idem, *Plotted, Shot and Painted,* 129–74. JSOTSup 215. Sheffield: Sheffield Academic, 1996.

Farmer, William R., Sean McEvenue, A. J. Levoratti, David L. Dungan, and André LaCocque, editors. *The International Bible Commentary.* Collegeville, Minn.: Liturgical, 1998.

Fewell, Danna Nolan, and David M. Gunn. "Boaz, Pillar of Society: Measures of Worth in the Book of Ruth." *JSOT* 45 (1989) 45–59.

———. *Compromising Redemption: Relating Characters in the Book of Ruth.* LCBI. Louisville: Westminster John Knox, 1990.

———. "Is Coxon a Scold?" *JSOT* 45 (1989) 39–43.

———. "Judah and Tamar: Genesis 38." In idem, *Narrative in the Hebrew Bible,* 35–45. OBS. Oxford: Oxford Univ. Press, 1993.

———. "'A Son Born to Naomi': Literary Allusions and Interpretation in the Book of Ruth." *JSOT* 40 (1988) 99–108.

Fisch, Harold. "Ruth and the Structure of Covenant History." *VT* 32 (1982) 425–37.

Fischer, Irmtraud. "The Book of Ruth: A 'Feminist' Commentary to the Torah?" In *Ruth and Esther: A Feminist Companion to the Bible,* edited by Athalya Brenner, 24–49. FCB 2/3. Sheffield: Sheffield Academic, 1999.

————."Eine Schwiegertochter—mehr wert als sieben Söhne! (Ruth 4,15)." In *Mit allen Sinnen Glauben: Feministische Theologie Unterwegs,* edited by Herlinde Pissarek-Hudelist and Luise Schottroff, 30–44. Gütersloh: Gütersloher, 1991.

Fishbane, Michael. *Biblical Interpretation in Ancient Israel.* Oxford: Clarendon, 1985.

Fishbane, Mona DeKoven. "Ruth: Dilemmas of Loyalty and Connection." In *Reading Ruth: Contemporary Women Reclaim a Sacred Story*, edited by Judith A. Kates and Gail Twersky Reimer, 298–308. New York: Ballantine, 1994.

Flanagan, James W. "Chiefs in Israel." *JSOT* 20 (1981) 47–73.

————. "Succession and Genealogy in the Davidic Dynasty." In *The Quest for the Kingdom of God: Studies in Honor of George E. Mendenhall*, edited by Herbert B. Huffmon et al., 33–55. Winona Lake: Eisenbrauns, 1983.

Frankiel, Tamar. "Ruth and the Messiah." In *Reading Ruth: Contemporary Women Reclaim a Sacred Story*, edited by Judith A. Kates and Gail Twersky Reimer, 321–35. New York: Ballantine, 1994.

Frick, Frank. "Widows in the Hebrew Bible: A Transactional Approach." In *A Feminist Companion to Exodus to Deuteronomy,* edited by Athalya Brenner, 139–51. FCB 1/6. Sheffield: Sheffield Academic, 1994.

Frymer-Kensky, Tikva. *In the Wake of the Goddess.* New York: Free Press, 1992.

Gadamer, Hans Georg. *Truth and Method.* Rev. ed. Translated by Garrett Barden and John Cumming. New York: Continuum, 1988.

Gage, Warren Austin. "Ruth upon the Threshing Floor and the Sin of Gibeah: A Biblical-Theological Study." *WTJ* 51 (1989) 369–75.

Garsiel, Moshe. *Biblical Names: A Literary Study of Midrashic Derivations and Puns.* Ramat Gan: Bar-Ilan Univ. Press, 1991.

Gerstenberger, Erhard S. "Covenant and Commandment." *JBL* 84 (1965) 38–51.

————. *Wesen und Herkunft des 'apodiktischen Rechts.'* WMANT 20. Neukirchen-Vluyn: Neukirchener, 1965.

Gilmore, David. "Anthropology of the Mediterranean Area." *ARA* 11 (1982) 175–205.

Ginzberg, Louis. *The Legends of the Jews.* Translated by Henrietta Szold. 7 vols. Philadelphia: Jewish Publication Society, 1909–38.

Gitay, Zefira. "Ruth and the Women of Bethlehem." *A Feminist Companion to Ruth,* edited by Athalya Brenner, 178–90. FCB 1/3. Sheffield: Sheffield Academic, 1993.

Glanzman, George S. "The Origin and Date of the Book of Ruth." *CBQ* 21 (1959) 201–7.

Globe, Alexander. "Folktale Form and National Theme, with Particular Reference to Ruth." In *Approaches to Teaching the Hebrew Bible as Literature in Translation,* edited by Barry N. Olshen and Yael S. Feldman, 127–32. New York: Modern Language Association, 1989.

Glueck, Nelson. *Ḥesed in the Bible.* Translated by Alfred Gottschalk. Cincinnati: Hebrew Union College Press, 1967. (German ed. 1927.)

Goethe, Johann Wolfgang von. *Westöstlicher Diwan, Noten und Abhandlungen: Hebräer.* Goethe's Werke. Vol. 21. Reprint, Frankfurt: Suhrkamp, 1927.

Goitein, Shlomo Dov. "Women as Creators of Biblical Genres." *Prooftexts* 8 (1988) 1–33.

Goldin, Judah. "The Youngest Son or Where Does Genesis 38 Belong?" *JBL* 96 (1977) 27–44.

Gordis, Robert. "Love, Marriage, and Business in the Book of Ruth: A Chapter in Hebrew Customary Law." In *A Light unto My Path*: *Old Testament Studies in Honor of Jacob M. Myers,* edited by H. N. Bream et al., 241–64. Philadelphia: Temple Univ. Press, 1974.

Gordon, Cyrus H. "Paternity at Two Levels." *JBL* 96 (1977) 101.

Gosse, Bernard. "Le Livre de Ruth et ses liens avec II Samuel 21,1-14." *ZAW* 108 (1996) 430–33.

———. "Subversion de la législation du Pentateuque et symboliques respectives des lignées de David et de Saül dans les livres de Samuel et de Ruth." *ZAW* 110 (1998) 34–49.

Gottwald, Norman K. *The Hebrew Bible: A Socio-Literary Introduction with CD-ROM.* Minneapolis: Fortress Press, 2002.

———. *The Tribes of Yahweh: A Sociology of the Religion of Liberated Israel, 1250–1050 B.C.E.* Maryknoll, N.Y.: Orbis, 1979.

Goulder, Michael D. "Ruth: A Homily on Deuteronomy 22–25?" In *Of Prophets' Visions and the Wisdom of Sages: Essays in Honor of R. Norman Whybray on His Seventieth Birthday,* edited by Heather A. McKay and David J. A. Clines, 307–19. JSOTSup 162. Sheffield: JSOT Press, 1993.

Gow, Murray D. *The Book of Ruth: Its Structure, Theme and Purpose.* Leicester: Apollos, 1992.

Grant, Reg. "Literary Structure in the Book of Ruth." *BSac* 148 (1991) 424–41.

Green, Barbara. "The Plot of the Biblical Story of Ruth." *JSOT* 23 (1982) 55–68.

Greenstein, Edward L. "Reading Strategies and the Story of Ruth." In *Women in the Hebrew Bible,* edited by Alice Bach, 211–31. New York: Routledge, 1998.

Gunkel, Hermann. "Ruth." In idem, *Reden und Aufsätze,* 65–92. Göttingen: Vandenhoeck & Ruprecht, 1913.

———. "Ruthbuch." In *RGG* 4:2180–82.

Hals, Ronald M. "Ruth, Book of." In *IDBSup,* 758–59.

———. *The Theology of the Book of Ruth.* Facet Books 23. Philadelphia: Fortress Press, 1969.

Hanson, K. C. "BTB Reader's Guide: Kinship." *BTB* 24 (1994) 183–94.

———. "The Herodians and Mediterranean Kinship. Part 1: Genealogy and Descent." *BTB* 19 (1989) 75–84.

Harris, P. "Woman in the ANE." In *IDBSup*, 960–63.

———. "Woman in Mesopotamia." In *ABD* 6:947–51.

Harvey, Dorthea Ward. "Ruth, Book of." In *IDB* 4:131–34.

Hollyday, Joyce. "You Shall not Afflict: A Biblical Perspective on Women and Poverty." *Sojourners* 15.3 (1986) 26–29.

Honig, Bonnie. "Ruth the Model Emigrée: Mourning and the Symbolic Politics of Immigration." In *Ruth and Esther: A Feminist Companion to the Bible,* edited by Athalya Brenner, 50–74. FCB 2/3. Sheffield: Sheffield Academic, 1999.

Hubbard, Robert L. Jr. "*Ganzheitsdenken* in the Book of Ruth." In *Problems in Biblical Theology: Essays in Honor of Rolf Knierim,* edited by H. C. Sun et al., 192–209. Grand Rapids: Eerdmans, 1997.

———. "Ruth iv 17: A New Solution." *VT* 38 (1988) 293–301.

Humbert, Paul. "Art et leçon de l'histoire de Ruth." *RTP* 26 (1938) 257–86. Reprinted in *Opuscules d'un hébraïsant,* 83–110. Neuchâtel: Secrétariat de l'Université, 1958.

Hunter, Alastair. "How Many Gods Had Ruth?" *SJT* 34 (1981) 427–36.

Hurvitz, Avi. "Ruth 2.7—'A Midrashic Gloss'?" *ZAW* 95 (1983) 121–23.

Hyman, Ronald T. "Questions and the Book of Ruth." *HS* 24 (1983) 17–25.

———. "Questions and Changing Identity in the Book of Ruth." *USQR* 39 (1984) 189–201.

Isserlin, B. S. J. *The Israelites.* Minneapolis: Fortress Press, 2001.

Jacobs, J. "Levirate Marriage." In *JE* 8:45–46.

Jenni, Ernst. *Das hebräische Pi'el: Syntaktisch-semasiologische Untersuchung einer Verbalform im Alten Testament.* Zurich: EVZ, 1968.

Jensen, Jane Richardson. "Ruth according to Ephrem the Syrian." In *A Feminist Companion to Ruth,* edited by Athalya Brenner, 170–76. FCB 1/3. Sheffield: Sheffield Academic, 1993.

Jepsen, Alfred. "Das Buch Ruth." *TSK* (1937–38) 416–28.

Jobling, David. "Ruth Finds a Home: Canon, Politics, Method." In *The New Literary Criticism and the Hebrew Bible,* edited by J. Cheryl Exum and David J. A. Clines, 125–39. JSOTSup 143. Sheffield: JSOT Press, 1993.

Johnson, A. R. "The Primary Meaning of the Root *g'l*." In *Congress Volume: Copenhagen, 1953,* 67–77. VTSup 1. Leiden: Brill, 1953.

Johnson, Marshall D. *The Purpose of the Biblical Genealogies, with Special Reference to the Setting of the Genealogies of Jesus.* 2d ed. SNTSMS 8. Cambridge: Cambridge Univ. Press, 1988.

Johnson, Willa M. "Ethnicity in Persian Yehud: Between Anthropological Analysis and Ideological Criticism." In *SBLSP 1995,* 177–86. Atlanta: Scholars, 1995.

Kampen, John. *The Hasideans and the Origin of Pharisaism: A Study in 1 and 2 Maccabees.* SBLSCS 24. Atlanta: Scholars, 1988.

Kates, Judith A. "Women at the Center: Ruth and Shevuot." In *Reading Ruth: Contemporary Women Reclaim a Sacred Story*, edited by Judith A. Kates and Gail Twersky Reimer, 187–98. New York: Ballantine, 1994.

———, and Gail Twersky Reimer, editors. *Reading Ruth: Contemporary Women Reclaim a Sacred Story*. New York: Ballantine, 1994.

Kessler, Rainer. "Zur israelitischen Löserinstitution." In *Schuld und Schulden: Biblische Traditionen in gegenwärtigen Konflikten,* edited by Marlene Crüsemann and Willy Schottroff, 40–53. KT 121. Munich: Kaiser, 1992.

Klagsbrun, Francine. "Ruth and Naomi, Rachel and Leah: Sisters under the Skin." In *Reading Ruth: Contemporary Women Reclaim a Sacred Story*, edited by Judith A. Kates and Gail Twersky Reimer, 261–72. New York: Ballantine, 1994.

Klingenstein, Susanne. "Circles of Kinship: Samuel's Family Romance." In *Reading Ruth: Contemporary Women Reclaim a Sacred Story*, edited by Judith A. Kates and Gail Twersky Reimer, 199–210. New York: Ballantine, 1994.

Klugel-Nash, Nomi. "Standing in the Sandals of Naomi." In *A Psychological Interpretation of Ruth,* Yehezkel Kluger. Eisenach: Daimon, 1999.

Kluger, Yehezkel. *A Psychological Interpretation of Ruth: In the Light of Mythology, Legend and Kabbalah.* Eisenach: Daimon, 1999.

Knauf, Ernst. "Ruth la moabite." *VT* 44 (1994) 547–48.

Köhler, Ludwig. *Hebrew Man.* Translated by Peter R. Ackroyd. Nashville: Abingdon, 1956.

Kristeva, Julia. *Étrangers à nous-mêmes.* Paris: Gallimard, 1991.

———. *Nations without Nationalism.* Translated by Leon S. Roudiez. New York: Columbia Univ. Press, 1993.

Kronholm, Tryggve. "The Portrayal of Characters in Midrash Ruth Rabbah: Observations on the Formation of the Jewish Hermeneutical Legend Known as 'Biblical Haggadah.'" *ASTI* 12 (1983) 13–54.

Kruger, Paul A. "The Hem of the Garment in Marriage: The Meaning of the Symbolic Gesture in Ruth 3:9 and Ezek. 16:8." *JNSL* 12 (1984) 79–86.

Kutscher, Yehezkel. *The Language and Linguistic Background of the Isaiah Scroll (1QIsa).* Edited by Elisha Qimron. STDJ 6A. Leiden: Brill, 1974.

Labuschagne, C. J. "The Crux in Ruth 4,11." *ZAW* 79 (1967) 364–67.

LaCocque, André. *The Book of Daniel.* Translated by David Pellauer. Atlanta: John Knox, 1979.

———. "Date et milieu du livre de Ruth." *RHPR* 59 (1979) 583–93.

———. "Une descendance manipulée et ambiguë (Genése 29,31—30,24)." In *Jacob: Commentaire à plusieurs voix de Gen. 25–36. Mélanges offerts à Albert de Pury,* edited by Jean-Daniel Macchi and Thomas Römer, 109–27. MB 44. Geneva: Labor et Fides, 2001.

———. *The Feminine Unconventional: Four Subversive Figures in Israel's Tradition.* OBT. Minneapolis: Fortress Press, 1990.

———. *Romance, She Wrote: A Hermeneutical Essay on Song of Songs*. Harrisburg, Pa.: Trinity, 1998.

———. "The Stranger in the Old Testament." *Migration Today* 15 (1970) 55–60.

———, and Pierre LaCocque. *The Jonah Complex*. Atlanta: John Knox, 1981.

———, and Paul Ricoeur. *Thinking Biblically: Exegetical and Hermeneutical Studies*. Translated by David Pellauer. Chicago: Univ. of Chicago Press, 1998.

Laffey, Alice. *An Introduction to the Old Testament: A Feminist Perspective*. Philadelphia: Fortress Press, 1988.

Lamparter, Helmut. *Das Buch der Sehnsucht*. BAT 16/2. Stuttgart: Calwer, 1962.

Landy, Francis. "Ruth and the Romance of Realism, or Deconstructing History." *JAAR* 62 (1994) 285–317.

Lang, Bernhard. *Wisdom and the Book of Proverbs: A Hebrew Goddess Redefined*. NewYork: Pilgrim, 1986.

Larkin, Katrina J. A. *Ruth and Esther*. OTG. Sheffield: Sheffield Academic, 1996.

Leach, Edmund. *Genesis as Myth and Other Essays*. London: Cape, 1969.

Leggett, D. A. *The Levirate and Go'el Institutions in the Old Testament, with Special Attention to the Book of Ruth*. Cherry Hill, N.J.: Mack, 1974.

Lemaire, André. "Une inscription phénicienne decouverte récemment et le mariage de Ruth la Moabite." *Eretz-Israel* 20 (1989) 124*–29*.

Levenson, Jon. "Liberation Theology and the Exodus." *Reflections* 86.1 (1991) 2–12.

Levine, Baruch A. "In Praise of the Israelite *Mišpāḥâ*: Legal Themes in the Book of Ruth." In *The Quest for the Kingdom of God: Studies in Honor of George E. Mendenhall,* edited by H. B. Huffmon et al., 95–106. Winona Lake, Ind.: Eisenbrauns, 1983.

Levine, Étan. "On Intra-familial Institutions of the Bible [review of Leggett, *Levirate*]." *Bib* 57 (1976) 554–59.

Levine, Nachman. "Ten Hungers/Six Barleys: Structure and Redemption in the Targum to Ruth." *JSJ* 30 (1999) 312–24.

Lipiński, E. "Le mariage de Ruth." *VT* 26 (1976) 124–27.

Loader, James A. "Of Barley, Bulls, Land and Levirate." In *Studies in Deuteronomy: In Honour of C. J. Labuschagne on the Occasion of His Sixty-fifth Birthday,* edited by F. García Martínez et al., 123–38. VTSup 53. Leiden: Brill, 1994.

———. "Yahweh's Wings and the Gods of Ruth." In *Wer ist wie du Herr, unter den Göttern? Studien zur Theologie und Religionsgeschichte Israels: Für Otto Kaiser zum 70. Geburtstag,* edited by Ingo Kottsieper et al., 389–401. Göttingen: Vandenhoeck & Ruprecht, 1994.

Loretz, Oswald. "Poetische Abschnitte im Rutbuch." *UF* 7 (1975) 580–82.

———. "The Theme of the Ruth Story." *CBQ* 22 (1960) 391–99.

———. "Das Verhältnis zwischen Rut-story und David-Genealogie im Rut-Buch." *ZAW* 89 (1977) 124–26.

Lusseau, H. "Ruth." In *Introduction to the Old Testament,* edited by André Robert and André Feuillet, 447–52. Translated by Patrick W. Skehan et al. New York: Desclee, 1968.

Lys, Daniel. "Residence ou repos? Notule sur Ruth ii 7." *VT* 21 (1971) 497–501.

Machinist, Peter. "Literature as Politics: The Tukulti-Ninurta Epic and the Bible." *CBQ* 38 (1976) 455–82.

Malamat, Abraham. "King Lists of the Old Babylonian Period and Biblical Genealogies." *JAOS* 88 (1968) 163–73.

Maldanado, Robert D. "Reading Malinche—Reading Ruth: Toward a Hermeneutics of Betrayal." *Semeia* 72 (1995) 91–109.

Manor, Dale. "A Brief History of Levirate Marriage." *ResQ* 27 (1984) 129–42.

Mathewson, Steven. "An Exegetical Study of Genesis 38." *BSac* 146 (1989) 373–92.

May, Herbert G. "Ruth's Visit to the High Place at Bethlehem." *JRAS* (1939) 75–78.

McCarthy, Carmel. "The Davidic Genealogy in the Book of Ruth." *PIBA* 9 (1985) 53–62.

———, and William Riley. *The Old Testament Short Story: Exploration into Narrative Spirituality*. MBS 7. Wilmington, Del.: Glazier, 1986.

McKane, William. "Ruth and Boaz." *Transactions of the Glasgow University Oriental Society* 19 (1961–62) 29–40.

Meinhold, Arndt. "Theologische Schwerpunkte im Buch Ruth und ihr Gewicht für seine Datierung." *TZ* 32 (1976) 129–37.

Merrill, Eugene H. "The Book of Ruth: Narration and Shared Themes." *BSac* 142 (1985) 130–41.

Mesters, Carlos. *Der Fall Rut: Brot, Familie, Land. Biblische Gespräche aus Brasilien*. ErT 87. Erlangen: Verlag der Evangelisch-Lutheranischer Mission, 1988.

Meyers, Carol. *Discovering Eve: Ancient Israelite Women in Context*. New York: Oxford Univ. Press, 1988.

———. "Guilds and Gatherings: Women's Groups in Ancient Israel." In *Realia Dei: Essays in Archaeology and Biblical Interpretation in Honor of Edward F. Campbell Jr. at His Retirement,* edited by Prescott H. Williams Jr. and Theodore Hiebert, 154–84. SPHS 23. Atlanta: Scholars, 1999.

———. *Households and Holiness: The Religious Culture of Israelite Women*. Facets. Minneapolis: Fortress Press, 2005.

———. "Returning Home: Ruth 1.8 and the Gendering of the Book of Ruth." In *A Feminist Companion to Ruth,* edited by Athalya Brenner, 85–115. FCB 1/3. Sheffield: Sheffield Academic, 1993.

———. "'To Her Mother's House': Considering a Counterpart to the Israelite *Bêt ʾāb*." In *The Bible and the Politics of Exegesis: Essays in Honor of Norman K. Gottwald on His Sixty-fifth Birthday,* edited by David Jobling et al., 39–51. Cleveland: Pilgrim, 1991.

———. "'Women of the Neighborhood' (Ruth 4.17)—Informal Female Networks in

Ancient Israel." In *Ruth and Esther: A Feminist Companion to the Bible,* edited by Athalya Brenner, 110–27. FCB 2/3. Sheffield: Sheffield Academic, 1999.

Miller, J. Maxwell. "Moab." In *ABD* 4:882–93.

Milne, P. J. "Folktales and Fairy Tales: An Evaluation of Two Proppian Analyses of Biblical Narrative." *JSOT* 34 (1986) 35–60.

Minc, R. "Le rôle du chœur féminin dans le livre de Ruth." *BVC* 77 (1967) 71–76.

Montherlant, Henry de. "La Reine morte" (1942).

Moor, Johannes de. "The Poetry of the Book of Ruth [2 parts]." *Or* 53 (1984) 262–83; 55 (1986) 16–46.

Moore, Michael S. "Ruth the Moabite and the Blessing of Foreigners." *CBQ* 60 (1998) 203–17.

———. "Two Textual Anomalies in Ruth." *CBQ* 59 (1997) 234–43.

Morgenstern, Julius. "The Book of the Covenant (Part 2)." *HUCA* 7 (1930) 19–258.

Morgenstern, Mira. "Ruth and the Sense of Self: Midrash and Difference." *Judaism* 48 (1999) 131–45.

Myers, Jacob M. *The Linguistic and Literary Form of the Book of Ruth.* Leiden: Brill, 1955.

Neher, André. *The Exile of the Word: From the Silence of the Bible to the Silence of Auschwitz.* Translated by David Meisel. Philadelphia: Jewish Publication Society of America, 1981.

———. *The Prophetic Existence.* Translated by William Wolf. South Brunswick, N.J.: Barnes, 1969.

Neufeld, E. *Ancient Hebrew Marriage Laws.* London: Longmans, 1944.

Neusner, Jacob. *The Mother of the Messiah.* Harrisburg: Trinity, 1993.

Newsom, Carol, and Sharon H. Ringe, editors. *The Women's Bible Commentary.* Louisville: Westminster John Knox, 1992.

Nicholson, E. W. "The Problem of חצן." *ZAW* 89 (1977) 259–65.

Niditch, Susan. "Legends of Wise Heroes and Heroines. " In *The Hebrew Bible and Its Modern Interpreters,* edited by Douglas A. Knight and Gene M. Tucker, 445–63. Philadelphia: Fortress Press, 1985.

———. "The Wronged Woman Righted: Genesis 38." *HTR* 72 (1979) 143–49.

Nielsen, Kirsten. "Le choix contre le droit dans le livre de Ruth." *VT* 35 (1985) 201–12.

———. "Intertextuality and the Hebrew Bible." In *Congress Volume: Oslo, 1998,* edited by André Lemaire and Magne Saebø, 17–31. VTSup 80. Leiden: Brill, 2000.

Nowell, Irene. *Women in the Old Testament.* Collegeville, Minn.: Liturgical, 1997.

Osgood, S. Joy. "Women and the Inheritance of Land in Early Israel." In *Women in the Biblical Tradition,* edited by George J. Brooke, 29–52. Studies in Women and Religion 31. Lewiston, N.Y.: Mellen, 1992.

Ostriker, Alicia S. "The Redeeming of Ruth." In idem, *The Nakedness of the Fathers:*

*Biblical Visions and Revisions,* 169–75. New Brunswick, N.J.: Rutgers Univ. Press, 1994.

Otwell, John H. *And Sarah Laughed: The Status of Woman in the Old Testament.* Philadelphia: Westminster, 1977.

Oz, Amos. *The Story Begins*: *Essays on Literature.* Translated by Maggie Bar-Tura. New York: Harcourt Brace, 1999.

Ozick, Cynthia. "Ruth." In idem, *Metaphor and Memory,* 260–64. New York: Knopf, 1989.

Pardes, Ilana. *Countertraditions in the Bible: A Feminist Approach.* Cambridge: Harvard Univ. Press, 1992.

Parker, Simon B. "The Birth Annoucement." In *Ascribe to the Lord: Biblical and Other Essays in Memory of Peter C. Craigie,* edited by Lyle Eslinger and Glen Taylor, 133–49. JSOTSup 67. Sheffield: JSOT Press, 1988.

―――. "The Marriage Blessing in Israelite and Ugaritic Literature." *JBL* 95 (1976) 23–30.

Perdue, Leo G., Joseph Blenkinsopp, John J. Collins, and Carol Meyers. *Families in Ancient Israel.* The Family, Religion, and Culture. Louisville: Westminster John Knox, 1997.

Phillips, Anthony. "The Book of Ruth—Deception and Shame." *JJS* 37 (1986) 1–17.

Plum, Karin Friis. "Genealogy as Theology." *SJOT* 1 (1989) 66–92.

Porten, Bezalel. "The Scroll of Ruth: A Rhetorical Study." *GCA* 7 (1978) 23–49.

―――. "Structure, Style and Theme in the Scroll of Ruth." *AJS Newsletter* 17 (June 1976) 15–16.

―――. "Theme and Historiographic Background of the Scroll of Ruth." *GCA* 6 (1977) 69–78.

Pressler, Carolyn. *Joshua, Judges, and Ruth.* WBComp. Louisville: Westminster John Knox, 2002.

Price, I. "The So-called Levirate Marriage in Hittite and Assyrian Laws." In *Oriental Studies Published in Commemoration of the Fortieth Anniversary (1883–1923) of Paul Haupt as Director of the Oriental Seminary of the Johns Hopkins University, Baltimore, Md.,* edited by Cyrus Adler and Aaron Ember, 268–71. Baltimore: Johns Hopkins Univ. Press, 1926.

Prinsloo, W. S. "The Theology of the Book of Ruth." *VT* 30 (1980) 33–41.

Propp, Vladimir. *Morphology of the Folktale.* Translated by Laurence Scott. 2d ed. Austin: Univ. of Texas Press, 1968.

Putnam, Ruth A. "Friendship." In *Reading Ruth: Contemporary Women Reclaim a Sacred Story,* edited by Judith A. Kates and Gail Twersky Reimer, 44–54. New York: Ballantine, 1994.

Puukko, A. F. "Die Leviratsehe in der altorientalischen Gesetzen." *ArOr* 17 (1949) 296–99.

Rabinowitz, Louis I. "Levirate Marriage and Ḥaliẓah." In *EncJud* 11:122–31.

Rahlfs, Alfred. *Studie über den griechischen Text des Buches Ruth.* Mitteilungen des Septuaginta-Unternehmens 3/2. Berlin: Weidmann, 1922.

Rashkow, Ilona. "Ruth: The Discourse of Power and the Power of Discourse." In *A Feminist Companion to Ruth,* edited by Athalya Brenner, 26–41. FCB 1/3. Sheffield: Sheffield Academic, 1993.

Rauber, D. F. "Literary Values in the Bible: The Book of Ruth." In *Literary Interpretations of Biblical Narratives,* edited by Kenneth R. R. Gros Louis et al., 163–76. Nashville: Abingdon, 1974.

Reimer, Gail Twersky. "Her Mother's House." In *Reading Ruth: Contemporary Women Reclaim a Sacred Story,* edited by Judith A. Kates and Gail Twersky Reimer, 97–106. New York: Ballantine, 1994.

Rendsburg, Gary A. "Hebrew Philological Notes (I)." *HS* 40 (1999) 27–32.

Rendtorff, Rolf. *The Old Testament: An Introduction.* Translated by John Bowden. Minneapolis: Fortress Press, 1986.

Richardson, Jane. "Ruth according to Ephrem the Syrian." In *A Feminist Companion to Ruth,* edited by Athalya Brenner, 170–77. FCB 1/3. Sheffield: Sheffield Academic, 1993.

Richter, Hans-Friedemann. *Geschlechtlichkeit, Ehe und Familie im Alten Testament und seiner Umwelt.* BBET 10. Frankfurt: Lang, 1978.

———. "Zum Levirat im Buch Rut." *ZAW* 95 (1983) 123–26.

Robert, Marthe. *Kafka.* Paris: Gallimard, 1960.

Robertson, Edward. "The Plot of the Book of Ruth." *BJRL* 32 (1949–50) 207–28.

Rowland, Christopher, and Mark Corner. *Liberating Exegesis: The Challenge of Liberation Theology to Biblical Studies.* Louisville: Westminster John Knox, 1989.

Rowley, H. H. "The Marriage of Ruth." In *The Servant of the Lord and Other Essays on the Old Testament,* 171–94. Oxford: Blackwell, 1965. Reprint from *HTR* 40 (1947) 77–99.

Russell, Letty M. *Feminist Interpretation of the Bible.* Philadelphia: Westminster, 1985.

Rutledge, David. *Reading Marginally: Feminism, Deconstruction and the Bible.* BibIntSer 21. Leiden: Brill, 1996.

Sacon, K. K. "The Book of Ruth." *AJBI* 4 (1978) 3–22.

Sakenfeld, Katharine Doob. *Faithfulness in Action: Loyalty in Biblical Perspective.* OBT. Philadelphia: Fortress Press, 1985.

———. *The Meaning of Ḥesed in the Hebrew Bible: A New Inquiry.* HSM 17. Missoula, Mont.: Scholars, 1978.

———. "Naomi's Cry: Reflections on Ruth 1:20-21." In *A God So Near: Essays on Old Testament Theology in Honor of Patrick D. Miller,* edited by Brent A. Strawn and Nancy Bowen, 129–43. Winona Lake, Ind.: Eisenbrauns, 2003.

————. "Ruth 4: An Image of Eschatological Hope." In *Liberating Eschatology: Essays in Honor of Letty Russell,* edited by M. A. Farley and Serene Jones, 55–67. Louisville: Westminster John Knox, 1999.

————. "The Story of Ruth: Economic Survival." In *Realia Dei: Essays in Archaeology and Biblical Interpretation in Honor of Edward F. Campbell Jr. at His Retirement,* edited by Prescott H. Williams Jr. and Theodore Hiebert, 215–27. SPHS 23. Atlanta: Scholars, 1999.

Sasson, Jack M. "Divine Providence or Human Plan [review of Campbell, *Ruth*]." *Int* 30 (1976) 415–19.

————. "A Genealogical 'Convention' in Biblical Chronography?" *ZAW* 90 (1978) 171–85.

————. "Generation, Seventh." In *IDBSup,* 354–56.

————. "The Issue of *Ge'ullāh* in Ruth." *JSOT* 5 (1978) 52–64.

————. "Response to D. R. G. Beattie's 'Ruth III.'" *JSOT* 5 (1978) 49–51.

————. "Ruth." In *The Literary Guide to the Bible,* edited by Robert Alter and Frank Kermode, 321–28. Cambridge: Belnap, 1987.

————. "Ruth and Naomi." In *Encyclopedia of Religion,* edited by Mircea Eliade, 12:491–92. New York: Macmillan, 1987.

Saxegaard, Kristin Moen. "'More Than Seven Sons': Ruth as Example of the Good Son." *SJOT* 15 (2001) 257–75.

Scheftelowitz, Isidor. "Die Levirats-ehe."*AR* 18 (1915) 255.

Segond, Louis. *La Sainte Bible: Qui comprend l'Ancien et le Nouveau Testament.* Rev. ed. Paris: Billing, 1958.

Sheehan, John F. X. "The Word of God as Myth: The Book of Ruth." In *The Word in the World: Essays in Honor of Frederick L. Moriarty, S.J.,* edited by Richard J. Clifford and George W. MacRae, 35–43. Cambridge: Weston College, 1973.

Shepherd, David. "Violence in the Fields? Translating, Reading, and Revising in Ruth 2." *CBQ* 63 (2001) 444–64.

Smith, Mark S. *The Early History of God: Yahweh and the Other Deities in Ancient Israel.* 2d ed. Grand Rapids: Eerdmans, 2002.

Smith, Morton. *Palestinian Parties and Politics That Shaped the Old Testament.* New York: Columbia Univ. Press, 1971.

Smith, W. Robertson. *Kinship and Marriage in Early Arabia.* Reprinted, Boston: Beacon, 1963.

Smith-Christopher, Daniel. "The Mixed Marriage Crisis in Ezra 9–10 and Nehemiah 13." In *Second Temple Studies,* edited by Tamara C. Eskenazi and Kent H. Richards, 243–65. JSOTSup 175. Sheffield: Sheffield Academic, 1994.

Snell, Daniel C. *Life in the Ancient Near East.* New Haven: Yale Univ. Press, 1997.

Sohn, Seock-Tae. "'I Will Be Your God and You Will Be My People': The Origin and Background of the Covenant Formula." In *Ki Baruch Hu: Ancient Near*

*Eastern, Biblical, and Judaic Studies in Honor of Baruch A. Levine,* edited by Robert Chazan et al., 355–72. Winona Lake, Ind.: Eisenbrauns, 1999.

Speiser, E. A. "Of Shoes and Shekels." *BASOR* 77 (1940) 15–20.

Stamm, Johann Jakob. "Zum Ursprung des Namens der Ammoniter." In idem, *Beiträge zur hebräischen und altorientalischen Namenkunde,* edited by Ernst Jenni and Martin A. Klopfenstein, 5–8. OBO 30. Göttingen: Vandenhoeck & Ruprecht, 1980.

Staples, W. E. "The Book of Ruth."*AJSL* 53 (1936–37) 145–57.

Steinberg, Naomi. *Kinship and Marriage in Genesis: A Household Economics Perspective.* Minneapolis: Fortress Press, 1993.

Strouse, Evelyn, and Bezalel Porten. "A Reading of Ruth." *Commentary* 67.2 (1979) 63–67.

Tamisier, Robert. "Le livre de Ruth." In *La Sainte Bible: Texte latin et traduction française d'après les textes originaux; avec un commentaire exégétique et théologique,* edited by Louis Pirot. Vol. 3. Paris: Letouzey et Ané, 1946.

Thompson, Michael. "New Life Amid the Alien Corn." *EvQ* 65 (1993) 197–210.

Thompson, Thomas, and Dorothy Thompson. "Some Legal Problems in the Book of Ruth." *VT* 18 (1968) 79–99.

Tollers, Vincent L. "Narrative Control in the Book of Ruth." In *Mapping of the Biblical Terrain: The Bible as Text,* edited by Vincent L. Tollers and John Maier, 252–59. Lewisburg, Pa.: Bucknell Univ. Press, 1990.

Toorn, Karel van der. "The Significance of the Veil in the Ancient Near East." In *Pomegranates and Golden Bells: Studies in Biblical, Jewish, and Near Eastern Ritual, Law, and Literature in Honor of Jacob Milgrom,* edited by David P. Wright et al., 327–39. Winona Lake, Ind.: Eisenbrauns, 1995.

Trible, Phyllis. *God and the Rhetoric of Sexuality.* OBT. Philadelphia: Fortress Press, 1978.

———. "Ruth, Book of." In *ABD* 5:842–47.

Tsevat, Mattiyahu. "Marriage and Monarchical Legitimacy in Ugarit and Israel." *JSS* 3 (1958) 237–43.

VanGemeren, Willem A. "Ruth: Theology of." In *New International Dictionary of Old Testament Theology and Exegesis,* edited by VanGemeren, 4:1153–57. Grand Rapids: Zondervan, 1997.

Vaux, Roland de. *Ancient Israel: Its Life and Institutions.* Translated by John McHugh. 2 vols. New York: McGraw-Hill, 1961.

Vellas, B. M. "The Book of Ruth and Its Purpose." *Theologia* [Athens] 25 (1954) 201–10.

Vesco, Jean-Luc. "La date du livre de Ruth." *RB* 74 (1967) 235–47.

Volgger, David. "Yhwh gab Rut Empfängnis und sie gebar einen Sohn (Rut 4,13): Zur Interpretation der Rut-Erzählung." *BN* 100 (1999) 85–100.

Vuilleumier, René. "Stellung und Bedeutung des Buches Ruth im alttestamentlichen Kanon." *TZ* 44 (1988) 193–210.

Waard, Jan de, and Eugene A. Nida. *A Translator's Handbook on the Book of Ruth.* 2d ed. UBS Handbook Series. London: United Bible Societies, 1992.

Waetjen, Herman. "The Genealogy as the Key to the Gospel according to Matthew." *JBL* 95 (1976) 205–30.

Walsh, J. T. "Two Notes on Translation and the Syntax of *Ṭerem*." *VT* 49 (1999) 264–66.

Weinfeld, Moshe. "Ruth." *EncJud* 14:518–19.

Weiss, David. "The Use of *qnh* in Connection with Marriage." *HTR* 57 (1964) 243–48.

Wendland, Ernst R. "Structural Symmetry and Its Significance in the Book of Ruth." In *Issues in Bible Translation,* edited by P. C. Stine, 30–63. UBSMS 3. London: United Bible Societies, 1988.

Wénin, André. "La stratégie déjouée de Noémi en Rt 3." *EstBib* 56 (1998) 179–99.

Westbrook, Raymond. "The Law of the Biblical Levirate." *RIDA* 24 (1977) 65–87.

———. *Property and the Family in Biblical Law.* JSOTSup 113. Sheffield: Sheffield Academic, 1991.

———. "The Redemption of Land." *Israel Law Review* 6 (1971) 367–75.

Westermann, Claus. *Genesis 12–36.* Translated by J. J. Scullion. CC. Minneapolis: Augsburg, 1985.

———. "Structure and Intention of the Book of Ruth." Translated by Frederick J. Gaiser. *WW* 19 (1999) 285–302.

Williams, James G. *Women Recounted: Narrative Thinking and the God of Israel.* BLS 6. Sheffield: Almond, 1982.

Wills, Lawrence M. *The Jewish Novel in the Ancient World.* Ithaca, N.Y.: Cornell Univ. Press, 1995.

Wilson, Robert R. *Genealogy and History in the Biblical World.* YNER 7. New Haven: Yale Univ. Press, 1977.

———. "The Old Testament Genealogies in Recent Research." *JBL* 94 (1975) 169–89.

Witzenrath, Hagia Hildegard. *Das Buch Rut: Eine literaturwissenschaftliche Untersuchung.* SANT 40. Munich: Kösel, 1975.

Wojcik, Jan. "Improvising Rules in the Book of Ruth." *PMLA* 100 (1985) 145–53.

Wolde, Ellen van. "Texts in Dialogue with Texts: Intertextuality in the Ruth and Tamar Narratives." *BibInt* 5 (1997) 1–28.

Wong, Wai Ching. "History, Identity and a Community of *Ḥesed*: A Biblical Reflection on Ruth 1:1-17." *Asia Journal of Theology* 13 (1999) 3–13.

Wright, G. R. H. "The Mother-Maid at Bethlehem." *ZAW* 98 (1986) 56–72.

Yerushalmi, Yoseph Hayim. *Zakhor: Jewish History and Jewish Memory*. Seattle: Univ. of Washington Press, 1982.

Yoder, Christine Roy. "The Woman of Substance (אשת חיל): A Socioeconomic Reading of Proverbs 31:10-31." *JBL* 122, no. 3 (2003) 427–47.

Zimmermann, Frank. "The Births of Perez and Zerah." *JBL* 64 (1945) 377–78.

Zimolong, Bertrand. "Zu Ruth II,7." *ZAW* 58 (1940–41) 156–58.

Zornberg, Avivah. "The Concealed Alternative." In *Reading Ruth: Contemporary Women Reclaim a Sacred Story,* edited by Judith A. Kates and Gail Twersky Reimer, 65–81. New York: Ballantine, 1994.

Zyl, A. H. van. *The Moabites*. Pretoria Oriental Series 3. Leiden: Brill, 1960.

# Scripture Index

# Scripture Index

## Scripture Index

## Scripture Index

## Scripture Index

# Index of Names

## Index of Names